THE GREAT SLIDE SHOW BOOK

Dedication

To my parents, who gave me everything a budding slide-show maker could want: a camera, a projector, a white wall, and the most important ingredient of all — enthusiasm.

Acknowledgements

Writing a book, like creating a slide show, is far more of a team effort than many people realise: and my team for *The Great Slide Show Book* has given me as much support as any writer could ask for. Phil Gardner has been an unfailing source of support and encouragement from the very beginning. Doug and Krystyna Hewitt have taken rough sketches and vague suggestions and turned them into sharp, clean artwork and design, and Jim Barker's cartoons are, as always, a welcome complement to the text.

I am very grateful to the many manufacturers and suppliers who went to such trouble to find pictures for me, especially Mayfair Photographic and Harmon UK, and to the many people who made time to talk to me about equipment and techniques, especially David Pollock, of Pollock Audio-Visual, Richard Watson of R.C.W., and the staff at Turnkey. Special thanks, too, to Kodak for valuable comments and information, and the free use of material from the *Thames Calendar* programme; and to Woodmansterne Ltd, where I worked for eight years as an AV producer, gaining much of the experience used in this book — and making several of the programmes used as examples.

Finally a general 'thank you' to everyone who helped me make the slide programmes themselves, especially Mike Scott Rohan, who sweltered in a warm sweater in mid-August for *Witchwood*; Ann Ramsay, who spent half an hour in an icy gale for three vital shots; Kerry and Michael, who put up with me for two hours while we shot *Guess Who's Coming to Dinner*; Adrienne Bunn, the voice of *Joan of Arc*; Colin Prior, master of strange medieval instruments; and Tim Phillips and Colin Michaels, masters of equally strange modern ones. Jeremy Marks gave valuable help with additional photography, Ralph Dearden of R.C.W. produced a virtuoso set of rostrum shots for *Star of the Sea*, and the I.T.P. production team gave me soundtracks to be proud of. And finally a special word for 2-year-old Kath, who turned a dismal day at Whipsnade into an event.

THE GREAT SLIDE SHOW BOOK

Allan Scott

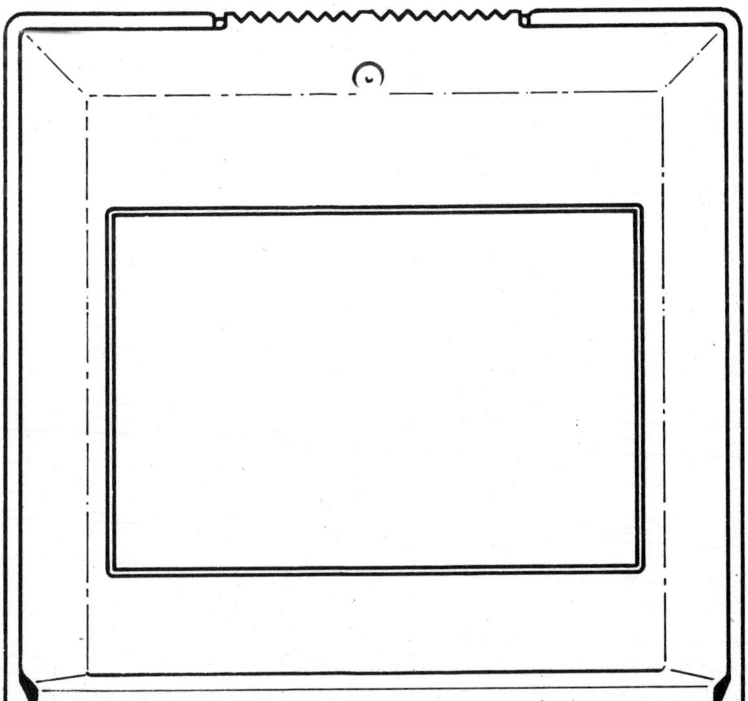

Adam & Charles Black

First edition 1984

Scott, Allan J. J.
The Great Slide Show Book
1. Slides (Photography)
I. Title
001.55'34 TR505

ISBN 0-7136-2461-2 Pbk

Published by
A & C Black (Publishers) Limited
35 Bedford Row, London WC1R 4JH

Design: Krystyna Hewitt
Illustrations: Douglas Hewitt

Photographic credits

Jean Coquin: 80–81 (top)
Derek Forss: 98
ITP slide library: 102–4
James Julius: 18 (left-hand sequence)
Kodak Ltd: 77–9, 82 (top)
Jeremy Marks: 30, 56 (bottom), 57, 73
Howard C. Moore: 39 (bottom)
Sir George Pollock: 12–13 (bottom), 99
Len Scott: 7 (middle, bottom), 9, 11, 32–3, 38 (top), 48 (right-hand sequence), 58–9 (middle and right-hand pairs), 61, 111 (colour shots)
Richard C. Watson: 83
Woodmansterne Ltd: 16 (Nick Servian), 31 (Howard C. Moore, top, Clive Friend, bottom), 43, 112 (Jeremy Marks), 54 (NASA, Nicholas Servian), 55 (NASA, Nicholas Servian).

The photograph of Simone Genevois, 33 (middle left), is taken from *La Merveilleuse Vie de Jeanne d'Arc* (made in 1929, directed by Marco de Gastyne).

Thanks also to the many manufacturers and distributors who have supplied pictures of their products.

The author wishes gratefully to acknowledge permission to reproduce the photographs listed above. All other photographs are by the author.

Typeset by PFB Art & Type Limited, Leeds, England

Printed and bound in Great Britain by William Clowes Ltd, Caxton Works, Beccles, Suffolk.

ISBN 0-7136-2461-2

Contents

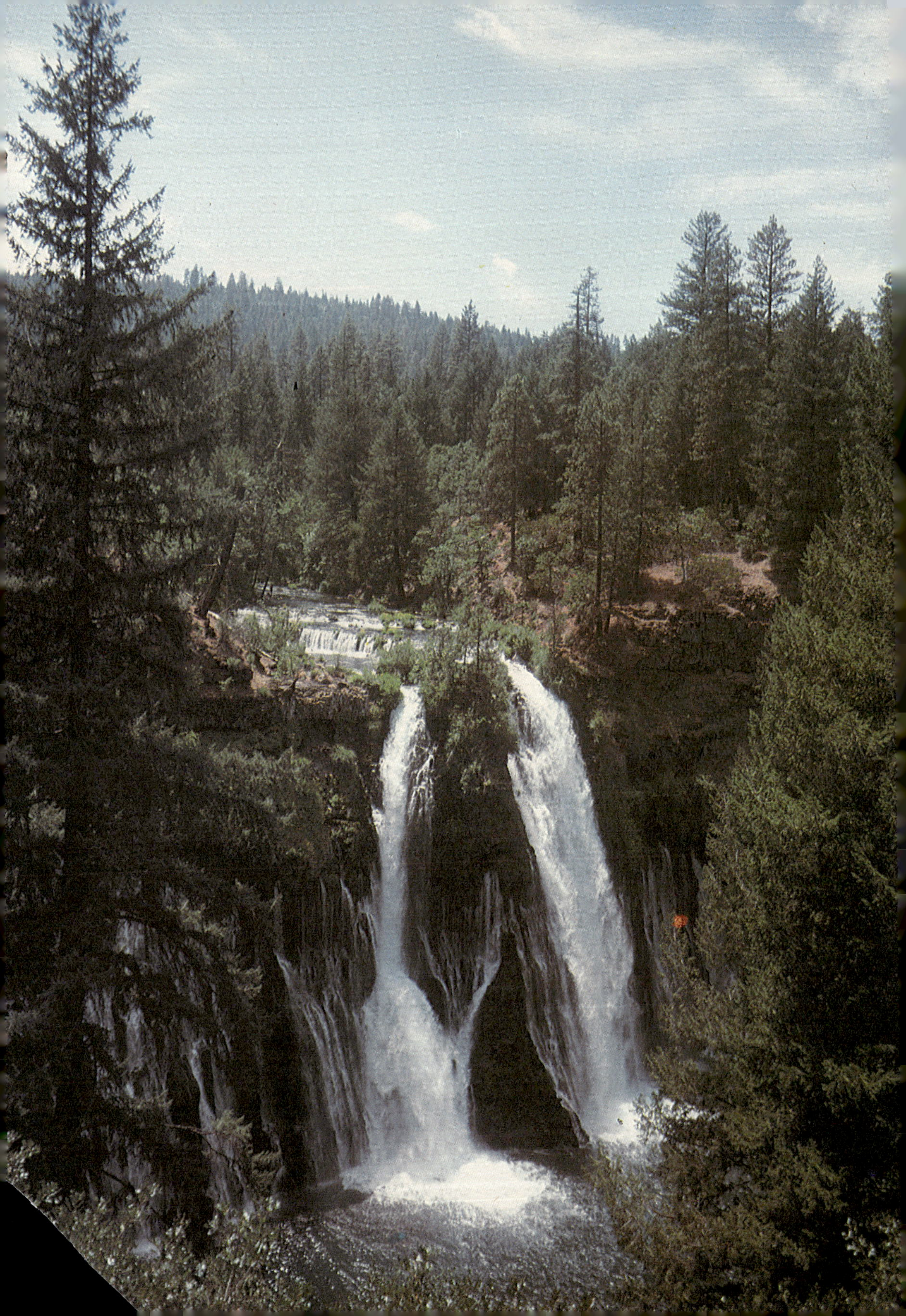

1

Who needs slide shows?

If you have a camera, and you're not using it to take colour slides, then you are missing something. And if you'd care to read the next paragraph or two, I'll tell you why.

Perhaps you have decided that colour slides are too much trouble. You prefer prints, in an album. But if you're serious about prints, you will also be serious about the way you present them. Before they are enshrined in the family album, you weed out the bad shots and the ones that didn't quite come off. The rest go in some kind of order, probably with short descriptive captions. You may even write longer captions that turn your album into a personal picture-book. After all, there's nothing like a good picture-book for a fireside browse in the winter, especially if there's only rubbish on TV. On the other hand, if there's a good film on, who needs picture-books?

Switch to colour slides, and things could be very different.

Think of the advantages. Your picture can be as large — or as small — as you wish. With a large screen (or even a large white wall) you can at last see your landscape shots as they were meant to be seen — at picture-window size. But do be careful not to walk out into that beautiful sunset. Walls can be very hard.

Landscapes like this deserve the sharpness, colour and sheer size that only a projected colour slide can give.

Again, think of close-ups. A projected slide will show every tiny detail of a flower or an animal — a typical colour slide registers up to 40 times more detail than a TV picture.* If you've never seen it before, it will be like going into a new world.

And in a way, you are.

*Comparison between a typical reversal image and a standard PAL domestic TV receiver.

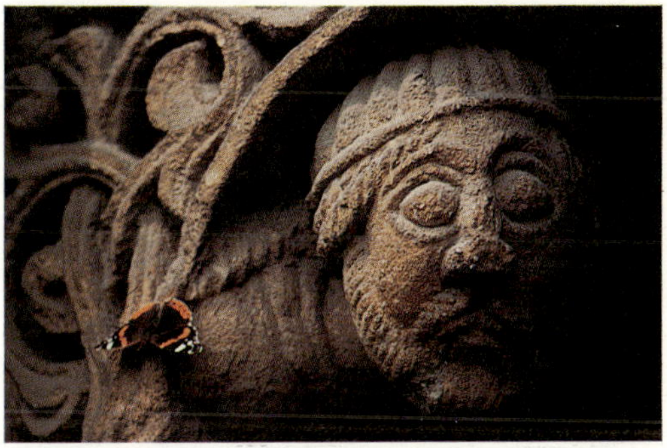

One day in eternity — a close-up shot that makes the most of the fine detail on 35mm slide film, and its intense colour.

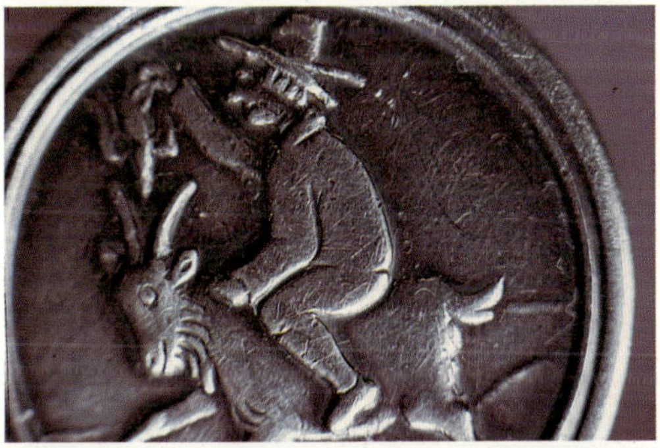

This child's silver spoon is only 25mm across. The slide, especially on projection, shows even the tiniest marks and scratches on the spoon.

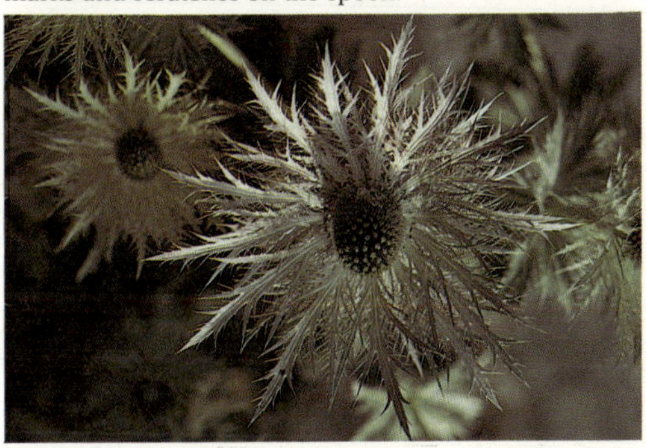

Filling a wall with a flower close-up like this one will impress any audience.

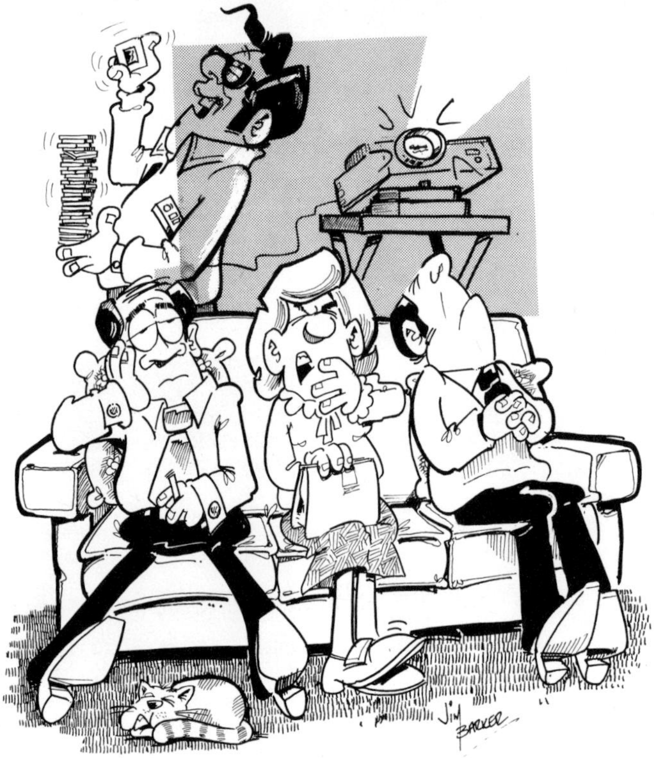

"Actually I'm not sure — it might be Mabel in Corfu, or it *could* be . . ."

The film of the book

Apart from their stunning visual effect, colour slides have another big advantage over prints — the same one your much-abused TV has over the printed book. With slides, you can put on a *programme* — a carefully-constructed sequence of pictures. Your audience, like the TV audience, is in a constant state of suspense because they don't know what's coming next. After all, they can't turn the page! And a good slide show is a constant succession of small surprises.

Of course, I did say a *good* slide show. Many people (perhaps including you) have been put off slide shows because many of them are very bad. It just isn't good enough to pull out a tray-full of unsorted slides, run them through the projector in any old order, and try to remember what they show and where you took them as you go along. No audience in the world will stand for it, not even your own family. Before long they'll be bored, the slides will disappear into a drawer or mysteriously vanish, and no one will ever look at them again.

Which is a pity. Because some of those pictures might have been assembled into an excellent programme. And anyone who can put together a half-decent photo album can make a half-decent slide show.

It's a bit like making the film of the book.

So how much will it cost?

Starting out in the world of colour slides doesn't have to be expensive. All you need to start working through this book is a camera — any camera that can take colour slides — and a projector. Nothing elaborate — if you like, try the second-hand shops, or the classified ad columns in the local paper. Your first screen can be a clean sheet, or a white wall. I know one very serious amateur who still uses the wall: he says it gives him bigger pictures. And when you see your first pictures you, too, will realise just how exciting slides can be.

Video versus slides

With more and more video recorders about, spending money on slide projectors may seem wasteful. It isn't — and I have no axe to grind, because I earn part of my living by making videos. If you, as an amateur, want to make videos anywhere away from the house, then you will have to use a portable. Even the lightest of these is a lot heavier than a 35mm camera; and for the price of the video recorder alone (without the video camera) you could probably buy two projectors, an electronic dissolve unit, and a perfectly good single-lens reflex camera!

And then there's the quality. No amateur can produce material that will match what you see on TV every night. Even the best equipment is not up to it — after all, the professional has enormously expensive cameras, editing suites and studio facilities at his disposal, and you don't. The funny thing is that a good slide show can defeat video on its own ground, at a fraction of the cost — as more than one of my clients has discovered!

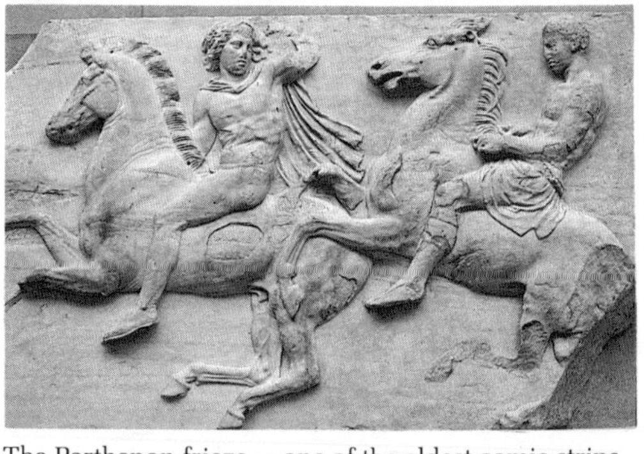

The Parthenon frieze — one of the oldest comic strips in the world.

The wide-screen all-colour comic strip

The art of making visual programmes is basically the art of the comic strip. Whether it's a cinema film, a commercial, a TV programme or a slide show it uses a series of images strung together by a storyline and supported (sometimes) by words. Not all programmes need words, and many work better without them — so you don't need to be today's answer to Will Shakespeare. Music and sound effects can add an extra dimension, but in the end everything depends on the pictures.

If the comic strip sounds like rather a low form of art, remember that the Athenians put one around the Parthenon. And even considering such illustrious competition, a slide show is a very special kind of comic strip. Every frame can fill an entire wall, it's in full colour, and it's *yours*; no one else could ever make the same programme. And slide shows, at no extra cost, can achieve a range of effects that would cost a TV producer thousands of pounds. Take a sneak preview of Chapter 5 and you'll see what I mean.

Putting your talent to work

Of course, the best pictures in the world are not necessarily going to make a good programme. That takes talent. But it's a talent many people have. A reasonably good photographer already knows how to put together a picture in a way that satisfies him and pleases others. To make a slide show, you need only learn how to put together a *series* of pictures so that the sum of the parts becomes greater than the whole.

And that's why the early chapters of this book do not deal with equipment. As I said, all you need is a camera and a projector. The most sophisticated equipment in the world is useless unless you know what to do with it, so we begin with a look at basic communication skills — how to put your ideas, whatever those ideas may be, into a form your audience will understand and enjoy.

What can I make programmes about?

If you can't, at this moment, think of anything to make a programme about, don't worry. The next chapter should give you a head start. And it'll take you a lifetime to run out of ideas once you *have* started. Like the TV producer, you can make many kinds of programme — documentaries, dramas, features, sketches, biographies, anything you like. But there's more. You can afford to make a programme that could never appear on television, but is certain to interest one particular audience. You can try things that

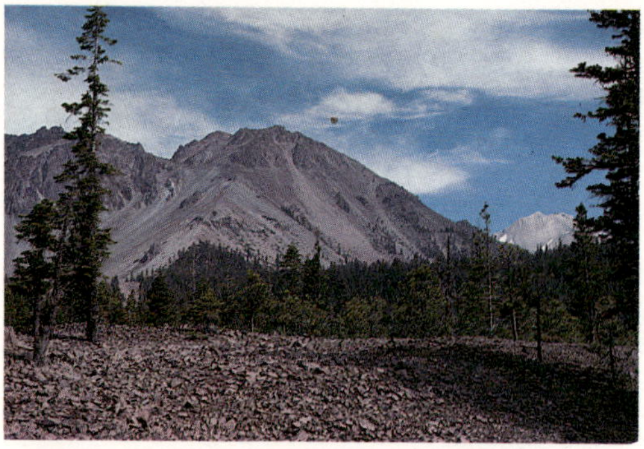

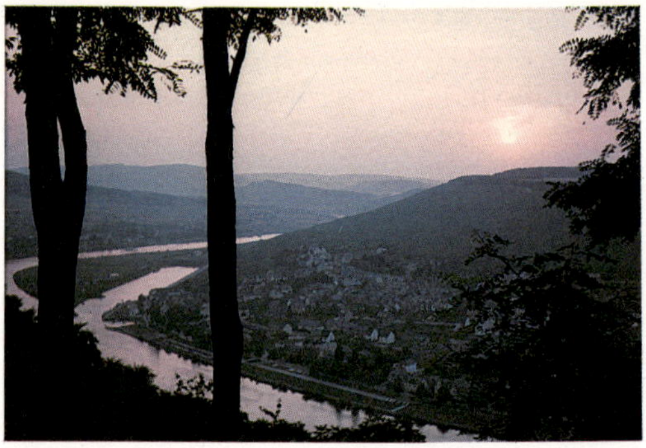

Travel shots like these lose most of their impact in a book! On a large screen it is far easier to appreciate them — and if they're part of a well-made sequence, they'll come across even better.

have never been done before for little more than the price of the film.

Making it pay

If you're still doubtful, remember that slide shows are big business. Major companies use them regularly because they're an effective, economical way of passing on information. Some of these professional programmes use up to forty projectors, but more than half the commercial shows made in any given year use two or perhaps three projectors — well within the range of the serious amateur.

The standard entry to the profession is through a college course involving audio-visual studies, but there are other ways. I never did a college course, and I now run a freelance audio-visual business of my own. It is possible. And there are other possibilities.

An increasing number of slide-show makers now tour the country with their work, often assisted by one or other of the major hardware companies. After all, what better demonstration of their equipment could there be? And at a time when people have more and more leisure, and photography is becoming more and more popular as a hobby, there are plenty of potential audiences. Those audiences could make you money. They might even finance the programmes you're making to impress that hard-headed business market.

In the slide-show business, as in any other business, there are no guarantees. But there is certainly room for talent. And the only way to find out if you have that talent is to start making programmes.

Besides, it's fun. And that's the most important fact of all.

2

Getting your act together

In pursuit of the Great Idea

You are watching the ultimate Boring Slide Show — Uncle Harry's holiday snaps of Benidorm. The commentary is straight out of the tourist brochure, full of 'smiling vistas' and 'delightful prospects'. Harry, being a technical type, has recorded the whole thing on tape, including electronic cues that change the projector automatically. Suddenly there is a major hitch. The screen goes dark. After much muttering in the shadows, the show starts all over again from the beginning. Only Harry has forgotten to reset the slide magazine — and as his pictures of the nudist beach come up on screen that bland, prerecorded commentary suddenly stops sounding bland . . .

One of the most enjoyable amateur slide shows I ever saw used this simple idea as its central theme. Of course, the whole show was prerecorded, including a lovely piece of comic dialogue in the middle, but a good presenter could have done it live. And as for the visual jokes wrung out of that innocent-sounding commentary — enough to say the audience was soon helpless with laughter.

Every good slide show starts with an idea, in this case one that turned a Boring Slide Show into a good one. But even if you are a comic genius, or the greatest writer since Tolstoy, you may still find it difficult to think of an original idea for a programme.

In fact, ideas are all around you — it is just that sometimes they are a little hard to recognise. The simplest things can be made into good slide shows. Take children's fantasies, for instance. Most children love to play with models, or dolls, or building bricks. A carefully-assembled series of slides can make it look as though the children are entering a miniature world. No need for complex 'special effects' shots, unless you feel like trying them. You are not making the

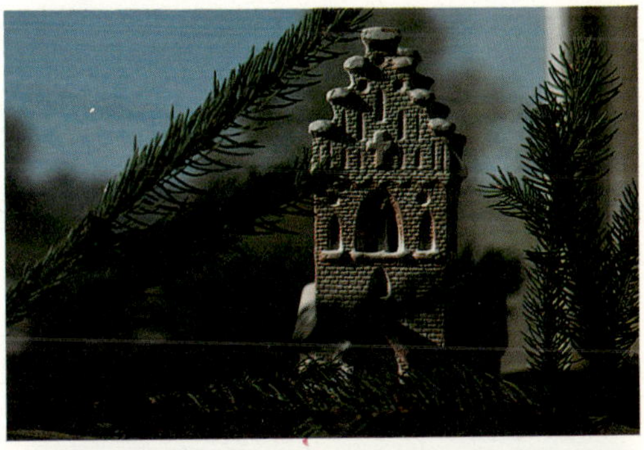

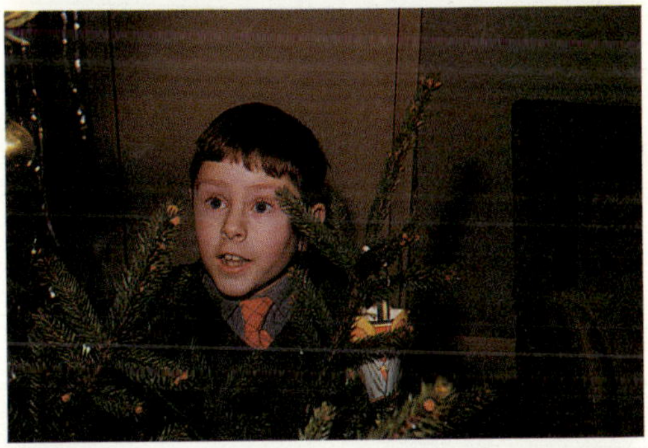

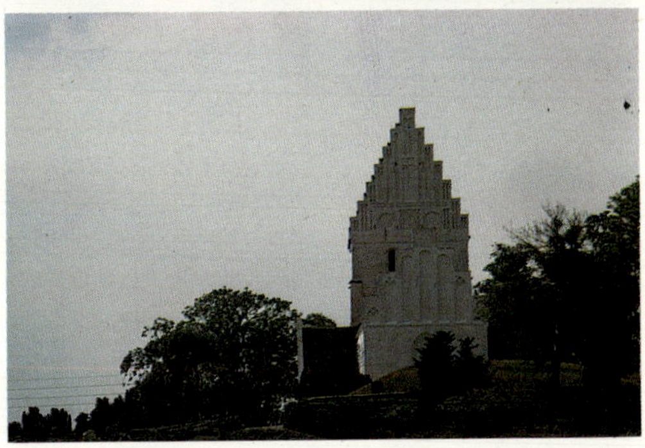

Part of a 'child's fantasy' sequence. The little boy imagines he can go into the model church by the Christmas tree — and suddenly it becomes a real church!

next episode of *Star Wars*. Just take a shot of, say, a model building from a low angle, and then a close-up of a child looking upwards. Let the commentary carry the storyline — or let the children themselves tell the story, if they want to!

On a more serious level, think of something that interests *you*. You probably have other hobbies besides photography; perhaps you collect matchboxes, or make model Roman chariots, or build Viking ships in the garden. Whatever you do, if *you* like it you can probably interest others, too. If so, good luck — but please read the rest of this chapter first!

A good rule for slide-show makers, and one that is constantly drummed into writers, is to work from what you know. I know something about slide shows, which is my excuse for writing this book. What do *you* know about? Cats? Manhole covers? Early Victorian crochet work? Can you make something *visual* of it? Then maybe it is slide-show material. Is there some place you know and love? Do you know enough about it to interest other people, or could you find out what you need to know? Then you can make a slide show about it. Or perhaps you know very little about it, but have simply shot reel after reel of film there, season after season. In that case why not look out a piece of music that captures the feel of that place for you, and build up a visual sequence to match the music? You don't have to *say* anything at all, and the idea will work just as well for Ionian temples on a distant Greek island as for the back streets of a northern town. But a word of warning: keep it *short*! Five to ten minutes is quite long enough for even the best slide show.

Still, that does suggest another idea — music and songs. Be careful, though. There are far too many would-be illustrations of Vivaldi's 'Four Seasons' about, and most of them are very long, very boring, and very uninspired. Pick a short song that you particularly enjoy, and see if you can come up with a new twist on it. Sir George Pollock

Still from Sir George Pollock's witty and imaginative two-projector slide sequence *Circles*.

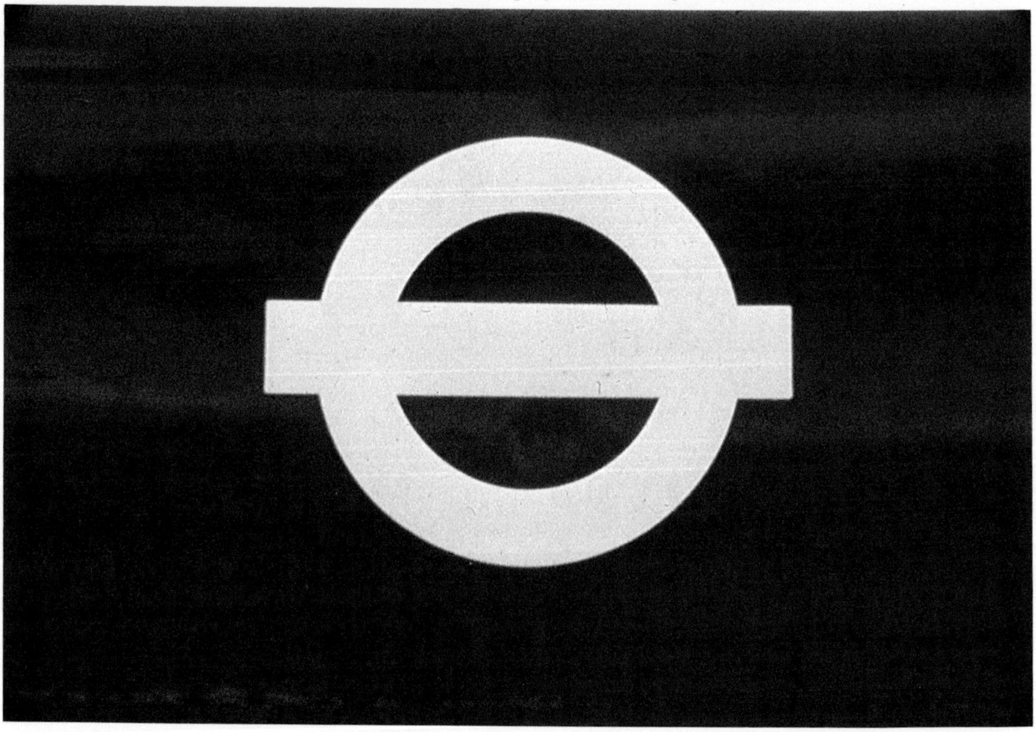

has produced a lovely show called *Circles*, shot entirely on location on the London Underground. The pictures add a new dimension to the song by telling a story of their own. Each day, two people, a boy and a girl, come to the same station but get on Circle Line trains travelling in opposite directions. Finally they both get on the same train. Simple, touching, funny, effective — and such an uncomplicated idea!

Poetry is another possibility, but risky. Good poetry will not usually stand being straitjacketed into one rigid interpretation. Some Boring Slide Shows try to do just that, and the poetry wins every time. Best to leave poetry until you have more experience.

Holiday pictures have their place, but unless you have been somewhere really unusual and exciting, like the jungles of Borneo, most people will not want a day-by-day account of what you did. Look at a few TV documentaries and see how the writers make them interesting. And to keep it short, try to pick out some particular aspect of the

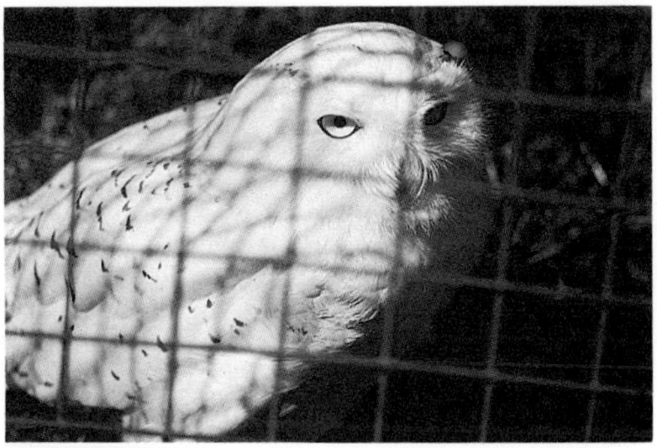

'And who do you think *you* are?' A canny owl from *Down at the Zoo*.

holiday that you have enjoyed. Do you like wandering round ruined Greek temples? Are you more interested in people? Everyday life? Unusual folk-customs? The antics of your fellow-visitors? Concentrate on one thing, and make the most of it.

Nearer home, what about a visit to your local zoo? Michael Tickner has made a wonderful programme comparing facial expressions on both sides of the bars. The

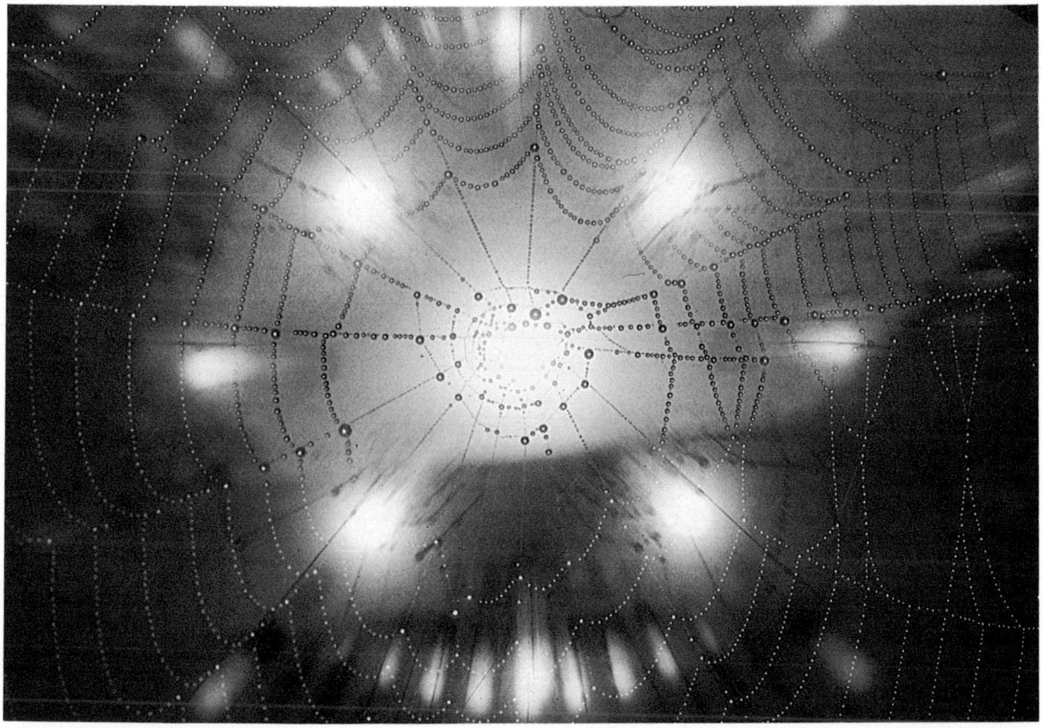

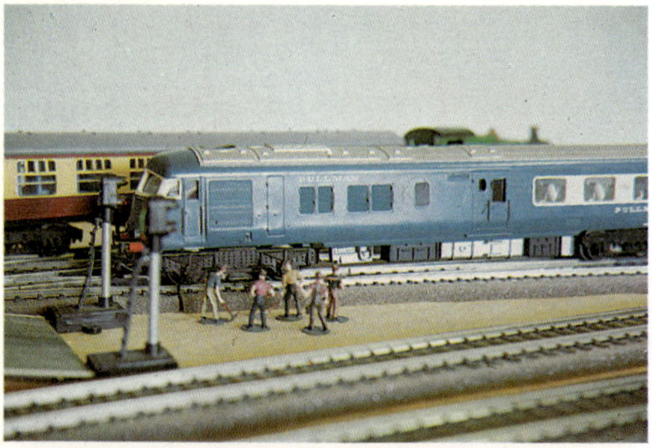

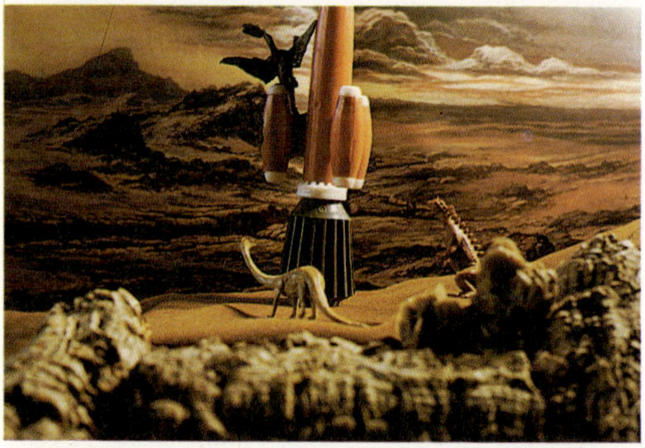

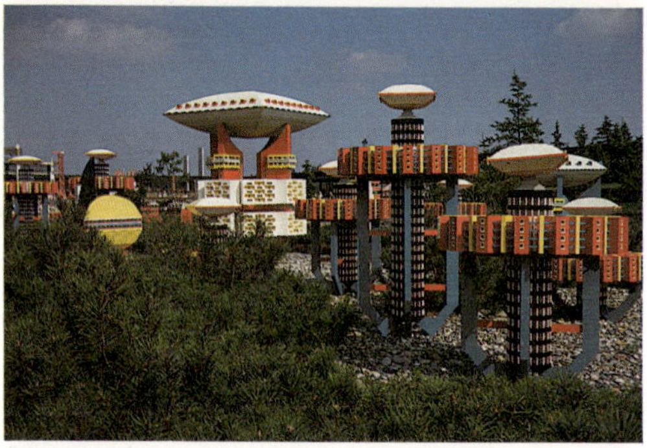

Other examples of fantasy at work: a model railway, an alien landscape made with models and a painting, and the 'City of the Future' exhibit from Legoland in Denmark.

animals seem to come out of it rather better than the visitors. A trip through your garden with a close-up lens may yield surprising results; that idea has produced at least one very entertaining TV series. Or perhaps there is someone you are very interested in, or very fond of, who would make a good subject for a short programme. Ask them if they would mind, and try it. If you are interested in local history, you could try doing this for one of your 'oldest inhabitants', perhaps illustrating it with period pictures (if you can get them) and modern views of the same places. If you have access to a tape recorder, you could even use a commentary made up of edited comments from your subject.

Do you have an artistic streak? Could you make up your own graphics, titles and drawings? (See p. 56 for some ideas on how to do this.) Perhaps you could put together a short programme using nothing but your own artwork: a story, or a 'how-to' programme, or even a 'how-not-to' programme . . .

I could go on, but by now you are probably thinking up some ideas of your own. If not, try a sneak preview of Chapter 10. In any case, don't rush for the camera just yet. Once you have a basic idea, you need to decide what you are going to do with it. In professional circles this is known as 'preparing a treatment', but I prefer to think of it as a branch of one of the oldest creative arts — storytelling.

Angling for attention

Storytelling is supposed to be an Art. But like a good many other Arts, it is also a Craft — and, as with any Craft, the basics can be taught; and learned. For instance, try this sentence:

'On the fourth of December, at precisely ten-thirty in the evening, David decided he would have to kill Joanna.' If you picked up a book that started with a sentence like that, you might be tempted to buy it. At very least you might be curious. Who is David? Who is Joanna? What is their relationship? Why has he decided to kill her? And why did he take the decision at a particular time on a particular day? For that matter, did he manage it, and if so, should he have?

That sentence is a simple example of what I call the *hook* — and one of these days I shall think of a story to go with it. The point is that the hook is just as useful in slide shows as in short stories. In fact, you cannot do without it.

Whatever sort of programme you are making, you need to think about your audience. Who are they? Your family? Your friends? A room full of complete strangers? Think about them as you prepare your script. How would you normally talk to them? How much do they already know about your subject? How much will you need to tell them? Can you be sure they will understand everything they need to understand to follow your programme? Above all, can you be sure you will be able to keep their attention?

The hook is a way of getting their attention the moment you start. It is a very ancient technique. Homer used it in the *Iliad*, the Saxons used it in the epic poem *Beowulf*, Milton used it in *Paradise Lost*, and most TV police thrillers, especially American shows, use a highly sophisticated version of it as part of their opening credits.

So how do you use the hook for a slide show?

Imagine you are sitting in a darkened room, waiting for a programme to begin. The screen is empty. Some of the audience are still talking. Then, from the left, comes the distinct sound of an air-raid siren. The room goes quiet. A drone is heard — the drone of massed bombers, coming nearer

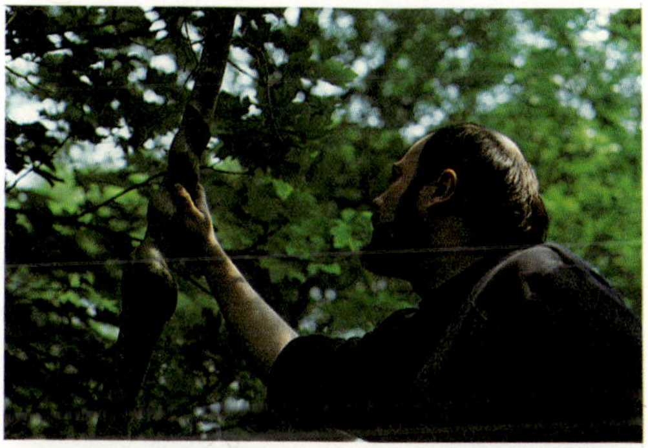

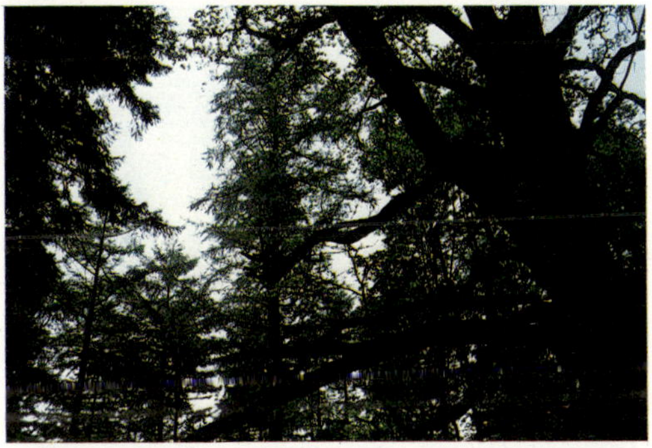

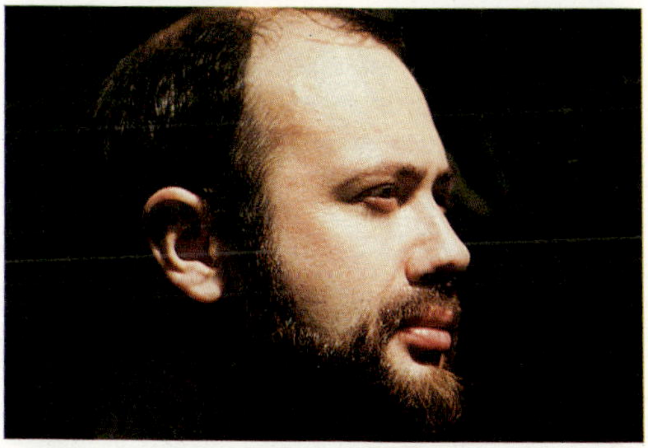

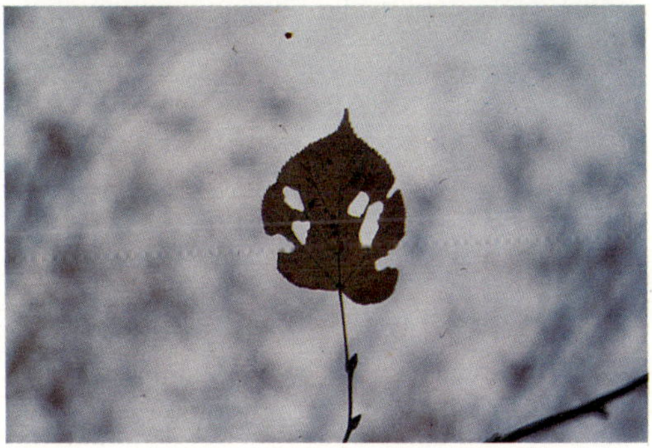

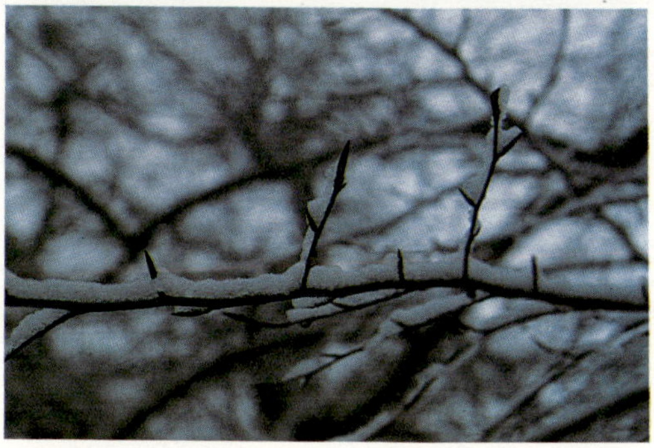

Selected shots from *Witchwood*, a sinister slide sequence in which a lone walker finds rather more than he bargained for on his morning stroll . . .

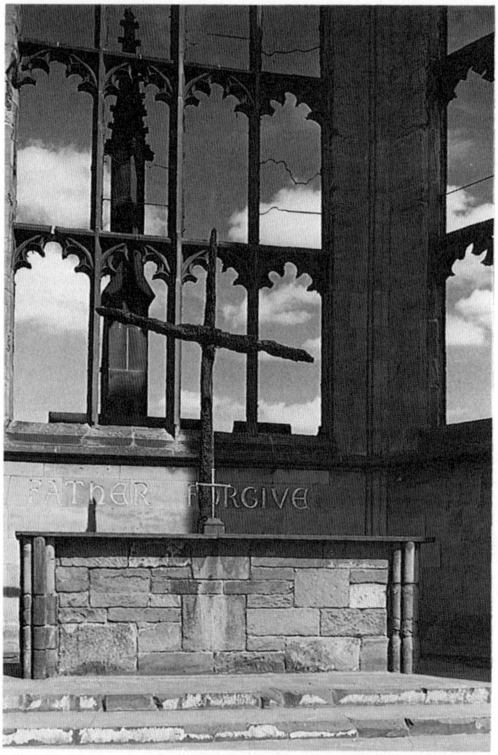

After the holocaust — the opening shot from *Coventry Cathedral* (Woodmansterne).

and nearer until they seem to be over your head. And behind them, increasingly, the stuttering roar of exploding bombs. A plane peels off and circles overhead. A crash of breaking timber — flames, louder and louder — and then underneath it all, but rising as all the other sounds fall away, a single tolling bell.

And on the screen appears the broken shell of a great cathedral.

For a few moments, there is only the ruin and the bell. And then a quiet, commanding voice says: 'This is the story of a cathedral reborn from the flames of war — Coventry Cathedral.'

That was how I started my first professional slide-tape programme — with a slightly over-stated hook, in this case using prerecorded sound. You can probably imagine the effect, especially on people old enough to remember those sirens for themselves. The rest of the show was a fairly straightforward description of the cathedral and the works of art it contains; but by then the audience was listening, and willing to be moved again.

The same technique can work in purely visual terms. Imagine, for instance, a gentle, not too pacy sequence showing a man walking through a wood in summertime. There is no commentary — just music. But as he walks, a change takes place. The music is becoming sinister, threatening — and the wood is changing, too. Although the man wears the same clothes, and walks the same path, the trees are dying, the summer colours have gone, and soon there is snow on the path. As he walks from warmth into winter, he begins to look frightened . . .

That is the opening of a short programme called *Witchwood* — of which more later.

Interesting developments

Having found your idea, and a hooking way to introduce it, the next stage is to develop it, using all the little tricks that this medium allows.

How can you do that?

Well, back on p. 9 I said that slide shows are very like comic strips — and many professionals use a modified comic strip to plan out their programmes. It's called a *storyboard*, and in the diagrams opposite and on p. 21 you can see two very different examples, one by Gerald Rogers and one by me. I'll discuss mine in more detail later. For the moment, let's look at Gerald's.

Flying start

This storyboard is beautifully put together. It has a consistent visual style. It has a neat visual gimmick — each shot almost 'turns into' the next. But, most important of all, it has a structure: the *hook* (little man dreams of flight), the *development* (his dream grows into a more and more complex reality), and the *resolution* (the astronaut unwittingly dreams of the very same image that started everything off).

This structure of hook, development and resolution is vital to any programme. The line you follow in developing them is up to you. Just make sure there *is* a line.

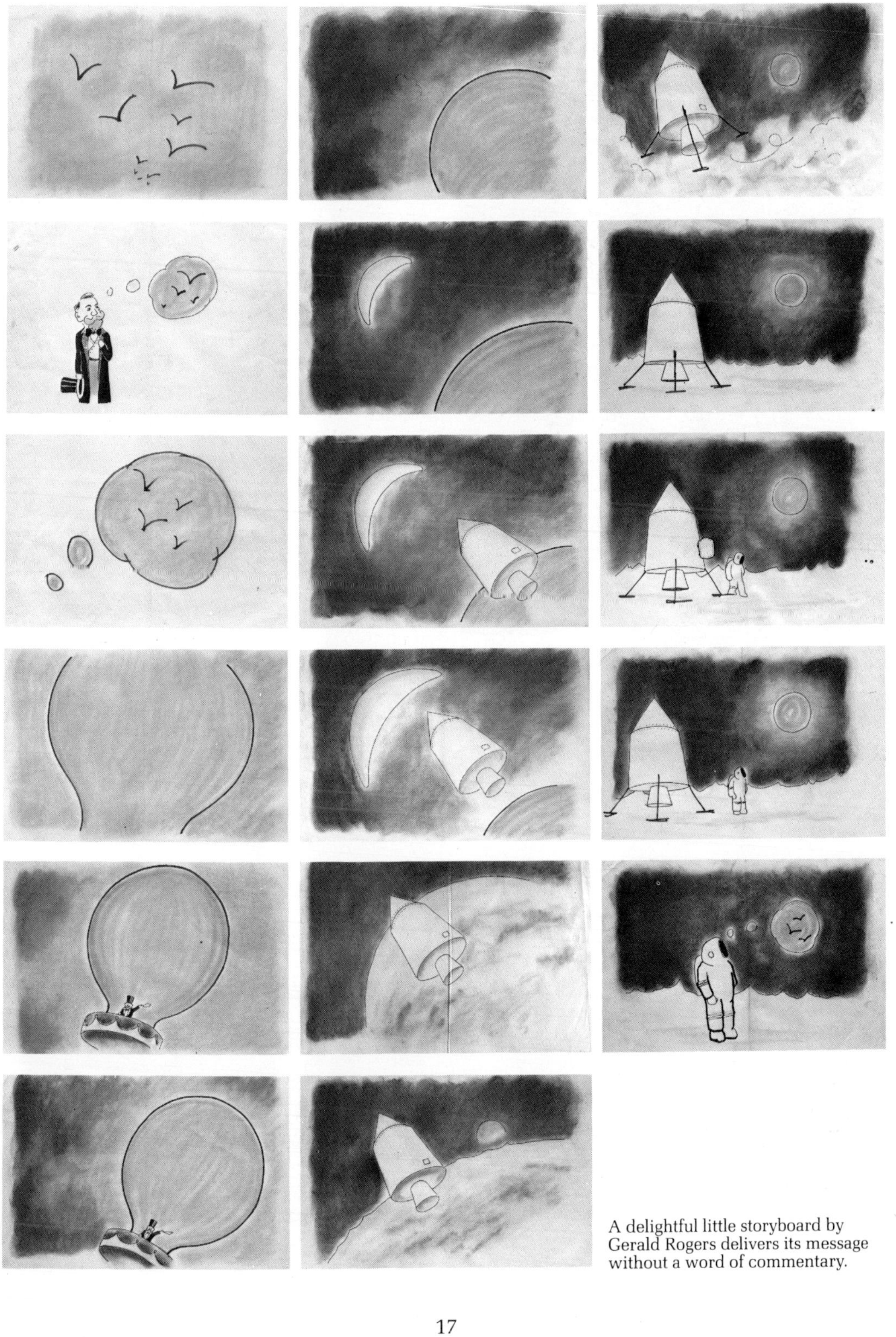

A delightful little storyboard by Gerald Rogers delivers its message without a word of commentary.

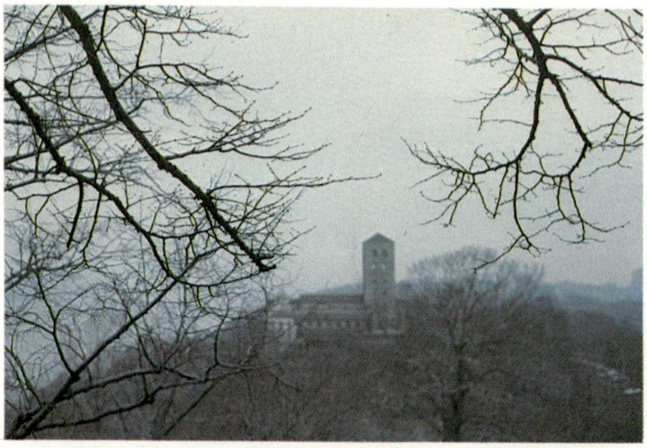

Oh, this was somewhere on Long Island. We didn't go in because it was closed. It's a bit out of focus, isn't it?

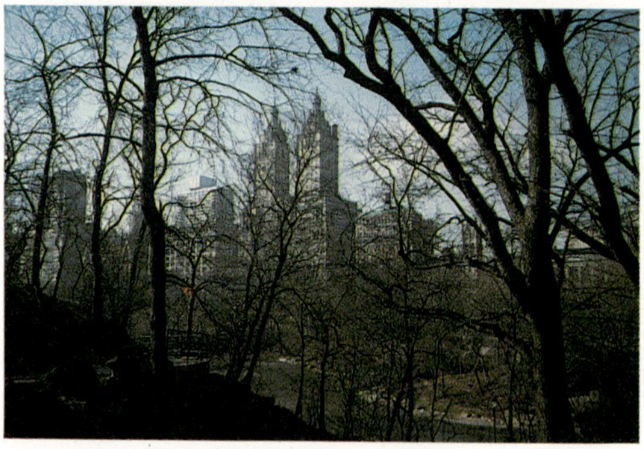

This is that place in the middle of New York. You know, the park place.

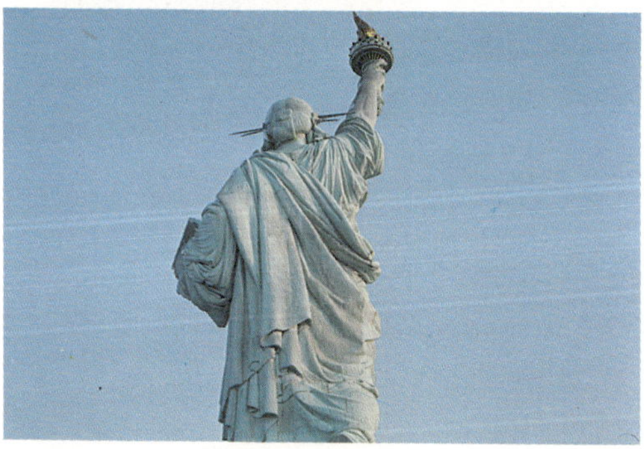

Oh, yes, this is the Statue of Liberty. We didn't go up because Mary doesn't like heights.

The sequence above is how not to do it. How many times have you suffered a commentary like this? It's of very little interest, and tells you nothing important about what you are seeing. At the top of p. 19, the pictures are explained rather more from a historical viewpoint — the programme tells you things you are unlikely to know. On the right here, the writer has approached his subject with more humour, concentrating entirely on entertainment value. But both sequences have a narrative line — they are going somewhere. The only question is, how fast?

Drive safely through your slide show

A slide show can go at any pace that is suitable at the time. A slow, sentimental sequence could leave a picture on screen for as long as thirty seconds. It would have to be a very good one, though. An 'action' sequence could involve changing slides as fast as the projector can move them. Most sequences, of course, will take a pace varying between these extremes without actually reaching them. But the key word is 'varying'. A sequence that uses the same pace uniformly throughout is doomed to be dull.

Gerald's flight sequence, for instance, would start out fairly slowly. Balloons are not exactly fast. As the balloon changes into the moon-rocket, the slide changes would come faster, suggesting speed and high technology. But the last couple of frames, with the astronaut dreaming of birds and blue skies, would be slow again.

Planning for pace is far easier with a storyboard. It gives a clear idea of the pictures you want, and the job each of them has to do. For instance, you may find that a picture in a fast sequence is carrying a long commentary. At storyboard stage you can either cut down the commentary or add a couple of extra pictures. By the time you

Even at Yosemite it's hard to get away from the salesmen . . .

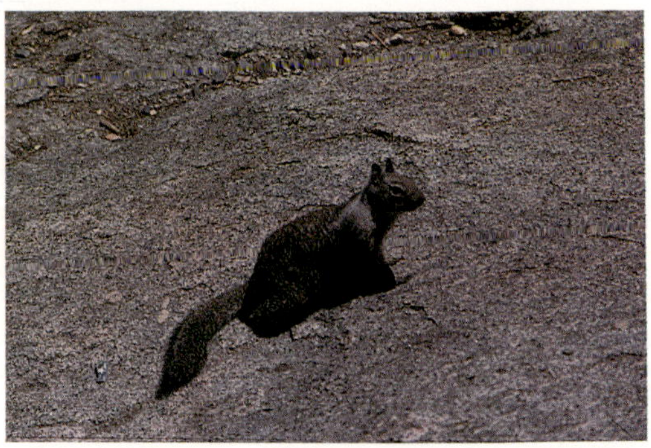

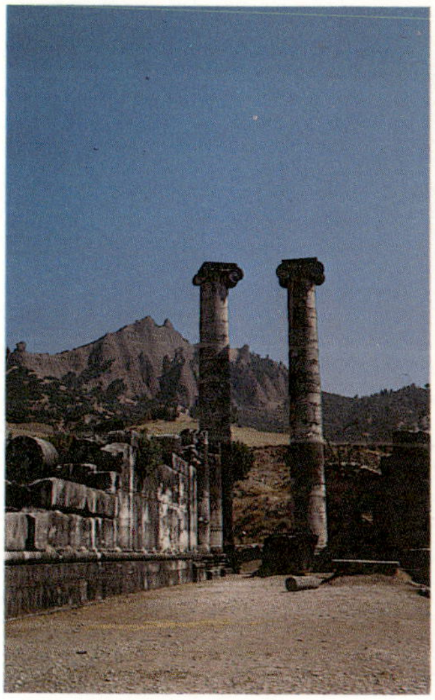

Sardis, in Turkey, on a dusty September day . . .

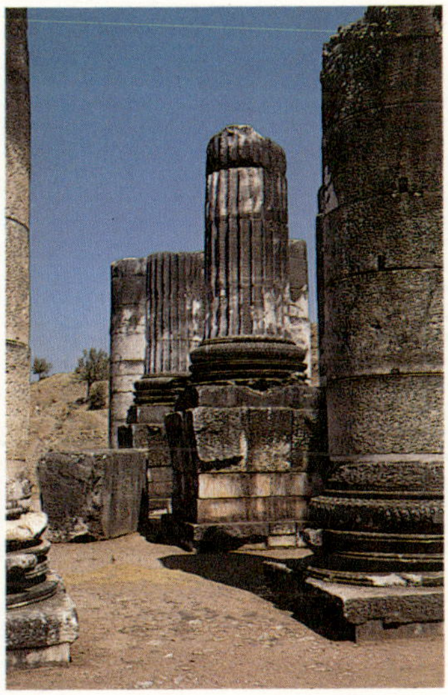

Hard to believe that these ruins once formed a vital link on one of the world's richest trade routes . . .

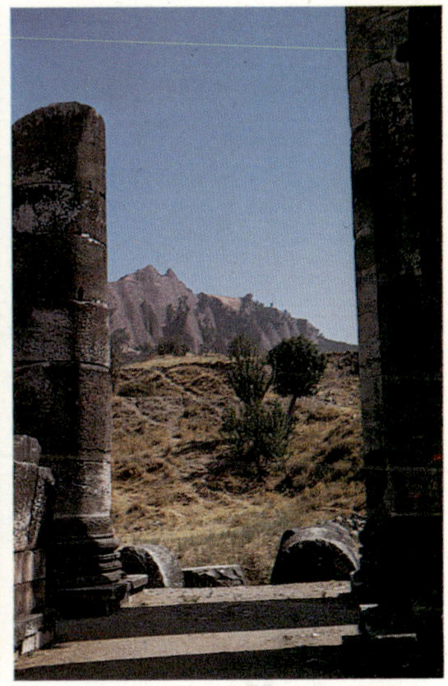

Or that the idea of money was born amid these brown and barren peaks.

have finished you will have a very good idea of what pictures you are going to need — and if you are travelling a long way to get your material, that could be very important.

Hollywood on the front lawn

Before you start work on your epic slide show with the five exotic locations and the cast of thousands, it is probably worth sitting down with a notebook and planning a couple of short, sharp sequences that you can shoot and produce in a couple of days. To show you what I mean I'll discuss a little show called *Guess Who's Coming to Dinner*, based on a children's science-fiction story I wrote for an anthology. Cast and locations were pretty easy to find — I just needed one ordinary family, one ordinary garden, one ordinary house — and one plastic alien!

Stage 1: Concept and Storyline

For this show I chose a style based on the BBC children's programme *Jackanory*. A narrator reads the story while simple still illustrations appear on screen. Unlike a TV camera, of course, a 35mm camera cannot create the illusion of movement by zooming and panning. With two projectors I could have beaten the problem, but I wanted my 'models' to have a copy of the programme

But the squirrel was only selling the view, so we gave him some food anyway. After all . . .

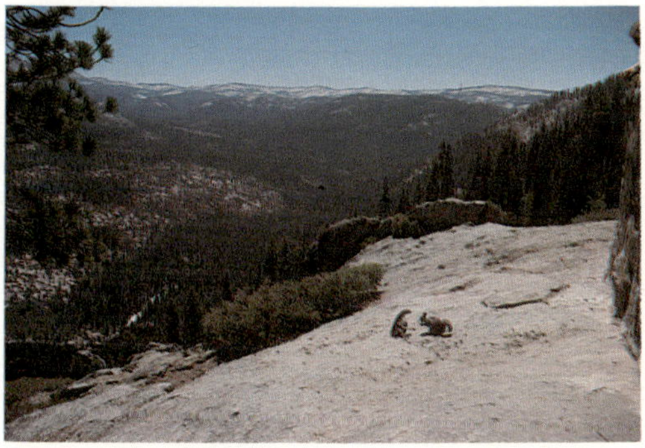

. . . it isn't every day you get the chance to see 9,000 feet of mountain neatly sliced in half by a glacier.

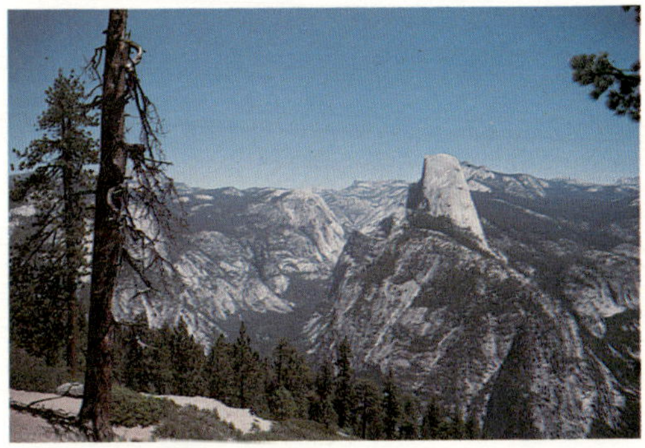

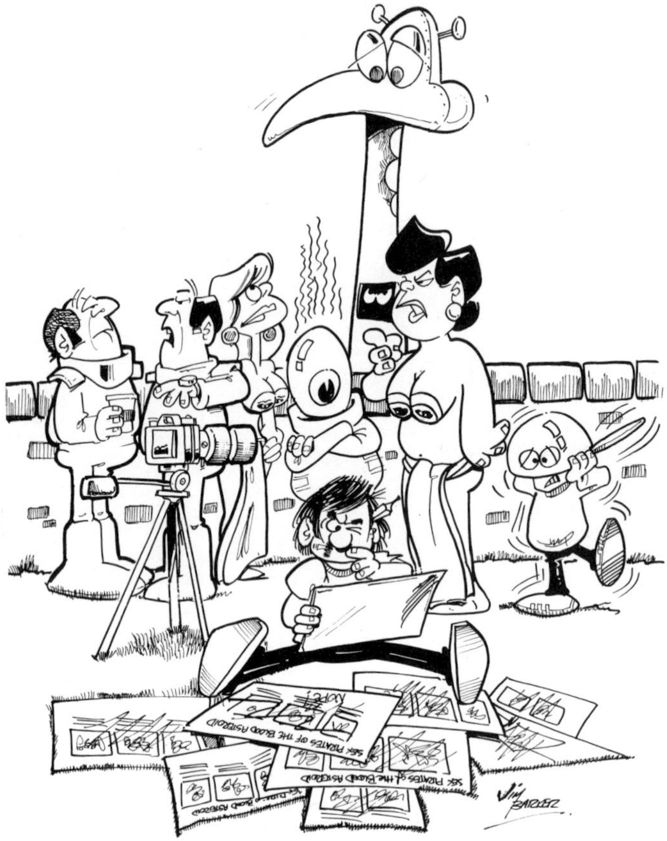

themselves, so I decided to use a single projector. I also decided that the script would be written for reading aloud by the projectionist, so he would not need a tape recorder.

The original story was cut down dramatically to make a five-minute slide show. It begins with the ominous words 'Edward was eating worms again' (hook) and goes on to detail a conversation between Edward (2), Adrian (9), and an alien called Caterpillar that says it likes to eat calcium and silicon but looks as though it wants to eat Adrian. Adrian and Edward run away. Later they are led to believe that calcium is milk — so Adrian thinks the alien just wanted a glass of milk, and feels bad about it all evening. In the morning, Adrian's father wakes up to find the house in ruins, and Adrian in the middle of the chaos looking up 'calcium' and 'silicon' in the encyclopaedia. There he finds the explanation for what has happened. 'You know, Dad,' he says, 'I think Caterpillar must've been awfully hungry!' (How's that for a resolution?)

Stage 2: Storyboard

As you can see, the storyboard breaks down the original storyline into a series of shots, making it work *visually*. Remembering those remarks about pace, notice how the number of pictures per word increases as Caterpillar begins to look more and more dangerous. A storyboard can also tell you how many different locations you will need; in this case I needed a garden, a kitchen, Adrian's room, his father's room, and a demolished house for the last sequence. If the kitchen had turned up at two or three different times in the show, I could have done what movie producers do and taken all the pictures of the kitchen at the same time, out of sequence. If your storyboard involves half a dozen different locations in different parts of the country, this sort of detail can become very important.

Stage 3: Production

At this stage, as you can see, the script is pretty well finished. Changes can still be made during production, but when I actually load film into the camera I like to have a fairly clear idea of what I am going to take — right down to the way that individual figures appear in shot. Notice that the storyboard includes many different camera distances and angles. Like a film script, it

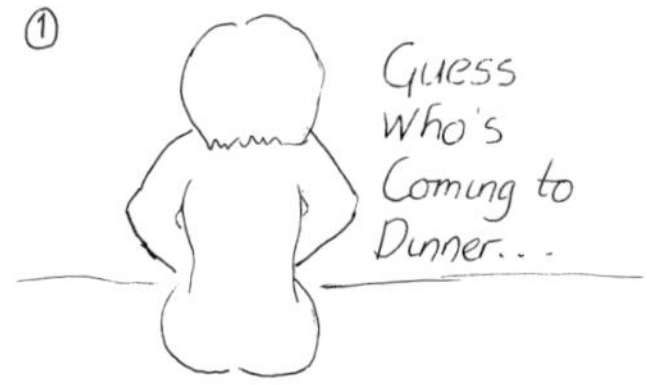

(Title slide)

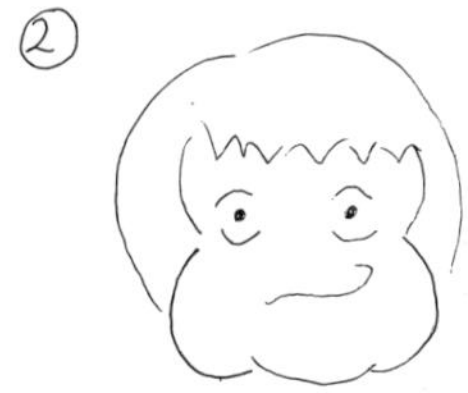

Edward was eating worms again.

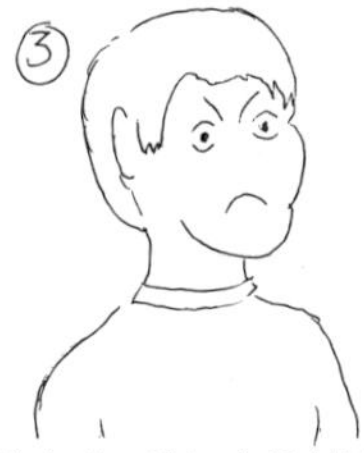

His brother Adrian decided that somewhere, on some tiry island on the other side of the world, there must be other people who ate worms -- But he couldn't think of anyone else in Woldingham who did. And now Edward was picking up another one...

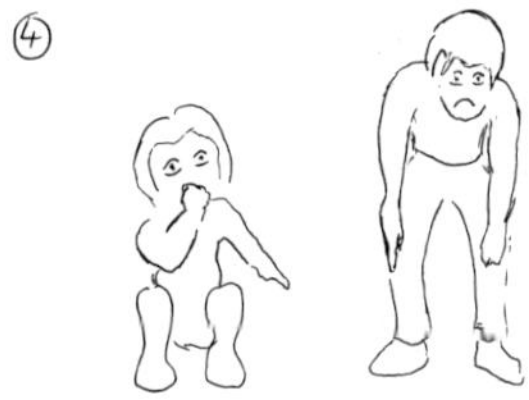

... only this time he dropped it. Adrian bent down to see why. What was so special about <u>this</u> worm?

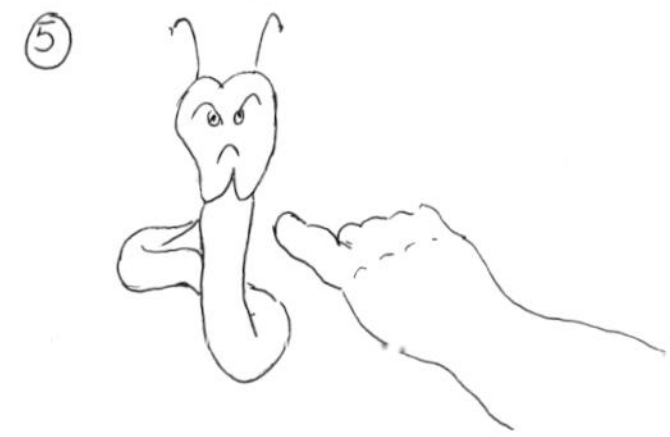

It certainly looked a bit odd -- something like a caterpillar, really, only about three sizes too big and brown.

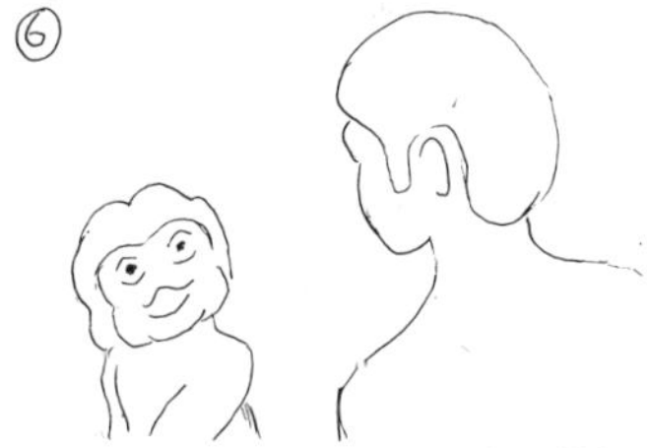

'Worm,' said Edward, cheerfully. 'Talks,' he added.

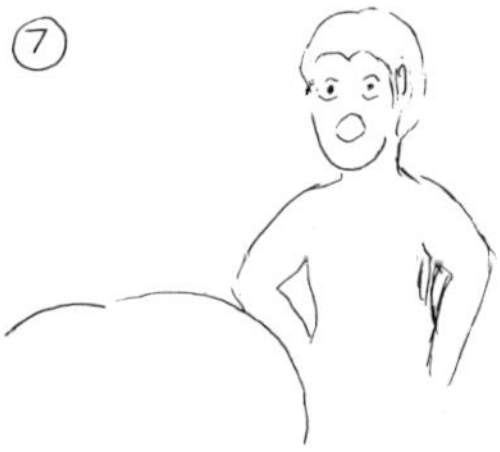

'Talks?' said Adrian. Edward came up with some pretty weird things sometimes, but this was weirder than most. He must have been watching too many cartoons on TV.

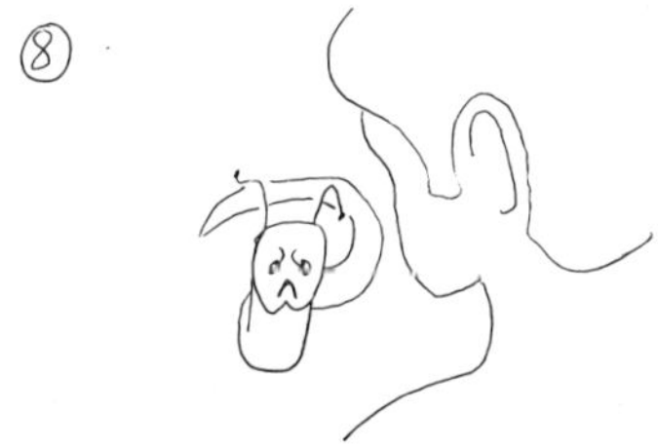

'It's not a worm, it's a caterpillar, you twit.' Adrian felt quite sure about this now. 'And caterpillars don't talk.' 'Talks,' said Edward, firmly.

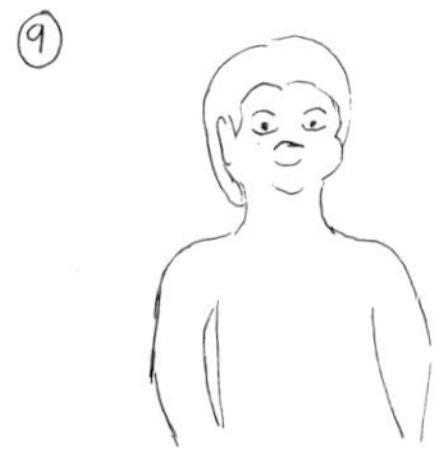

Adrian sighed. 'All right, have it your own way. Morning, caterpillar, if you are a caterpillar.'

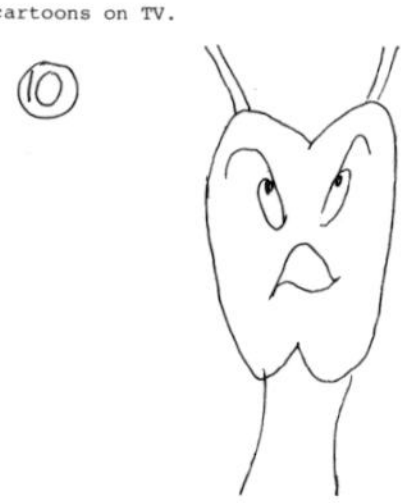

'Good morning,' said the caterpillar.

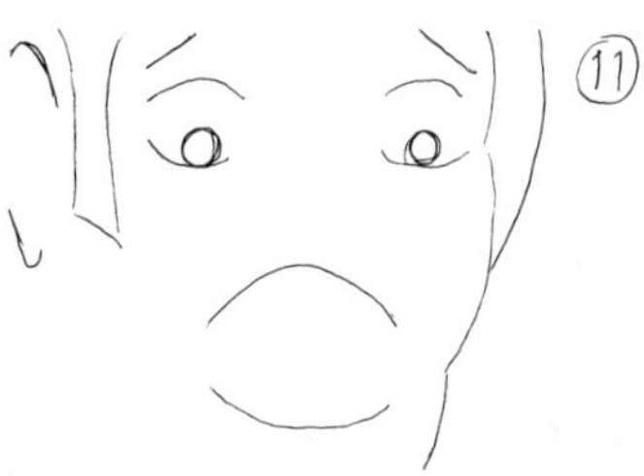

'P-p-pardon?' said Adrian.

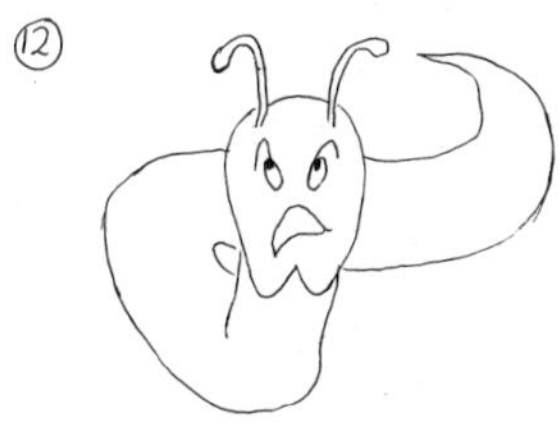

'I said "Good morning". Really, you young beings should clear out your hearing apparatus.'

Part of the storyboard for the author's single-projector programme *Guess Who's Coming to Dinner.* Some of the actual photographs from the sequence can be seen on p. 49.

uses a mixture of dramatic close-ups (such as Adrian's reaction to the talking alien) and explanatory long shots (such as the two children looking at the alien). In Chapter 5 I shall be talking about this subject in more detail, but for the moment you may find a few guidelines useful when you start to shoot your first programme.

1 Don't stay with one kind of shot. You must vary the shots as much as you vary the pace. The different types of shot, ranging from long shots to close-ups, are shown on p. 48. Use the full range, or your shows may become boring.

2 Learn how to build sequences. This programme opens with a long shot of Edward from the back, then a close-up of Edward's face, chewing, then another close-up of Adrian's disapproving frown. Only then do we have a 'two-shot' that shows where they are (in the garden) and how close to each other they are standing. In other words, the sequence starts in close-up and moves out.

3 Take care with composition and camera angles. During the conversation with Caterpillar, notice how the shots are framed. Only the two boys and the alien appear in shot — anything else would be distracting. And notice how the camera is tilted up or down to give the impression that we are looking through the eyes of the alien or of the boys.

Each of the shots in the storyboard has been composed in the way it has for a reason. As an exercise — and for fun — see if you can work out *why* I planned the shots the way I did. There are no prizes, and no answers at the back; but it may help you to start thinking about your own shots in the same way.

And once you've got the hang of it, you won't be *able* to make Boring Slide Shows!

Stage 4: Presentation

This show was made, as I said earlier, to be shown on a single projector with someone reading the commentary aloud from a prepared script. Notice that I thought about this even before I started drawing up the storyboard. Presentation is *important*. It's the only thing your audience sees. If you read your script badly, they are not going to care how brilliantly it was structured or how well it was written. If you created the world's most beautiful storyboard they won't care either — they will never see it. And if you are careless about the presentation, showing slides crookedly, upside-down, wrong way round or out of focus, they are not going to care how good the pictures really are. They will simply remember what they saw.

So the whole of the next chapter is about presentation. And because presentation is something you have to think about as soon as you start to plan a programme, we will also be looking very hard at the *way* that you write a script. If you are working by yourself, with limited equipment, your work will stand or fall on your ability to reach your audience. That's a challenge — it is also excellent practice. If you can succeed as a one-man band, you are well on the way to becoming a professional.

3 The one-man band

You're facing your very first audience, and you are about to present your first important slide show. You are feeling nervous, you are desperately hoping they will like what you have done, and you are desperately hoping that nothing will go wrong. At this stage, of course, it's far too late to worry. But take comfort. Although nothing in this world is guaranteed, there are ways of making sure that your worst nightmares never come true.

For the moment, let's assume you are still working with the basic equipment: a projector and yourself. I have often taken comfort from hiding behind my equipment and adjusting things. You can't. Everyone is looking at you with a rather blank expression, waiting for you to entertain them.

To succeed, there are a few very simple little tricks you will need to learn.

Who are you talking to?

In the last chapter we looked at some ideas for programmes, and saw how a simple programme could be put together. And the very first thing we discussed was involving the audience, and thinking about who they were likely to be. For instance, an audience of senior citizens will be annoyed if they can't hear you. So you will have to talk clearly, slowly and fairly loud — but not too loud, or they'll feel insulted! Schoolchildren never like being treated as 'children'. Treat them as young adults — they love it. In fact, you will never present the same programme in precisely the same way to two different audiences. And the changes will sometimes go much deeper than mere tone of voice or angle of approach — they may well affect the content of the programme itself.

The successful slide-show presenter has a whole series of different programmes up his sleeve. There may be a pretty, poetic

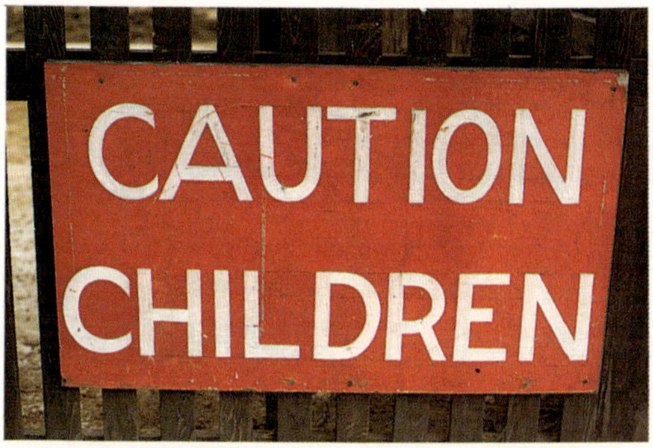

Children have little patience with slide shows! Give them short, colourful programmes with plenty of variety and plenty of excitement, but never underestimate their intelligence.

If you see your audiences like this, you're not alone — but it's worth learning how to win and hold their interest, and once you do you'll find them responsive and appreciative.

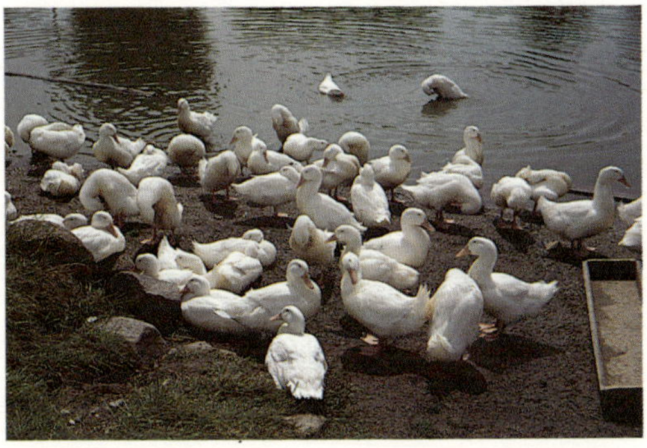

programme with very little commentary for the Old People's Club, and a fast-paced, action-packed sequence for the local school. He'll have his most pictorial sequence ready for the Camera Club, together perhaps with an experimental programme that may interest other club members aiming to test out the limits of slide work. For the church he might have a programme about someone like Francis of Assisi, perhaps based around holiday pictures. And for the gardening club there might be a pleasant but imaginative sequence featuring plenty of flower close-ups.

I am not suggesting for a moment that you will want to make all these programmes, or talk to all these audiences. Obviously you must make programmes that interest *you*. Do anything else, and your lack of knowledge and enthusiasm may well come through to the audience — which means guaranteed failure. On the other hand, when you're making programmes do try to think about the people who might want to see them, even if those people are only your own family and friends.

The face in the crowd

Talking about 'an audience' is dangerous. It tends to make you think of a large mass of people all reacting in exactly the same way to everything you present to them. That kind of thinking turns you into a lecturer — a bad lecturer. You are an entertainer, and your job is to remember that your audience consists of many individual people, each reacting in his or her own way to what you are showing. Whether you are running a fully automatic six-projector spectacular or talking your way through a series of slides presented on a battered second-hand magic lantern, it is always worth striking up some sort of personal relationship with your audience before you start. And that means talking to them as individuals. Suppose you're going to show them a programme about the Lake District. Before you start, find out if anyone comes from that area, or has been there on a visit. With luck, someone will say something you can turn into an introduction to the programme — and you will in any case have set up a relaxed atmosphere that is bound to help make your show a success.

Of course, these things can go too far. If the atmosphere is *too* relaxed, people will start to interrupt the show with questions. That will throw you out of gear, and break up the flow of the programme. Better to tell them beforehand that you will be very happy to answer questions — *afterwards*.

In the end, the best guarantee against interruptions is an absorbing and interesting programme. In the last chapter we looked at the overall structure of a programme: hook, development, and resolution. Now it's time to put some flesh on those bones, and to consider how you can prepare and deliver a script that will hold and entertain your audience. And that's not just a matter of structure — it's also a matter of style.

That was no lady . . .

Watch a successful stand-up comic and you'll soon see why he's successful. He knows how to hold an audience. And quite often he does it in the way I just described, by talking directly to individual people. But aside from that, he's also developed a natural style. He talks to them in an easy, conversational way that sounds relaxed and relaxes them.

That style is the essence of a successful programme.

This book, as you may have noticed, tends to be written in a rather conversational style. I use words like 'you're' and 'I'm'. And I'm not above beginning sentences with 'and'. I write like this because I've been hopelessly corrupted by years of slide-show scripting. I can't easily write any other way. In fact, most of what I write sounds pretty natural if it's read aloud. Try this paragraph and see.

If a style like this doesn't come easily to you, or if the ghost of your old English teacher comes up to haunt you, then it may be worth investing in a cheap cassette tape recorder (or, if you can afford it, an expensive reel-to-reel tape recorder) and skipping ahead to the next chapter. In any case, I'll be coming back to this subject later on — it's extremely important.

Most of us are not gifted with marvellous memories, so you will almost certainly be reading your commentary (if you have one at all) from a prepared script. Never fall into the trap of writing a script without reading it as well — and by 'reading' I mean reading *aloud*. If what you have written *sounds* wrong — if it doesn't sound like normal, relaxed, conversational English — then change it. And when you've finished, read it through from beginning to end, several times, until you are sure you can deliver it without any hesitations, mistakes, or deviations. Rather as if you were entering the radio panel game *Just a Minute*. Which brings me to another important topic: length.

Small is beautiful

Many slide shows are too long. Very few are too short. In fact the easiest way to keep an audience happy is to present them with an assortment of programmes, none of which lasts much longer than five minutes. Short shows need less planning, less scripting and less photography. The gaps between shows can be used to answer questions. A selection of different shows gives you a better chance of putting on something to interest everyone, or almost everyone, in your audience. You can arrange for a few programmes that won't need a commentary to be shown when you want to rest your voice. And you have at least a chance to be flexible — if one kind of programme doesn't

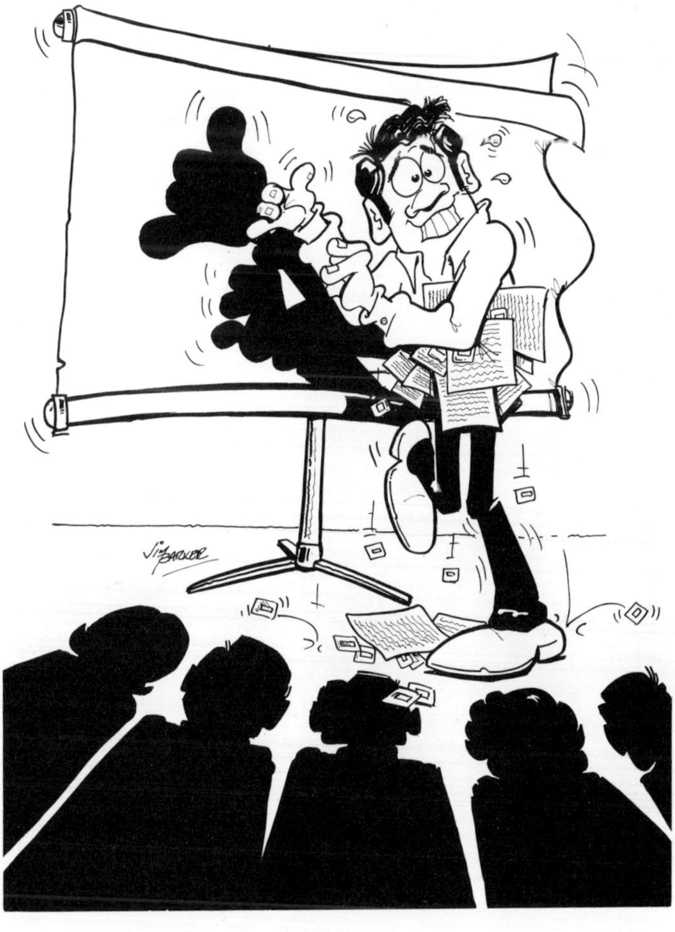

seem to be going down too well, pull out a couple of spares that have a different approach, and try them instead. Above all, your audience will never have time to be bored. Your aim should be to leave them clamouring for 'just one more' — and then say you'll be delighted to show them some more. Next time.

The trouble with a short slide show is that it has to be just right. Mistakes glare.

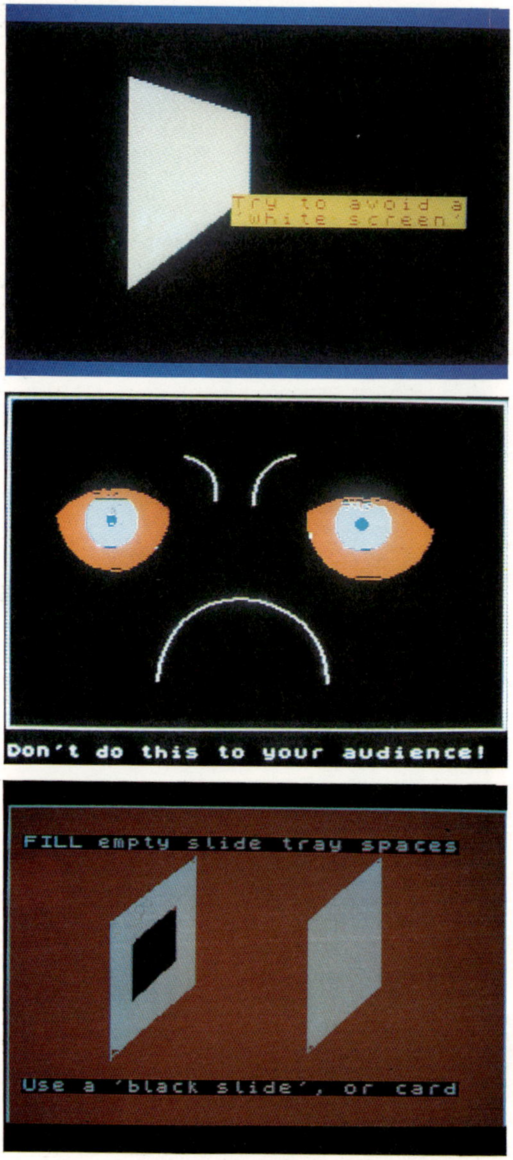

Shots from *How to Make a Slide Show*.

Woolliness shows. Bad pictures are remembered, because the audience will not have enough time to forget them. As a result, short shows often demand as much effort from you as the long half-hour spectaculars. On the other hand, you *are* learning a new and potentially very profitable skill. Quite aside from the fact that you are far less likely to produce yet another Boring Slide Show.

It'll be all right on the night . . .

Part of your job, and a part that is very important to your audience, is to be professional as a presenter. Of course, Murphy's Law applies, and anything that can go wrong sooner or later will go wrong. You can't help that — but you can be prepared.

The first essential is rehearsal. Practise delivering your programme several times before the day itself. Be confident that you can do it — this helps you as much as it will please the audience. Make sure all your slides are marked as shown opposite, to minimise the risk of putting one in upside-down or back-to-front. If your slides are in a magazine, be sure to check for sequence and alignment just before you leave for the show. And check your projector. Make sure it has no operating problems, and try, if you can, to have a backup available (perhaps a friend's projector). Always carry the essentials — spare fuses, spare lamps, a screwdriver, and a soft brush for cleaning the slides. Just as important, *know how to use them*. Be thoroughly familiar with your equipment, so you can deal with any problems *quickly*.

Setting up a public slide show demands care and pre-planning. If you do not have a screen of your own, you must make sure that one is available at the venue. If it isn't, arrange to borrow one, or hire one from your local audio-visual dealer (try Yellow Pages if the camera shop can't help you). Ideally, visit the venue at least a week before the show and check it out for yourself. That way you will know where the screen will be, and how high the projector will have to stand to reach it.

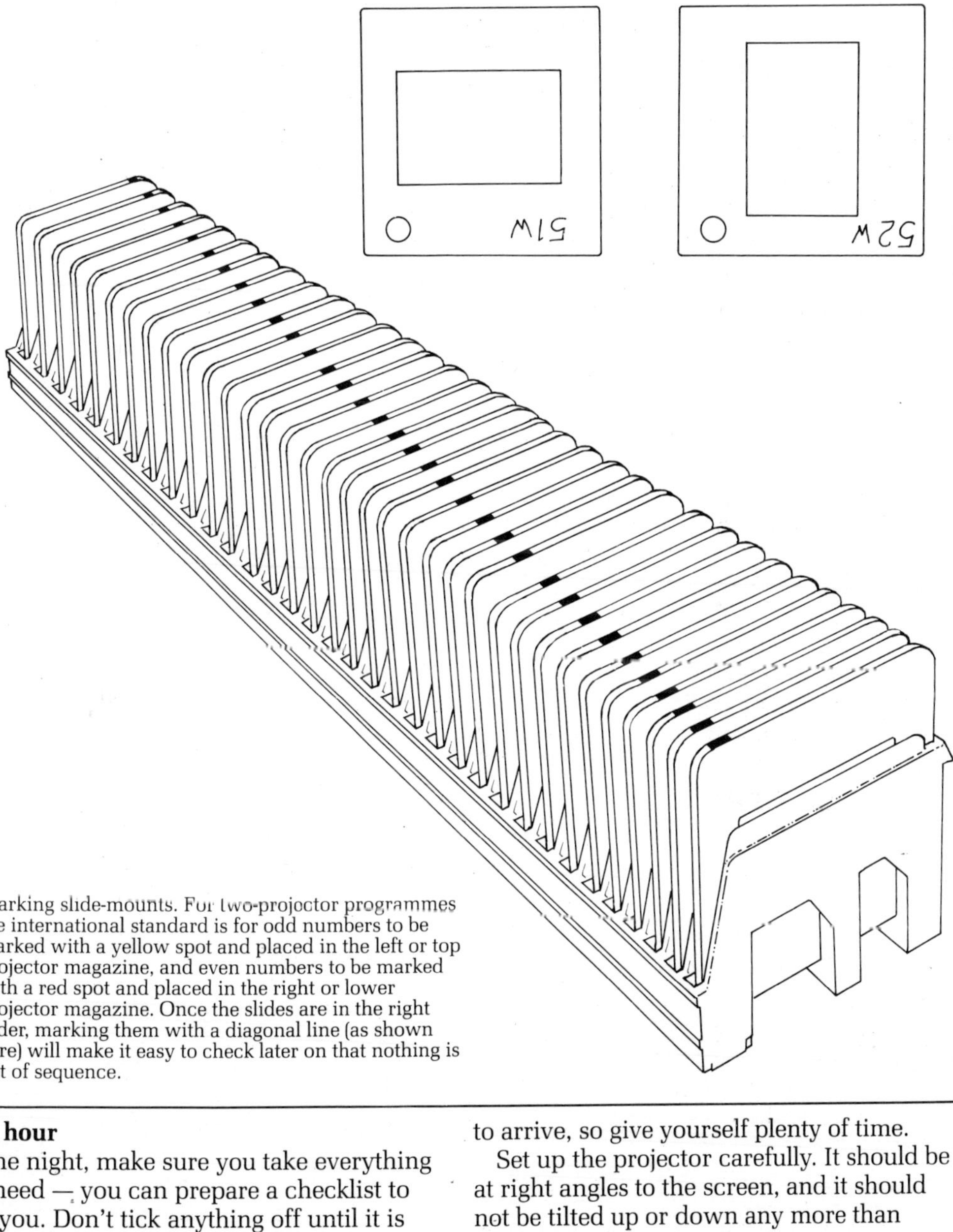

Marking slide-mounts. For two-projector programmes the international standard is for odd numbers to be marked with a yellow spot and placed in the left or top projector magazine, and even numbers to be marked with a red spot and placed in the right or lower projector magazine. Once the slides are in the right order, marking them with a diagonal line (as shown here) will make it easy to check later on that nothing is out of sequence.

Zero hour

On the night, make sure you take everything you need — you can prepare a checklist to help you. Don't tick anything off until it is actually in the car! Make sure you have a good, long extension cable with a plug that will suit the mains supply at the venue. If necessary, fit an Adaptall-type plug that can be adjusted to suit different types of socket.

Try to get to the venue early — you should aim to be set up before the audience begins to arrive, so give yourself plenty of time.

Set up the projector carefully. It should be at right angles to the screen, and it should not be tilted up or down any more than absolutely necessary. The picture it produces should fill as large as possible an area of the screen — but if your show contains a mixture of upright and horizontal pictures, remember to allow room for both. Try to arrange your cabling so people will not trip over it; an accident could be

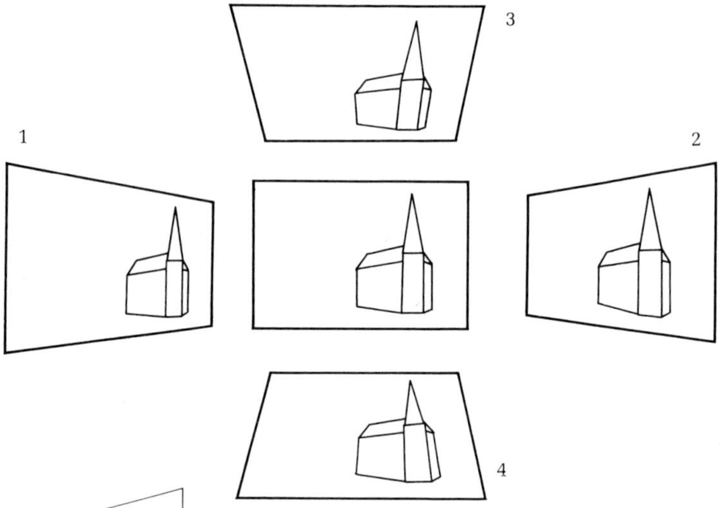

Keystoning is a distortion of the screen image caused by bad projector alignment.
(1) Projector twisted to the left
(2) Projector twisted to the right
(3) Projector tilted upwards
(4) Projector tilted downwards
In twin-projector shows a certain amount of keystoning is inevitable.

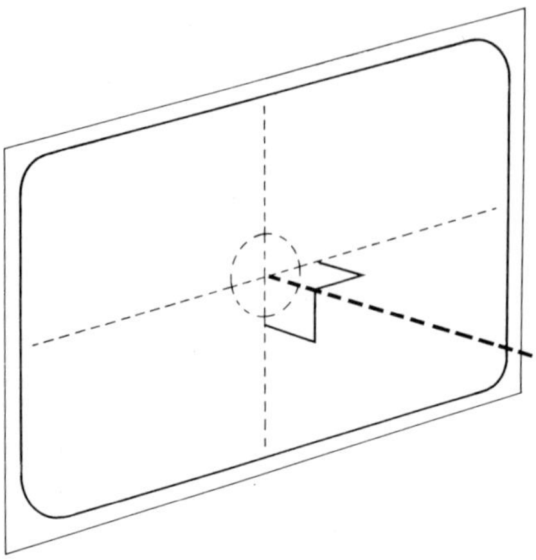

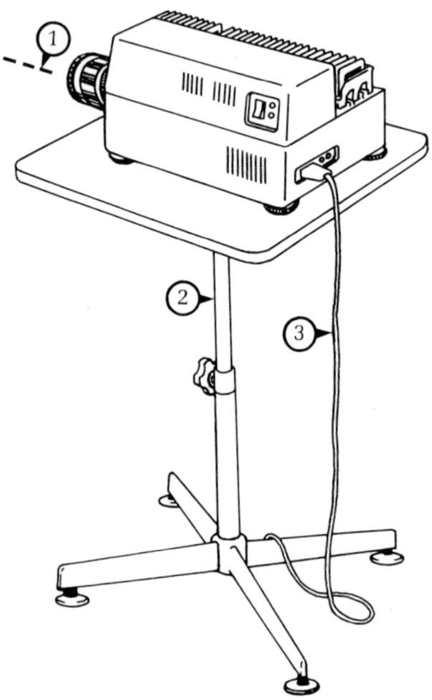

The three golden rules for good projection:
(1) Aim the projector directly at the centre of the screen, and parallel to it both vertically and horizontally.
(2) Use a firm, stable stand that will safely provide as much height as you need.
(3) Watch out for trailing cables — avoid connecting them until it is necessary to do so.

unpleasant both for the victim and for your projector. For the same reason, never plug in your equipment until the audience is seated and settled. Try to arrange the seating so that no one has their view of the screen blocked by the projector, and no one is sitting too far to one side of the screen — an ideal seating layout is shown below, and in Appendix 4 you'll find a chart showing the size of picture produced by different lenses at different distances from the screen.

Before the audience arrives, remember to check that no one will cast a shadow on the screen when they sit down — and allow for tall people! If your projector is small, it will probably be better to place it near the front of the hall, or your picture could be very dim. If possible, arrange for the hall to be properly blacked out. Stray light, especially on a long summer evening, can ruin a good programme.

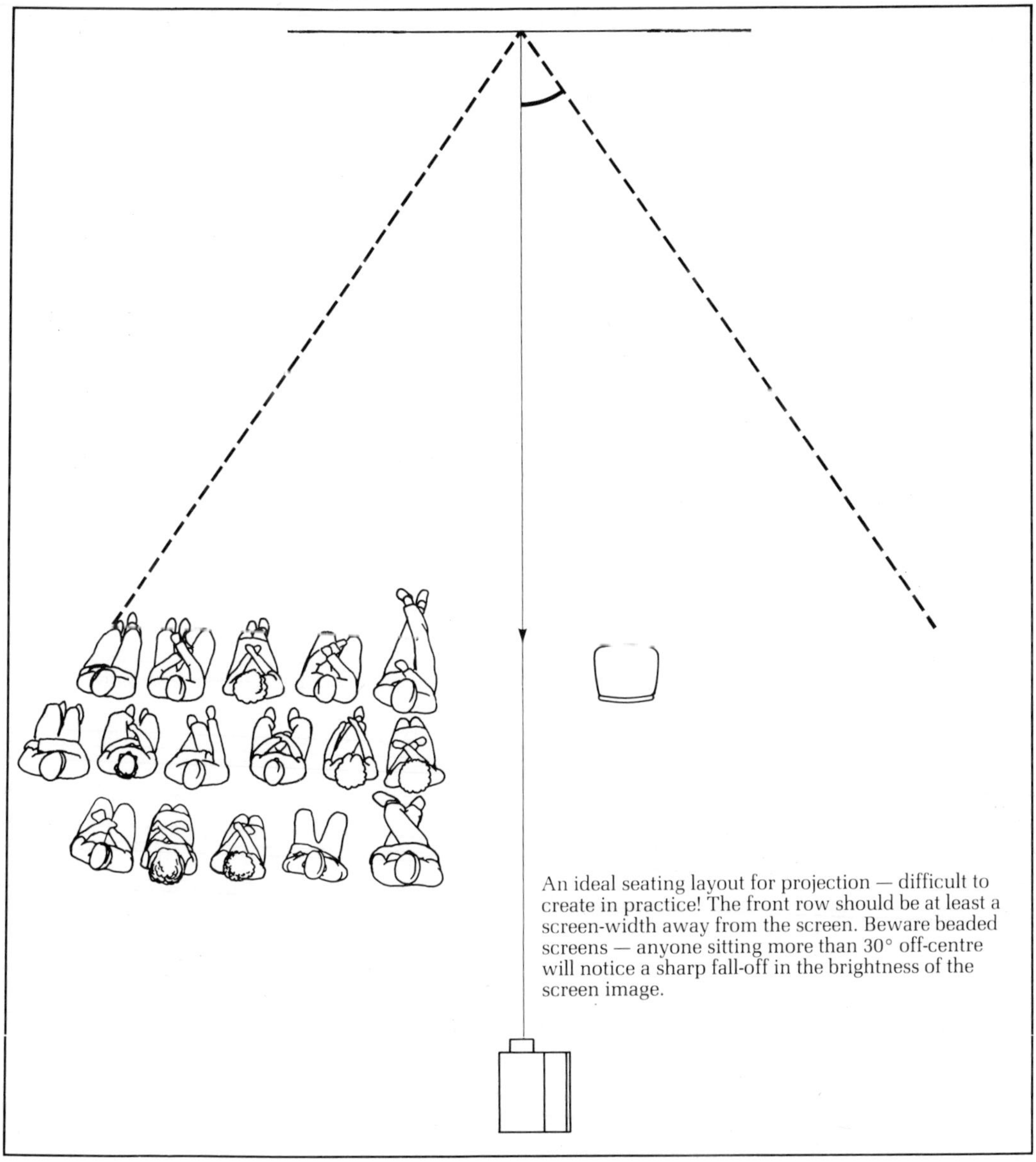

An ideal seating layout for projection — difficult to create in practice! The front row should be at least a screen-width away from the screen. Beware beaded screens — anyone sitting more than 30° off-centre will notice a sharp fall-off in the brightness of the screen image.

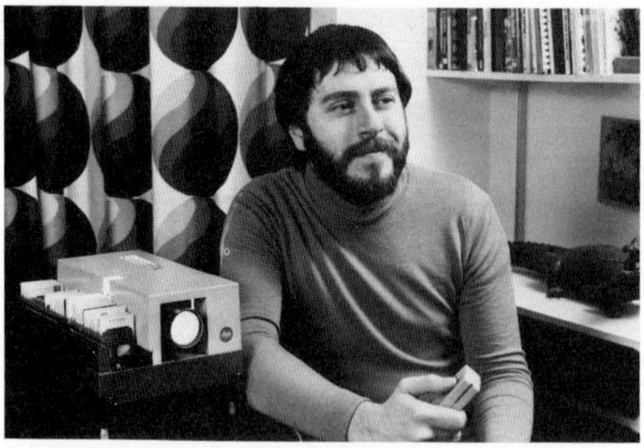
A remote control lead is a useful accessory. With an extension cable you can talk to even the largest audience from the front of the hall while keeping full control.

Useful extras

If you are delivering a live commentary, consider the advantages of a remote-control projector. A long remote-control lead will allow you to speak from a point near the screen, and facing your audience. It may well be worth the extra expense, and such a projector can probably be used later on as one of a matched pair for twin-projection work. If you are using a written script, make sure that your writing is large, neat and legible, even in poor light, and use a clipboard or a file to keep the sheets in order and stop them falling out. And *number the sheets*. There is nothing worse than losing your script halfway through a show and spending the next ten minutes trying to sort the pages into their proper order. Remember to take a small pocket torch to help you read your notes — you can even fasten it to the clipboard. And remember to put in a fresh set of batteries before every show — it pays!

If you are feeling ambitious, you might arrange to build a small portable lectern with its own lamp, shaded from the audience, and a stand to carry your notes. But remember that the lectern will need power as well — so again, make sure you have enough cable, and make sure you have all the necessary adaptors.

Making gremlins work for you

If disaster does strike, take it calmly. Projector lamps will always blow at the most inconvenient possible moment — accept that it has happened, tell the audience what is going on, and get someone to turn on the lights. By now you should be well drilled in how to replace a lamp, so go through the routine you have practised, settle the audience down, and start the show again, either from the beginning or from a logical point in the middle. Handle the situation calmly and professionally, and you can turn the disaster into a personal triumph. Audiences admire professionalism — and the bigger the problem, the better your chance to show them just how good you are.

Taking the next step

Before long, anyone performing live one-projector programmes will find himself (or herself) faced with two enormous temptations. The first is an overwhelming desire to tape-record the commentary. The second is an almost equally overwhelming desire to acquire another projector and some means of dissolving from one to the other. There is no doubt at all that the real art of slide-tape begins with two projectors, and that dissolving slides can successfully distract the audience from even the simplest of soundtracks. Equally, though, there is no doubt that most households are far more likely to have one projector and a hi-fi system than two projectors and a little black box of specialist electronics. This is why the next chapter deals with tape recording, and the one after that with twin projection.

If you are one of the lucky few who can start thinking about twin projection straight away, please do not ignore Chapter 4. You probably have most of the equipment you need to make full use of it.

If, on the other hand, twin projection seems little more than a pipe dream, take heart. Go down to your local camera club and make yourself known — and popular! The club may well have access to the equipment you need, and if they can't get it for you then one of their members may be prepared to let you try his. The same goes for sound equipment — but let it be said straight away that you can start work on the next chapter with nothing more complicated than a simple cassette tape recorder.

4

Getting it taped

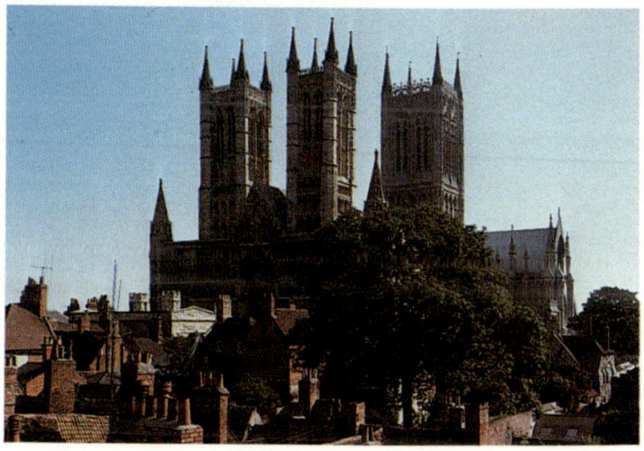

Darkness. In the distance, the sound of horses and wagons, drawing nearer, approaching, passing — and suddenly, towering high above the surrounding houses, the twin western towers of Lincoln Cathedral appear on the screen . . .

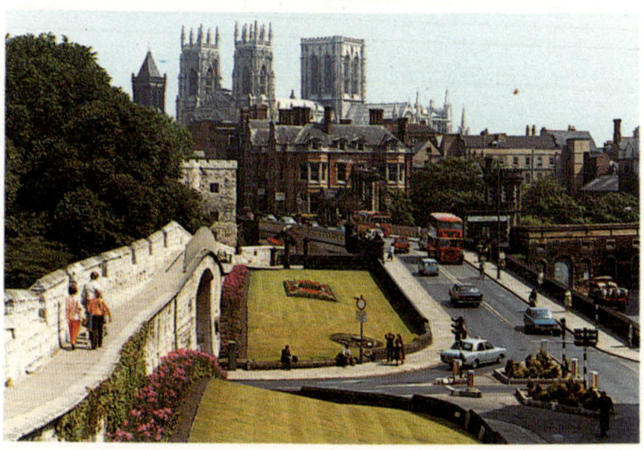

A view of York from the city walls, backed by the everyday sounds of the city. 'This is a very special place — a place where 1900 years of history are caught up in every building, every square foot of ground. In the streets of York, you can almost hear the voices out of its past . . .' And then the everyday sounds fade away, a deep, throbbing note fades in onto the soundtrack, and out of the past comes the voice of a long-dead Roman emperor. . .

A set of long, slow chords building slowly on a massive, echoing church organ. Out of the blackness on the screen comes the glittering spiral of a distant galaxy, framed in black. Then a globular cluster. And then — as though seen from millions upon millions of miles away — the earth and moon . . .

Three examples of what can be done with a prerecorded soundtrack, a little imagination — and a 24-track professional sound studio. They're really only here to whet your appetite, and to convince you (if you needed convincing) that a good soundtrack can be just as important to a successful slide show as good pictures.

Each of those programmes uses a different approach. The Lincoln show relies on sound effects. The York programme relies, at first, on the narrator — the complex electronic background effects are only there to highlight the arrival of the 'voice from the past'. The third programme uses music only — but the effect, when combined with the opening pictures, is extremely powerful.

Commentary, music, sound effects: the three elements of any fully-developed soundtrack. In this chapter we'll see how they can be used, even with the simplest equipment, to add a new dimension to your slide shows.

Talking to yourself

At this stage I suggest you find a quiet and private place where no one is likely to hear you or disturb you. Because the first technique you need to learn before you start recording the Greatest Slide Show Ever Made is talking to yourself.

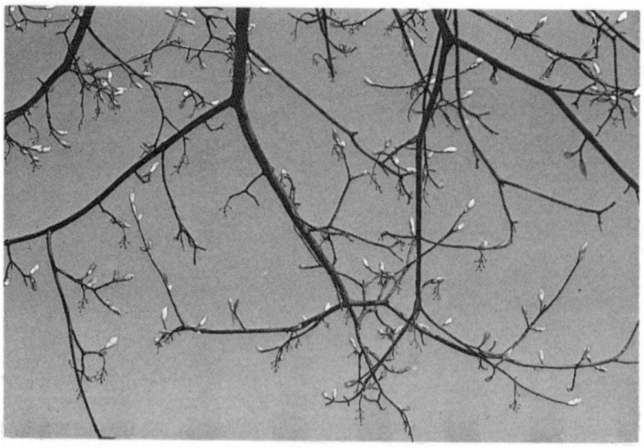

Birdsong

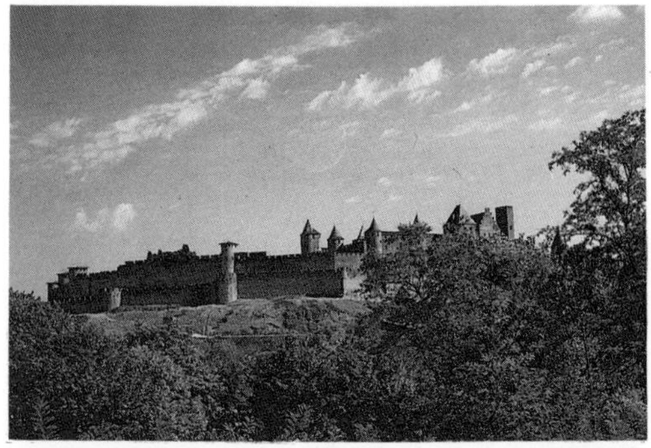

Lark singing . . .

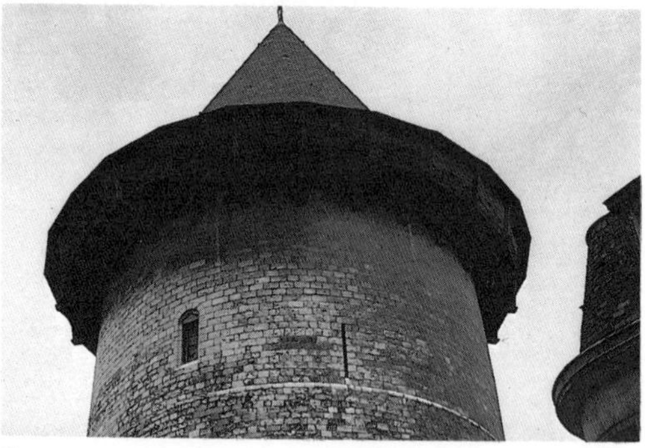

Crows cawing. Distant murmuring voices

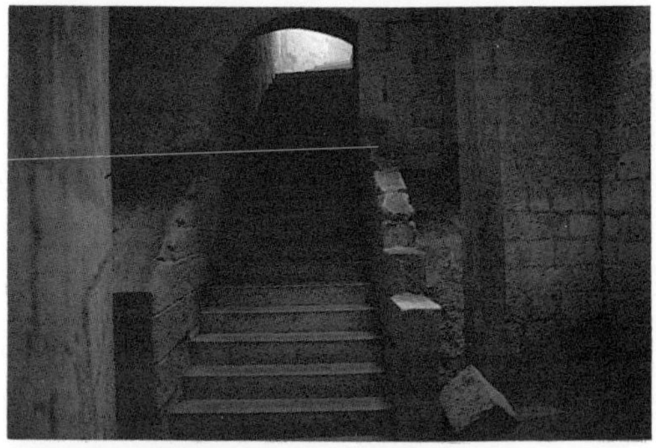

Footsteps echoing. Heavy door is unlocked

At the moment it doesn't much matter what kind of tape recorder you have. It may be a semi-professional reel-to-reel machine with a list of features as long as your arm. It may be the cassette recorder bit of the bedside radio. Whatever it is, just put its microphone within range of a chair you find comfortable, set it to record, start the tape, sit back, and talk to it about anything that happens to come into your head. If it helps, shut your eyes and imagine your best friend sitting just a few feet away, drinking in every word in rapt silence.

Once you stop feeling silly you will find this rather pleasant. Your imaginary friend doesn't talk back, interrupt, or ask awkward questions at the wrong moment. Then there's the hypnotic brilliance of what you're saying. The delightful sound of your own voice. Maybe you don't even notice when the tape runs out. Never mind. Just carry on till you feel like stopping, then wind back the tape and listen to what the *machine* heard.

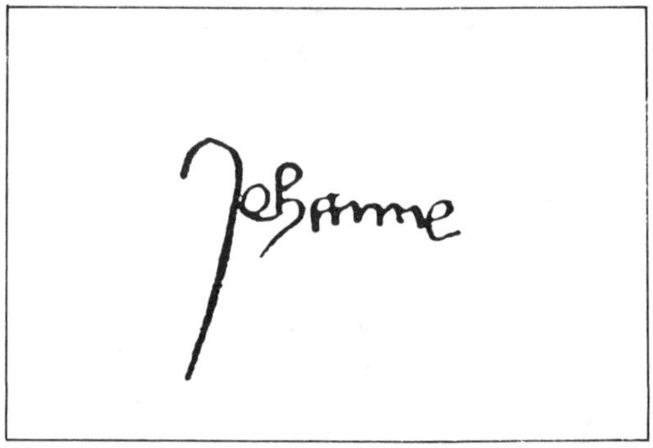

Her name was Jehanne, also called La Pucelle. We call her. . .

At this point you could be in for a shock. When I first tried it I couldn't believe that the piping treble coming out of the loudspeaker was really me. Admittedly I was ten years old at the time, but it was still a shock. It didn't sound right. In fact, it never does. The other major shock, unless you are a remarkably good impromptu speaker, is the staggering amount of hesitation you will hear — every sentence

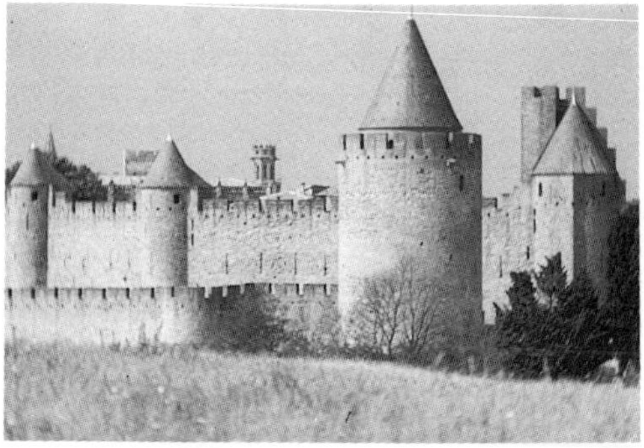

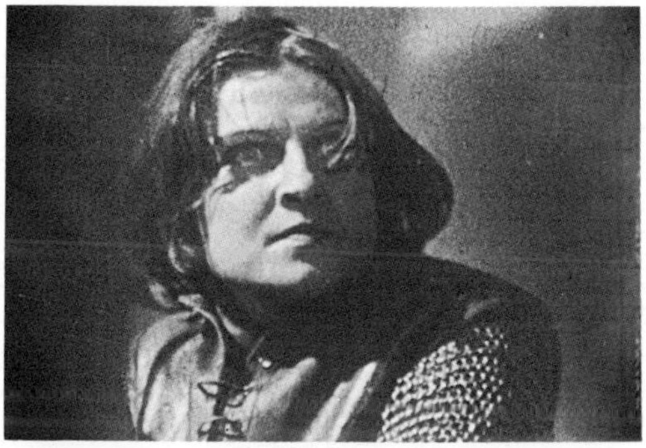

GIRL'S VOICE: No! I stand by what I have said! If I stood in the fire itself, I wouldn't say anything else!

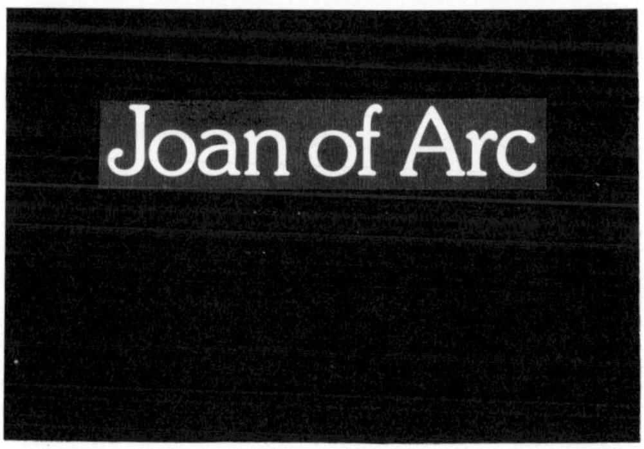

Joan of Arc.

will be peppered with 'ums' and 'ers'. It's normal — but it's also completely unacceptable in a slide-show commentary.

But count your blessings. If you have been talking like that to your audiences, imagine how *they* must have felt! Now you can put things right, and make a commentary that sounds exciting, flowing and completely professional.

In Chapter 3 we looked at ways of writing

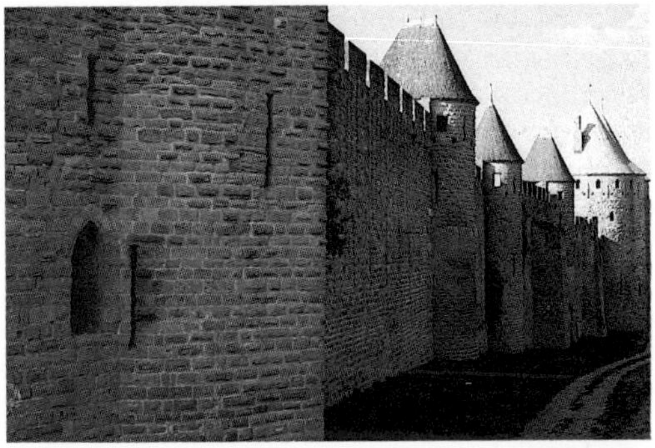

VOICE: In France, in the year 1431, a 19-year-old girl sat alone before 40 judges, accused of witchcraft and heresy.

your commentary so it sounds natural. A tape recorder helps you to check that it really does — like your camera, it doesn't lie (unless you fool it a little first!). And you can also see if your words really match the pictures. If you're reading from a prepared script, however well you know it, you tend to look at the script, not the pictures. If the commentary is taped you can watch to see precisely how your pictures fit it — and sometimes you may find that they don't. You can check timing, too — and that can make or break a show. Look at the sequence shown on these two pages. If the title slide comes early, the surprise effect of revealing Joan's name is destroyed. If the title slide is late, it's an anticlimax. If it appears at precisely the same moment as the word 'Joan', the surprise effect is amplified. Always be conscious of timing — it becomes even more important if you take the plunge and buy that second projector.

But your commentary needs good timing, too. Like the stand-up comic, you have to get the measure of your audiences. How long does it take them to react to what you say? How long before they laugh, or sigh, or grunt with surprise? If they do none of these things, your timing may be at fault. Or it may be your delivery.

How do you read your script? Do you sound as if you meant every word? If not, then your audience won't believe what you're trying to tell them. The most natural-sounding commentary ever written will have no effect except boredom if it's delivered in a low, flat monotone.

The trouble is, most of us are naturally reticent. We don't throw ourselves and our emotions all over the room. So when we read something aloud, we tend to do it as though what we were saying somehow embarrassed us.

So find that quiet corner again. Pick a poem or story you really like, and read it into your tape recorder. Then listen. Hard. Try to imagine how your favourite actor or actress would read it. Do you sound anything like them? If not, why not? What's different?

Very probably, your voice is too *level*. Actors, especially radio actors, put feeling into their voice by moving it up and down in pitch, making it louder and softer, or by varying the speed at which they read the words. Try it. To help you, I've included a diagram of the way I read one of my scripts. Obviously this is personal to me, but try it anyway. Does it sound more exciting, more as though you meant it? Try again — exaggerate a little more if anything. Now play back the tape. You may well find that what seemed over the top to you as you read the script sounds all right on tape — unless you've gone *too* far! Practise with some extracts of your own choice until you hit the level that sounds right. There are no hard and fast rules about this — you may well have to use different levels of 'drama' in different programmes. The only real crime is to be boring.

If you are using a cheaper cassette deck this could be the moment you fall foul of ARL — Automatic Recording Level. This neat electronic device alters the recording level of the machine according to the strength of signal coming through the inputs. It will certainly stop you recording at too high a level — but as soon as you stop talking, ARL boosts the recording level in a desperate search for something to record. This causes nasty little surges of background

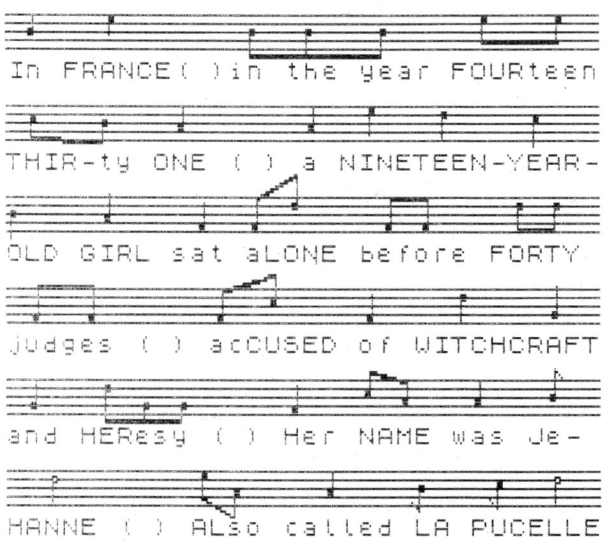

Reading a script. This extract from *Joan of Arc* shows emphasis (by capital letters) and a rough idea of rise and fall in pitch (the musical notation must not be taken literally!). Incidentally, this is an example of the computer-generated graphics mentioned on p. 109.

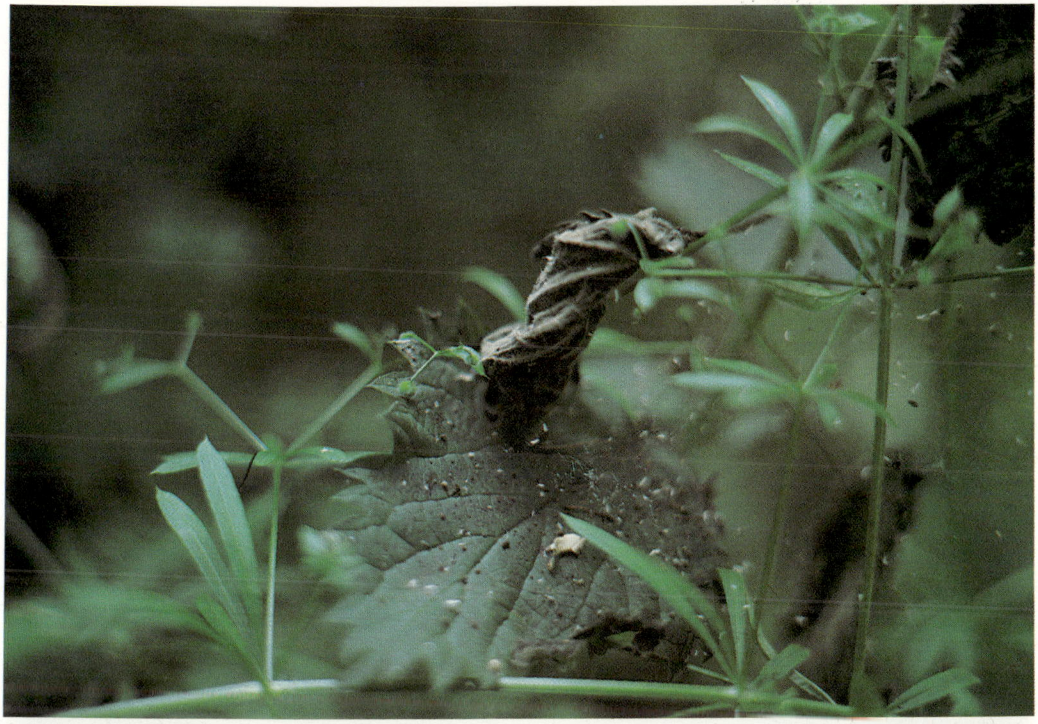

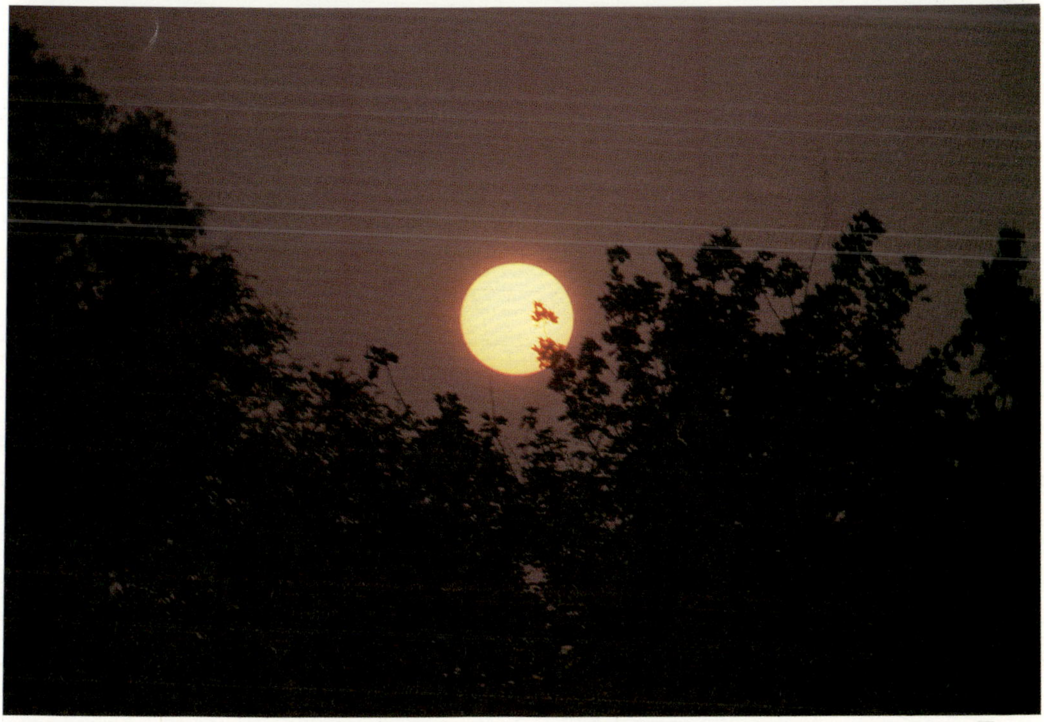

Atmosphere shots from *Witchwood*. With the addition of Tim Phillips' sinister music score, even these simple pictures begin to carry a suggestion of menace.

noise that become horribly evident as soon as you try to amplify your recording on a more sophisticated setup. For really serious work, ARL machines are a dead loss. Controlling recording level yourself is harder, and may lead to awful mistakes, but it's still the only way to do the job properly — and it's a skill well worth learning.

A final word on commentaries. Listen to the way the professionals do it, on TV, radio, disc and tape. Don't be afraid to copy a style you like — in time you'll develop your own. However, sooner or later you — and your audience — will get tired of the sound of your voice. Your soundtrack will need something else. Silence is one (much underrated) possibility. But the next logical choice is music.

Music, maestro!

Your choice of music could make or break a show. The right one may leave the audience crying their eyes out or rolling in the aisles with laughter (fine, as long as they were meant to). The wrong choice may irritate them, confuse them, or (horror!) bore them. So how do you choose?

The following six commandments are just for reference. All except the last can be broken, sometimes to excellent effect. But start off by following them to the letter and you will not go too far wrong.

1 Thou shalt not use a piece that has been done to death already. I know the man who first used *I am Sailing* for a show about yachts. That was before it was a hit. He won't use it again.

2 Thou shalt choose music that suits the subject — and not just reasonably well, but extremely well. Take time. Be fussy. Be downright awkward.

3 Thou shalt be willing to use different types of music for different types of show — but within a single show, try to use pieces that sit easily with one another. A hodge-podge of different musical styles is usually more irritating than effective.

4 Whereas it is easy to use too much music, it is harder to use too little.

5 Thou shalt learn to match music with slide changes, pacing them to fit the pace and direction of the music. A well-constructed pictorial sequence can actually heighten the emotional impact of a piece of music. Flicking slides past your audience at twenty a minute over a recording of a funeral march will only work if you *want* them to laugh.

6 Thou shalt at all times and in all places obey the laws of copyright. For details see Appendix 1. Ignore these rules and you make life harder for everyone, besides jeopardising your own chances should you decide to turn professional.

Concerto for slide-projector and . . . ?

In the end, your choice of music is entirely personal. Obviously it will depend a great deal on your own tastes. However, if your tastes are restricted to the current hit parade — or to the more sheltered reaches of classical music — it may be worth trying to broaden them a little. I have seen successful shows that used classical music, chartbound sounds, heavy metal, folk rock, twelve-tone music, electronic music, and music written and performed by the maker of the programme. If you have any talent in this direction, use it — you could save yourself a lot of trouble with copyright clearance! Or see if any of your musical friends are willing to help you, just for the fun of it. Colin

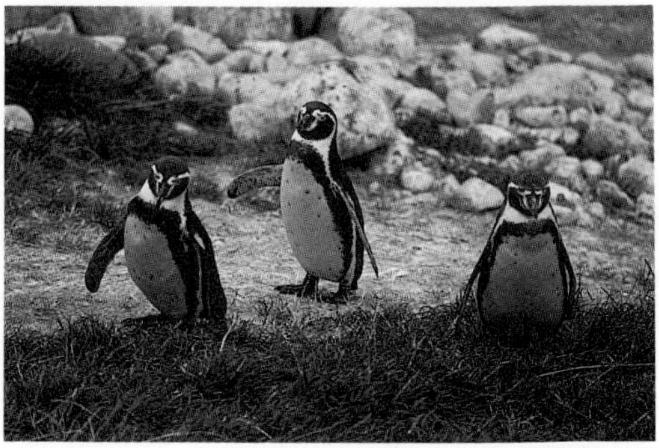

'See? He falls on his face even when he's dressed for the part.'

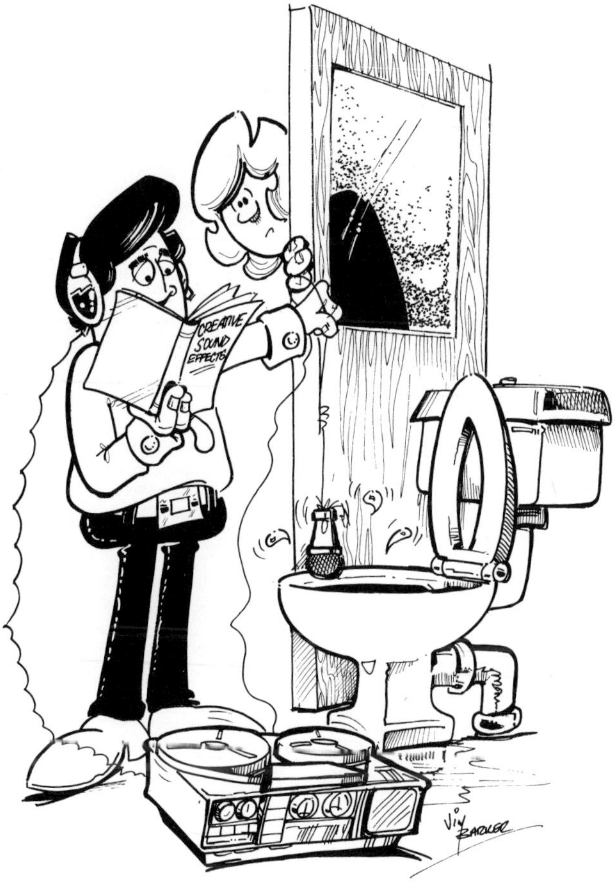

Michaels and Tim Phillips, who created the music score for *Witchwood*, not only gave me a sound that matched the pictures perfectly, but also taught me a lot about the way music is structured, and the many ways in which music and pictures can be linked. It was a very worthwhile experience and I'm very grateful to both of them.

Whatever you do, be open to new ideas, new styles and new associations. My own music collection is a ragbag of records from medieval popular music through most of the intervening centuries via grand opera to almost (but not quite) every different kind of modern music. Your taste in music need not be as perverse and contrary as mine — but remember that just as different audiences like different programmes, so they are likely to enjoy different music. If you can bend enough to accommodate them, and produce a first-class programme at the same time, you are going to be invited back again — and again.

Noises off

Back in Chapter 2 I showed you how sound effects could be used to create an unusual and arresting hook right at the beginning of a programme. This is not normally done, which is just as well. If everybody did it, it would lose its surprise value. Generally speaking, sound effects have three main uses within a show:

1 To help create a believable background (for instance, open country noises behind a commentary that is supposed to have been recorded out of doors).

2 For 'spot effects' (a thunderclap, a doorknob rattling, a train arriving in a station, and so on.)

3 To provide comic relief. (Many sound effects are funny. Others can be made funny by using them creatively.)

All of these uses really belong to the final section of this chapter, which looks at ways of mixing sound effects with music and speech. For the moment, though, let's consider them in isolation.

Sounding effective

A couple of years back the BBC broadcast a radio play called *The Revenge* that had no dialogue whatsoever. It consisted entirely of sound effects. To enjoy it to the full, of course, you needed to listen in stereo, ideally with headphones, but it worked — and worked well.

Few of us have the BBC's recources, yet even with a limited selection of effects you can achieve a surprising amount. For instance, think of animal sounds. Of course, you could use them as background sound for a series of pictures taken at the zoo. But suppose you turn it around? Use some conversations about the animals (either scripted and recorded at home, or picked up surreptitiously on the spot) and run those conversations against pictures of the *animals*. Then use the animal sounds against the pictures of their human (?) visitors. I tried this in a sequence called *Down at the Zoo*.

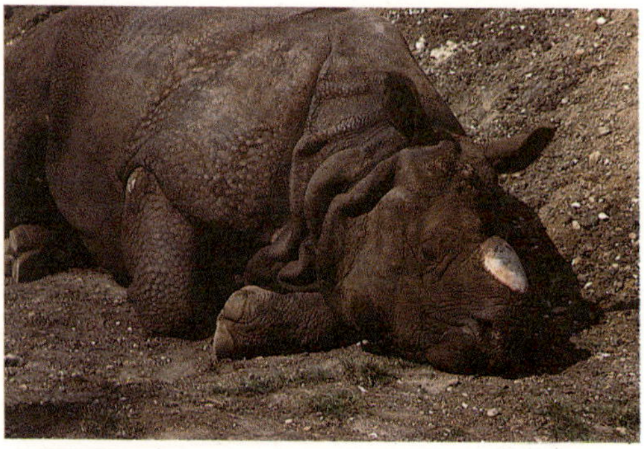

'Nothing like a nice nap in the sun when life seems a bit pointless.'

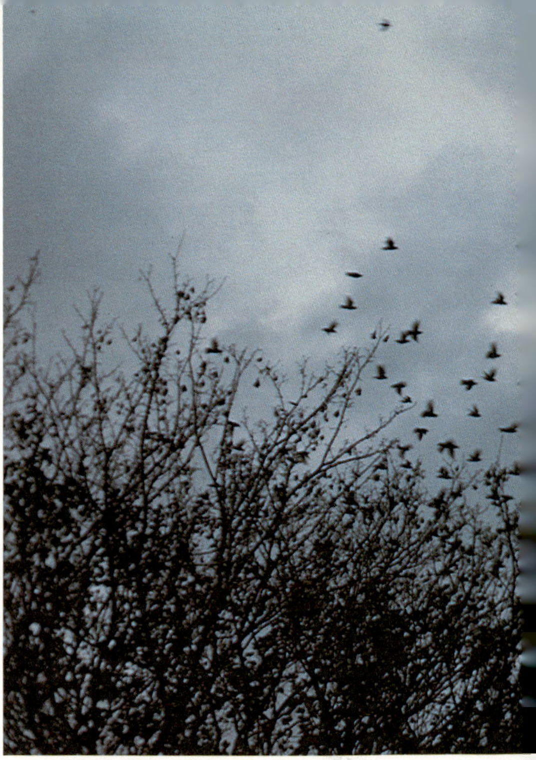

Another possibility is the careful use of selected sounds. One planned version of *Witchwood* used no music at all. There was simply the normal background sound of a wood in spring, with birds singing and a little wind in the trees. As the spring woods change to autumn and die, the birdsong dies with them. Only the wind is left, rising to a higher and higher note.

A range of prerecorded sound effects is available on disc from the BBC and from a number of other sources. Many of these are copyright-free for certain applications — but do check. And don't be afraid to go out and record your own effects. It's not as difficult as it may seem.

Reel magic

It's in this area — sound effects — that reel-to-reel tape decks come into their own. It's perfectly possible to create sound effects using a cassette recorder; it's just a lot more difficult. Cassette decks normally run at only one speed; most reel-to-reel decks offer a choice of speed, allowing you to record a sound at a very fast speed and play it back at a very slow one, or vice versa. A plastic egg-box crunched into oblivion and recorded at

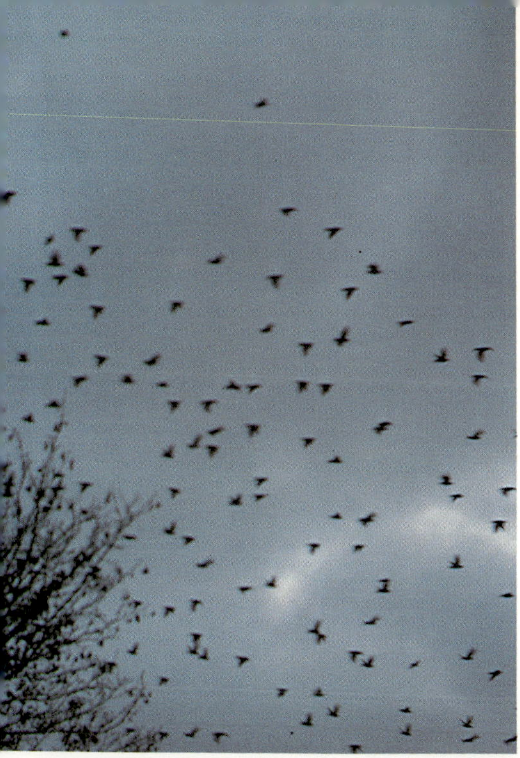

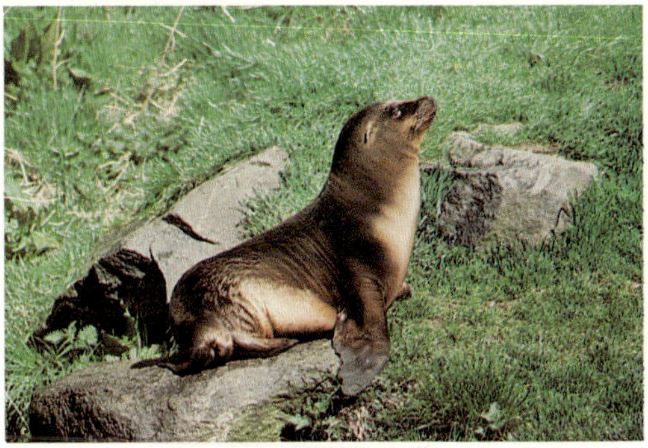

'Frankly, it all smells a bit fishy to me.'

◀ A flock of birds is startled from a tree in an early, sound-effects only, version of *Witchwood*.

The author on location with a Uher Stereo Report at the Rocket 150 Steam Cavalcade. Headphones are a must for checking precisely what is going onto the tape — even here, where some very noisy locomotives were passing within a few feet of the microphones!

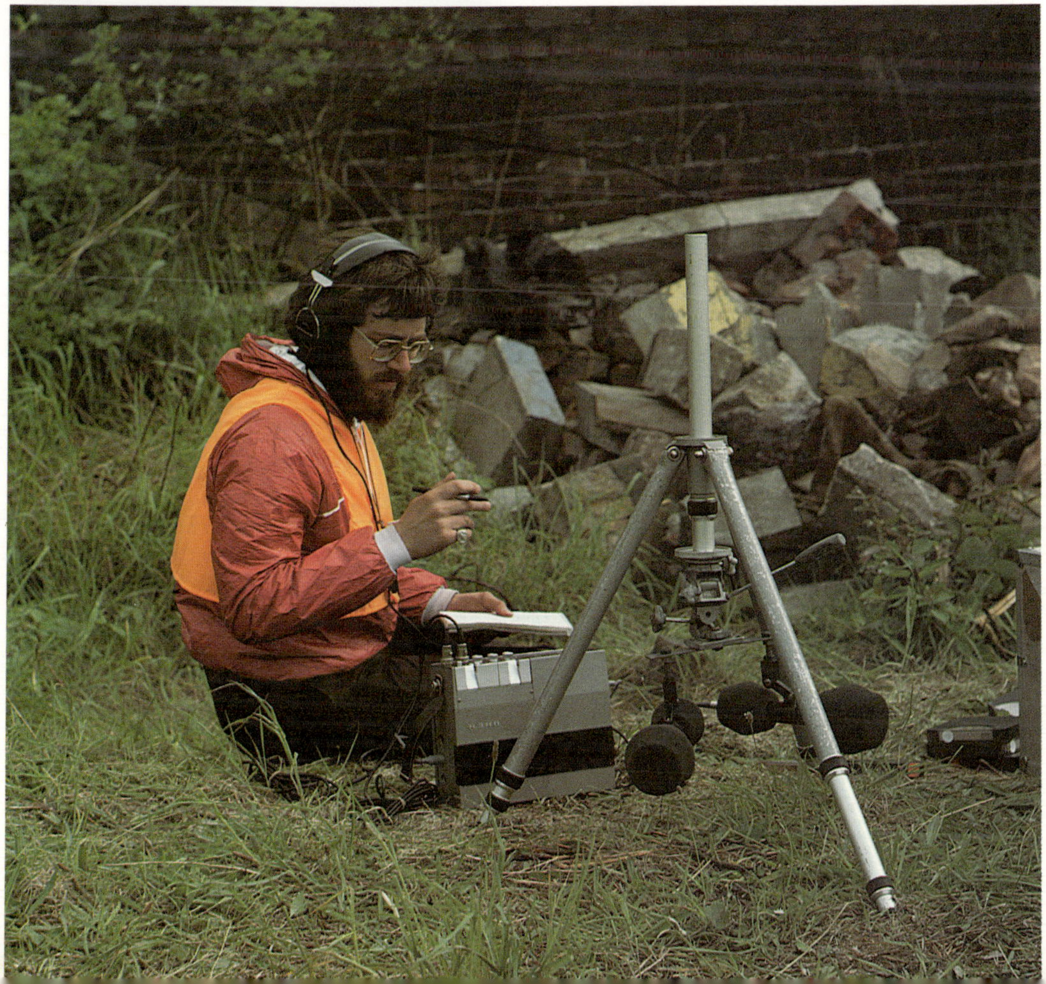

7½ips (inches per second) sounds rather different when played back at 1⅞ips — in fact, it sounds like massive timbers breaking, which is why I used it in my Coventry Cathedral programme.

The best sound effects always come from the most unlikely sources — in fact, it's worth spending a couple of free days just trying out the sound of different household objects in front of the microphone, and playing back your recordings at all sorts of different speeds. Even the professionals do this. Ben Burtt, sound designer for the *Star Wars* films, made a special trip to the White Sands missile testing range to pick up some effects. But the recordings he logged on the range proved far less useful than the sound of a faulty air-conditioning unit in his motel room — a sound used throughout the series for the engines of a space battlecruiser!

With sound effects the only limits are those of your own imagination and invention. The microphone will rarely hear precisely what you hear, especially in unusual environments (such as the bathroom). Changing playback speed adds a further range of new sounds. And if you want something special, don't give up. Spike Milligan, creator of the anarchic BBC radio comedy programme *The Goon Show*, once discovered to his amazement that the BBC effects library had no recording of howling wolves. So he, Peter Sellers and Harry Secombe did the howling themselves. On another occasion Milligan persuaded an innocent canteen lady to make him a bowl of custard — then took off his sock, poured the custard into it, and hurled the sock at the wall. 'Doesn't sound anything like it,' he muttered disgustedly. He'd been trying to simulate the sound of someone being struck down with a sockful of wet custard!

To spur yourself on, look out for 'quality' cartoons on TV. Most of them seem to be made in Eastern Europe, and most use no dialogue at all — only a sequence of sound effects. I can imagine no more effective way of breaking the language barrier.

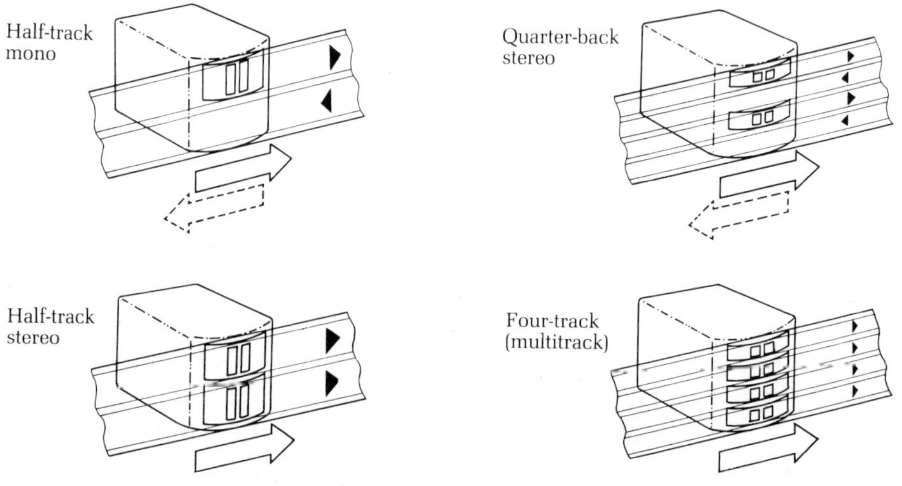

Reel-to-reel ¼-inch tape formats — a guide for the perplexed. Most domestic machines use quarter-track stereo: in one direction the left and right signals are recorded on tracks 1 and 3 respectively, and when you turn the tape over they are recorded on tracks 4 and 2. The half-track format is used on professional machines — most studio 2-tracks use half-track stereo. The four-track (multitrack) format was originally intended for quadraphonic work, but is regularly used for advanced creative soundtrack recording (see Chapter 8).

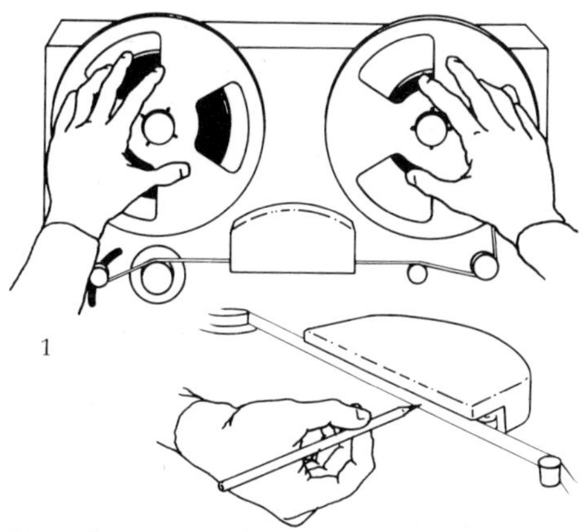

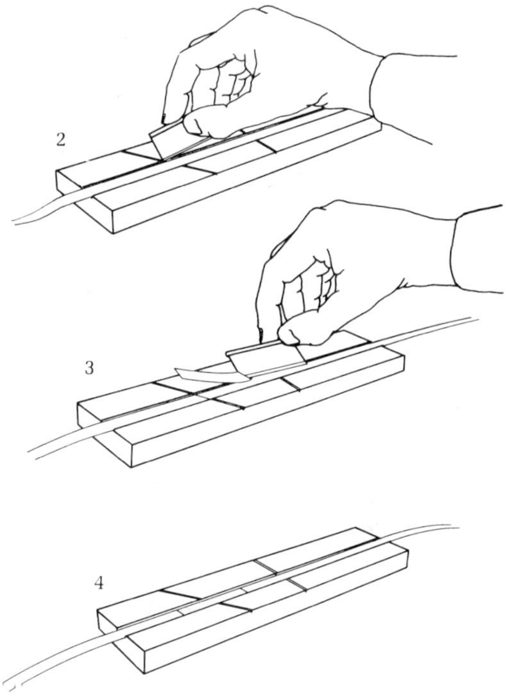

Tape editing on a reel-to-reel machine.
(1) Find the point where you wish to cut the tape by see-sawing the tape back and forth over the playback head while the PAUSE control is engaged. Mark the point with a chinagraph pencil.
(2) Lay the tape (shiny side up) on a cutting block and use a sharp blade to make a neat, accurate cut, following the grooves in the block. Repeat the process with the piece of tape that needs to be joined to this one.
(3) Butt the cut ends of the tape together in the cutting block until they just touch, then join them with a length of splicing tape as shown. Use ¼-inch wide splicing tape designed for the job!

Putting the pieces together

Recording commentary, music and sound effects separately is fairly simple. Making shows that use only one of these elements is good practice, and good exercise for the imagination. But before long you will want to put all three together in one soundtrack.

It is possible, but rather difficult, to do this with a simple cassette recorder. For instance, you could play the records you want to use on the gramophone at the same time as you record the commentary; but the quality of the final recording will not be good. If your music is 'live', you can do much the same — and the quality should be better, too. However, both you and your live musicians are likely to make mistakes. With a basic cassette deck, you will either have to leave the mistakes on the tape, or start again from the beginning. It is very difficult to rerecord a *part* of the tape without leaving an unpleasant clicking sound at the point where the new recording starts.

More sophisticated cassette decks, with electronic logic controls, can cope with this problem — but they will still not allow you to cut a section out of the tape entirely. This sort of editing can only be done on reel-to-reel decks, and is easiest when the tape has been recorded at high speed (i.e. at least 7½ips). By cutting up the tape, as shown above, you can literally piece together a

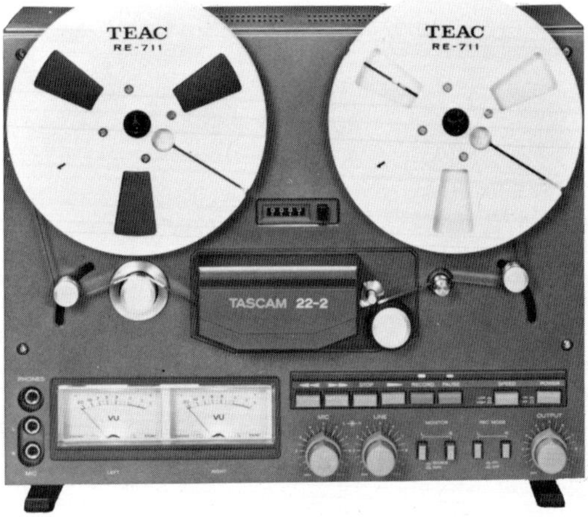

The Tascam 22-2 combines most of the features listed on p. 42.

perfect soundtrack, with all the music and effects cues precisely right and all the commentary clear and error-free — even if you only got it right after nineteen attempts. With the vast majority of cassette decks, you could only achieve the same result by rewinding the tape again and again to the precise point at which you needed to rerecord — and even then, the slightest error in starting the new section would require you to do it all over again. It *is* possible, and if you already own a quality cassette deck it may be worth trying. However, if your work with sound has got your imagination going, then now is the time to start thinking about a reel-to-reel deck. And if you want to use it creatively, there are certain features worth looking for.

1 It should be a stereo deck. This may seem obvious — less obvious is the fact that it should be able to record signals separately and at different times on right and left-hand tracks.

2 Ideally, you should be able to transfer a recording from one track to the other, while at the same time recording a new signal on the second track.

3 A *line input* socket is vital — it allows you to record signals from your cassette recorder or hi-fi. Ideally you should be able to use it *at the same time* as a signal is being recorded from the microphone input. To make full use of this facility you really need separate recording level controls for the microphone input and the line input.

4 You should be able to hear a signal when rocking the tape backwards and forwards across the playback head (see p. 41).

Machines with these facilities are not cheap; but for creative work, all are essential. Let me show you why.

Setting up the home studio

The machine I have just described will allow you to:

1 Record live sound (speech, music or effects) in mono and stereo.

2 Record live sound and mix it with recorded sound that is being picked up through the line input.

3 Record a complete soundtrack in mono and then add control impulses for your projector(s) on the other track.

4 Create multi-track recordings by 'additive mixing'.

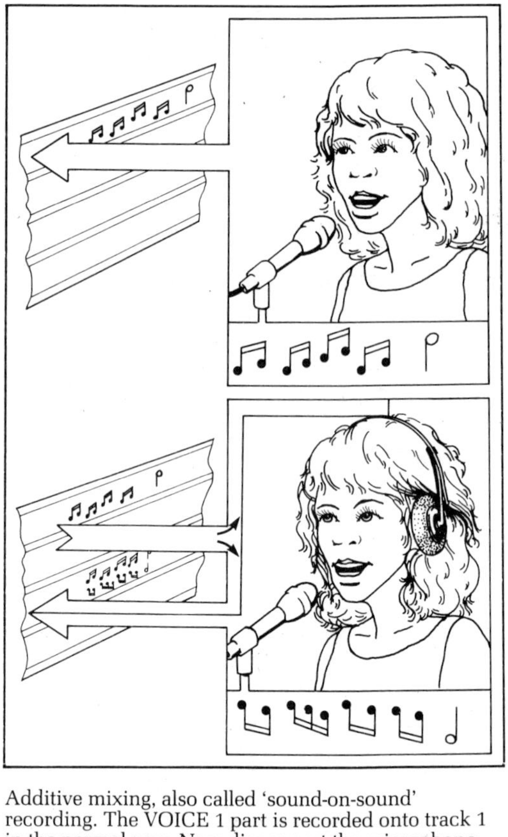

Additive mixing, also called 'sound-on-sound' recording. The VOICE 1 part is recorded onto track 1 in the normal way. Now disconnect the microphone and plug it into track 3. Set the SOUND-ON-SOUND switch on your tape deck to send signals from track 1 to track 3.

Now, as your singer records the VOICE 2 part, the SOUND-ON-SOUND facility copies the VOICE 1 part onto the same track. The resulting combination of VOICE 1 and VOICE 2 can be copied back onto track 1 in the same way while a third part is added — but watch out for tape hiss! Most tape decks of this type allow the singer to hear the previous part(s) on headphones while performing.

Number 4 may puzzle you. Say you want to record four different musical instruments — for example, three recorders and a piano. But only one member of your family is musical, and she can only play one instrument at a time! No problem. Start by recording the melody part on track 1. Rewind, start the tape again, but this time record on track 3. Your musician plays the second part while listening to the first part on headphones — and at the same time, you switch through the recording on track 1 so it is also picked up on track 3, together with the new live recording. Continue switching back and forth between tracks until all the parts are recorded. The diagram shows how it works — but do remember that each time you transfer from track to track, you are adding an extra layer of tape hiss, so don't try to record a one-man symphony orchestra. You must also take care that the recording being transferred is neither too loud nor too soft when mixed with the live recording. Always experiment before you 'go for a take' — and always check that the track you have just recorded is exactly right before you transfer back to the other track and wipe out the original recording on it.

Of course, you can use the same technique for mixing together commentary, music and sound effects. However, if you put down your commentary live, and add music or sound effects at the same time, through the line input, you can produce a stereo soundtrack — and, of course, stereo sound effects.

Stereo sound effects *can* be extremely useful. I have used them to simulate the Great Fire of London, the crowds at the 1981 Royal Wedding, the collapse of the central tower at Lincoln Cathedral, and the sound of an Underground train entering a station. But beware. Unless you are using two projectors it is very difficult to simulate movement in a slide show. If your soundtrack suggests that there *is* movement, your audience will feel something is wrong. In fact, they have been led to expect a

The Great Fire of London, from the BISFA award-winning *St Paul's Cathedral* (Woodmansterne). The effects used to build up the soundtrack included a slowed-down volcano, a burning department store, a street riot, assorted horse whinnies, a farm cart, falling rubble from a demolition site — and a couple of crushed eggboxes (see p. 38)!

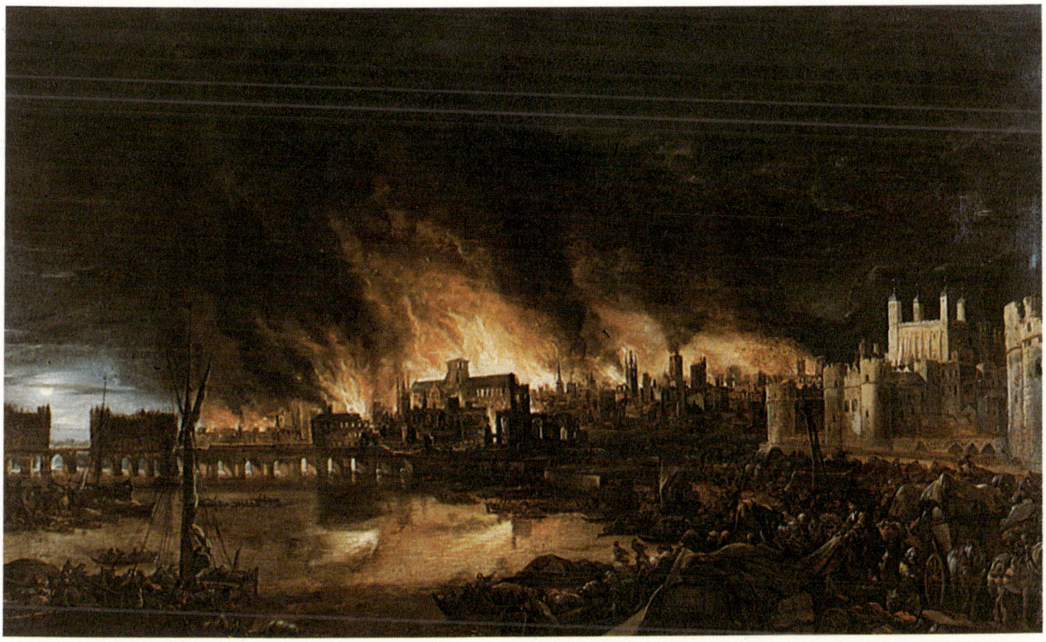

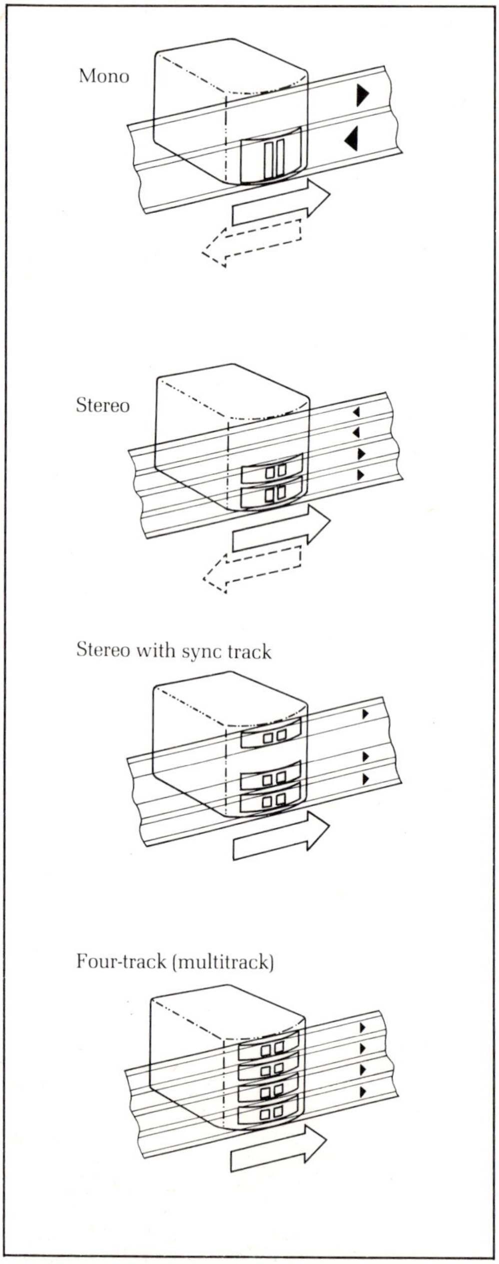

Cassette tracking formats. These look slightly more logical than the reel-to-reel formats on p. 40, except that the track numbering starts from the bottom! Notice how standard mono and stereo decks are in fact mutually compatible. The 'stereo with sync track' format can only be used in one direction, even though track 3 is left blank to stop control signals 'leaking' onto the soundtrack (and vice versa, which can be even worse!). The four-track format is not, essentially, different from the four-track reel-to-reel format.

moving picture — but they're not getting one. Stereo can always be made to work for you: but do use it carefully.

One final point. Never underestimate the power of silence. A good sequence of pictures with no soundtrack whatsoever can serve to point up an earlier passage that used a very busy soundtrack. And if one simple sound effect will do, then use that one effect — and nothing else. In the Coventry sequence described on p.15, the opening air-raid effects involved complex stereo mixing of seven different sound sources. But the rest of the programme was extremely simple — and for nearly a minute after the chaos had died away, the soundtrack consisted of the narrator's voice and a single tolling bell. Be economical. It makes your job simpler, and it will almost certainly achieve better results.

'Audio-visual' tape recorders

A number of specialist machines are designed specifically for use with slide projectors and/or electronic projector control systems. The simplest of these

Mastering machines — the next step up from the domestic reel-to-reel recorder, offering the finest sound reproduction with the convenience of cut-and-splice editing (see p. 41). Aside from the Revox range (still a name to conjure with) choices include the Tascam 32 (left), the Fostex A2 (centre) and the luxurious Otari (right). For the home recording buff, machines of this calibre are a very expensive luxury — for the serious creative sound producer they are a necessity.

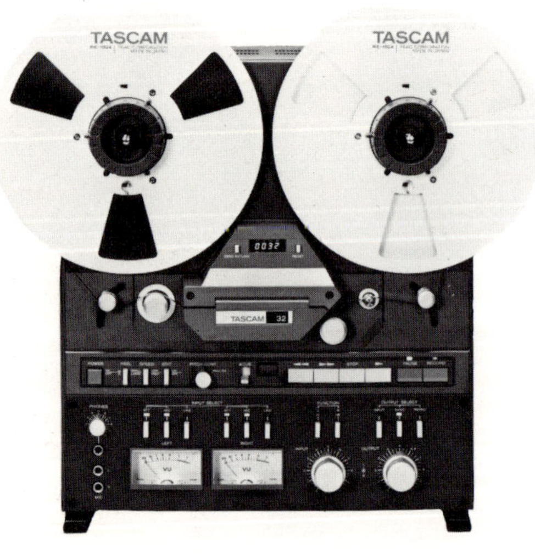

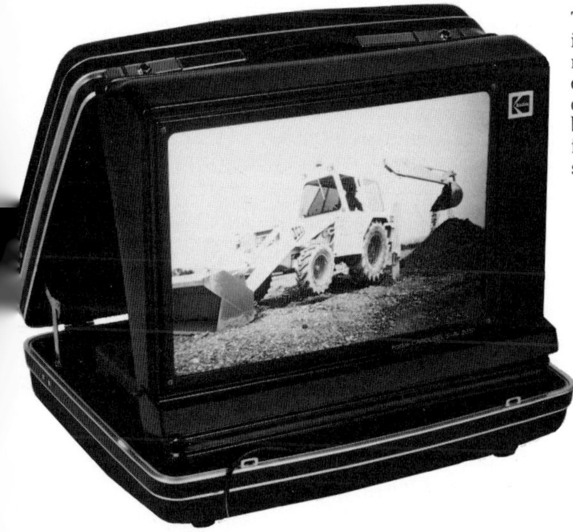

The Telex Caramate back-projection unit (below) includes a built-in cassette deck that you can use to record programmes *and* program slide changes. By opening the port at the front you can use the unit as a conventional projector. The Kodak Carousel S-AV 2010 back-projection unit (left) combines a Carousel and a fully programmable cassette deck in a single briefcase-sized unit.

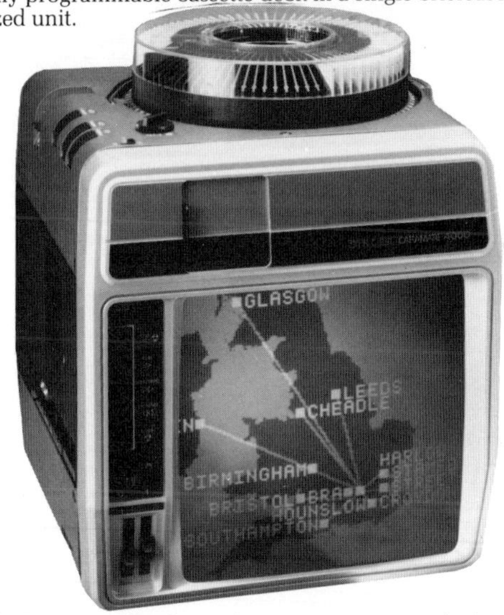

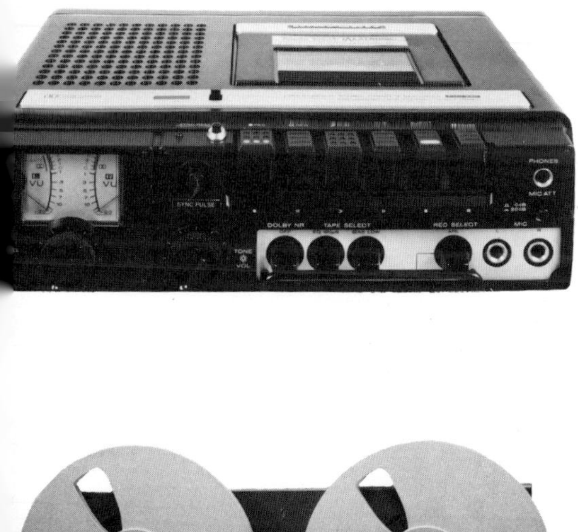

The Imatronic Triple Track is a stereo cassette deck with Dolby — but it also gives you full access to a third track that can record and replay control signals from electronic dissolve units. A built-in 1kHz pulse generator lets you control single-projector programmes, too. It has recently been replaced by a new model, so this could be a good second-hand buy.

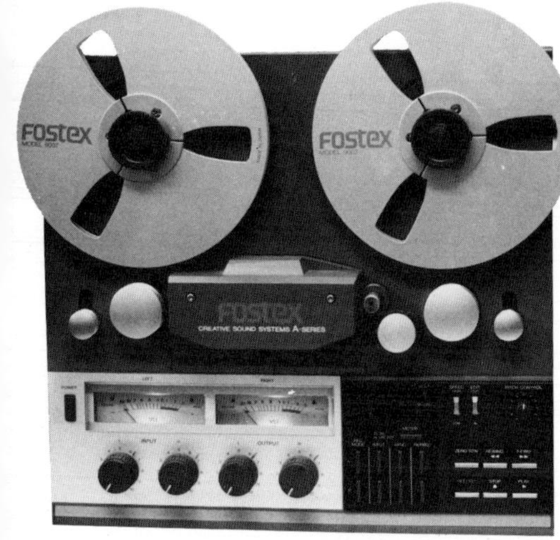

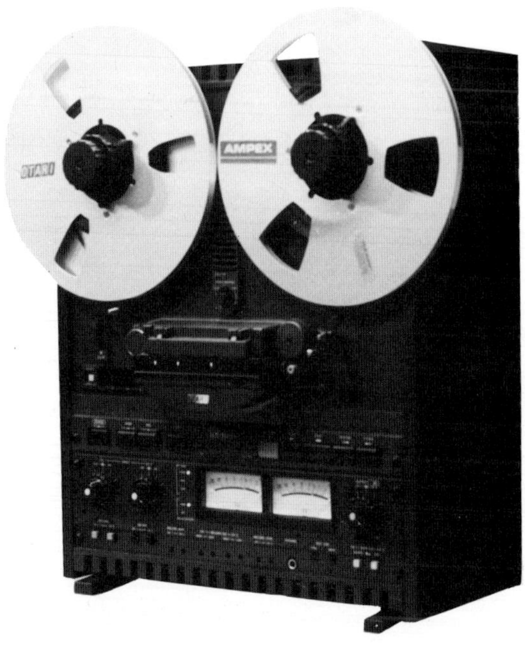

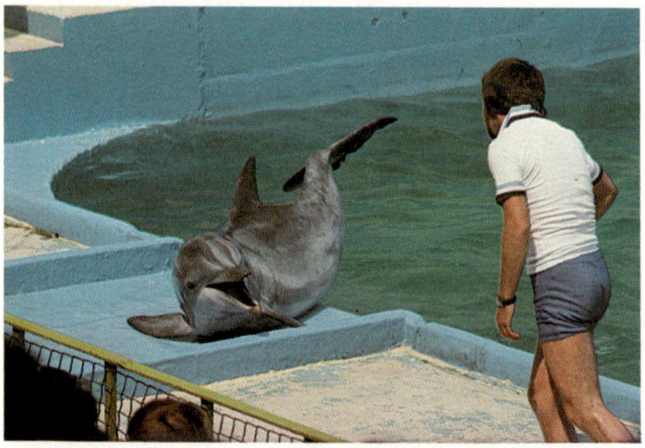

'Did you hear the one about the human in the swimming pool?'

machines usually combine a mono or stereo cassette recorder with a 'pulse generator' that records projector control signals onto track 4 of the cassette (see p. 44). Do make sure that your projector does not need any extra circuitry to respond to these control signals before you buy — *ideally take your projector to the shop and test it.*

Some machines actually combine a slide projector with a cassette tape deck. Some of these decks are playback-only machines (check!), but some are fully-equipped recorders that also let you program automatic slide changes. Most machines of this type have a small integral screen, but you can usually project onto a screen in the normal way if you want to. A word of warning, though. Such machines are not usually suitable for large halls, and the sound quality often leaves a lot to be desired. For simple single-projector voice-and-picture shows, they're fine. For anything else, they're less than ideal.

Some more advanced audio-visual cassette decks allow you full access to track 4 of the cassette, or even tracks 3 and 4. This means you can record either one or two separate control programs on these channels *from an outside source*. The decks are mostly used with specialist electronic dissolve equipment controlling two, three or more projectors. Before even considering such a machine, you will need unbiased professional advice. Talk to your local audio-visual dealer — and read the next chapter first. Some systems actually supply a machine of this type built into the dissolve control unit.

Exploring your tape recorder

This chapter can't pretend to be a complete guide to choosing and using a tape recorder. That would take another book — so I refer you to Appendix 2 on p. 115! However, by now you should have some idea of what *can* be done with different types of machine. It's up to you to decide how far you want to go with your soundtracks. If a simple cassette deck is all you need, why spend more? On the other hand, there's nothing (except, perhaps, your bank manager) to stop you setting up a complete home studio, with something like a four-track reel-to-reel tape deck and a semi-professional mixing console. I'll be talking about more elaborate setups of this kind in Chapter 8; though normally, of course, only clubs or small groups of enthusiasts can take things this far. But whatever machine you choose, use it to the full — and never be afraid to experiment.

You might surprise yourself.

5

Creating the right image

When we were at school, we were all taught to put words together into sentences according to a set of rules — the rules of English grammar. There is also a set of rules for putting pictures together into a sequence — and it's often referred to as 'shot grammar'. I'm assuming you already know how to take an acceptable photograph, so if you're not sure you do, try a couple of the basic books listed on p. 115. However, if you've long ago left such books behind you, you're more than ready to learn the next stage — photography's answer to the English essay.

Naming of parts

Shot grammar, like English grammar, uses technical words. Luckily, the technical words in shot grammar are very simple, and most explain themselves. The most important of them are shown visually on p. 48. We've used a human figure to define the different types of shot, because this is how they are normally defined — but do remember that the same terms can be applied to other subjects, too.

In Chapter 2 I suggested that one way to keep a programme lively was to vary the type of shot you were using across the full range between big close-up and long shot. I also showed you a few short sequences. So before I start talking about the extra possibilities offered by special-effects photography and the use of two projectors, let's see what can be done with an ordinary camera and a little imagination.

In normal still photography, we use close-ups and long shots without thinking of them as parts of a sequence. The sequence below shows how they can be. The first is a long shot showing the church framed in the arches of the bridge. This gives us a chance to understand how the building is set in the surrounding landscape. In the following shots, the camera moves closer and closer,

A sequence closing in on the inscription above Knaresborough Church clock: 'Redeeming the time'.

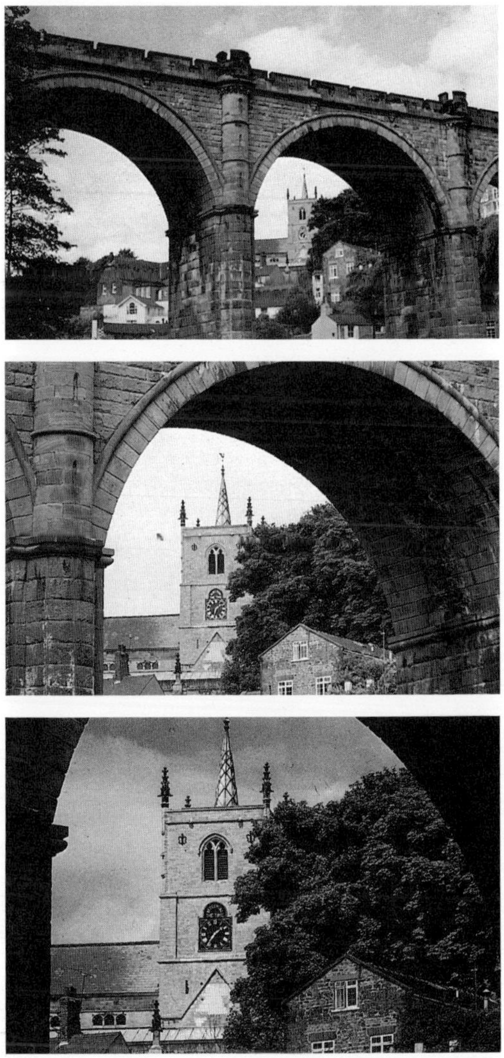

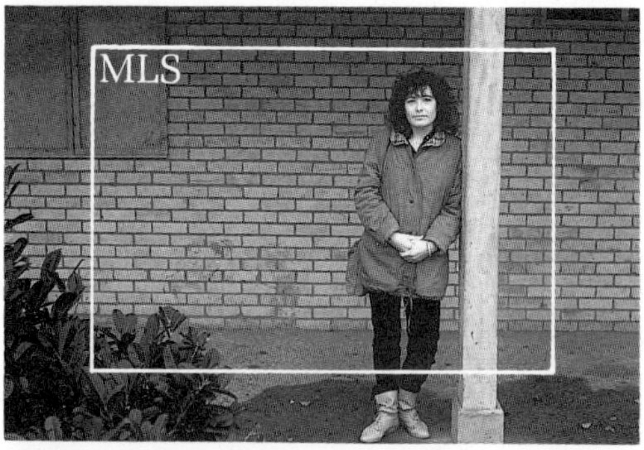

Long shot (LS) and Medium Long Shot (MLS)

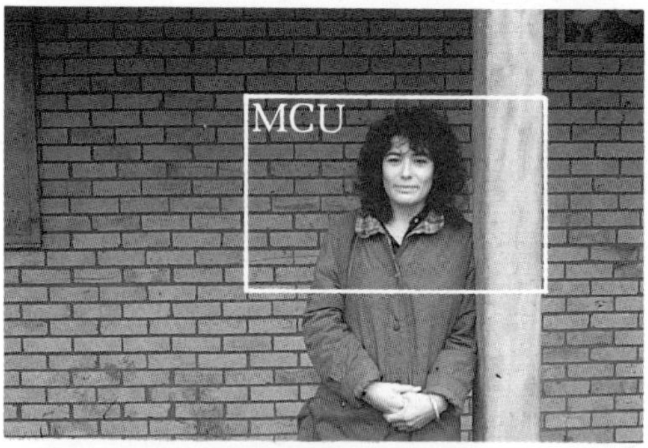

Mid shot (MS) and Medium Close Up (MCU)

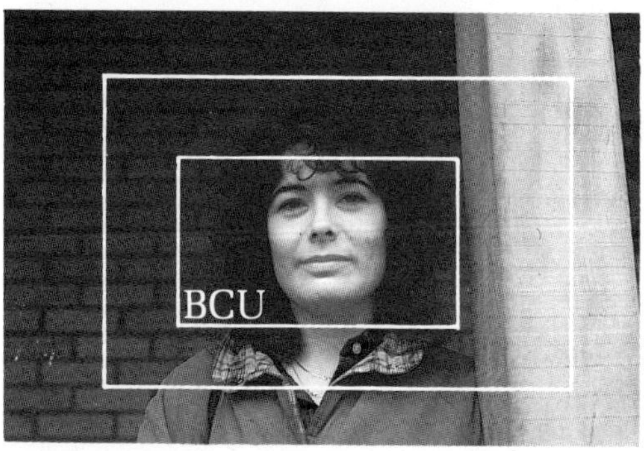

Close Up (CU) and Big Close Up (BCU)

until we can just see the inscription on the clock — a detail that will become the jumping-off point for the next sequence.

On the right here, you can see the opposite approach. From a curious and intriguing close-up we move out to see the carving of which it forms a part, and then the entire archway.

With a single-lens reflex camera, sequences like this can often be created by standing in one spot and either changing lenses, or closing in with a zoom lens. Those with less elaborate equipment will just have to put on their hiking boots (much healthier, really).

Notice that either of those sequences could have been put together in reverse order. What would the effect have been? What is the effect now?

By moving in on a particular detail, the sequence on p. 47 draws our attention to a *part* of the scene that is going to be

A grotesque medieval carving sets the scene for a programme about the Middle Ages.

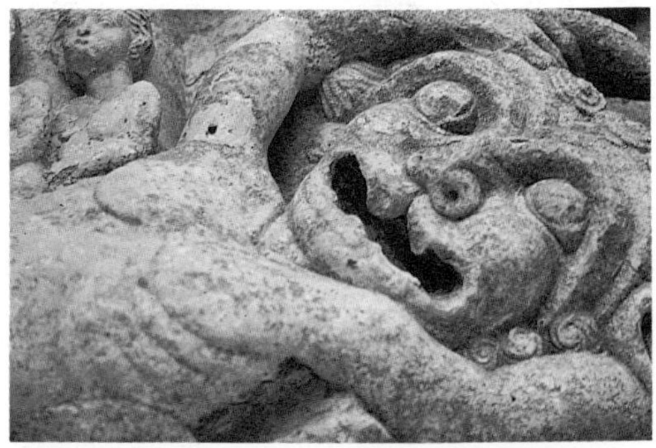

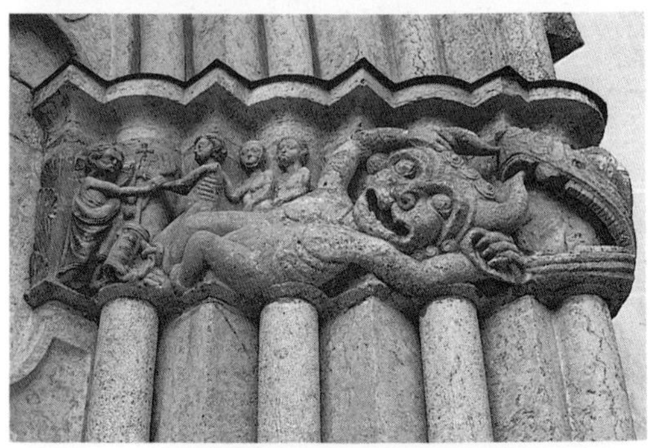

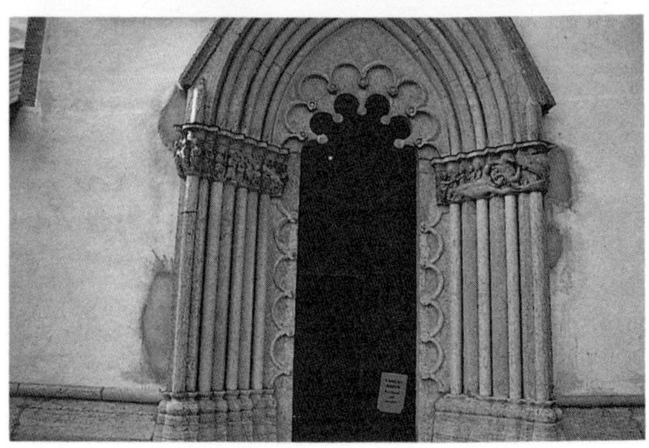

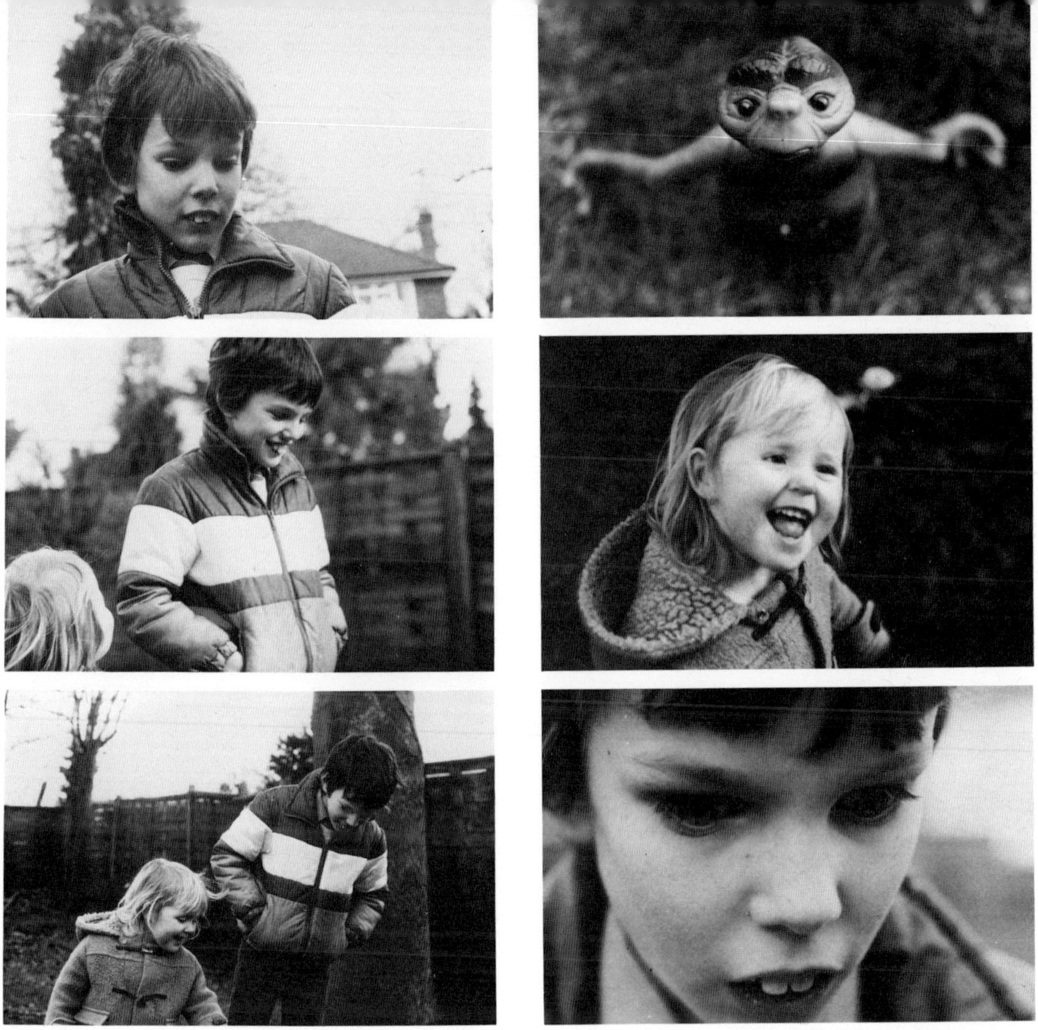

Shots from *Guess Who's Coming to Dinner*: notice the use of different camera angles and distances in this short sequence.

important. It's like being met by someone at a busy station in a town you don't know and being taken to the particular door that will get you to the taxi rank.

The second sequence intrigues by starting on an enigmatic close-up. What is this carving? Where is it? What significance does it have? In other words, it's a visual hook — a prime example of the way pictures can support, amplify or even totally replace a written commentary. Try to think of other ways in which your choice of shot can say as much as your commentary.

Now look here . . .

If there are people in your sequence, then you need to think about the *eyeline*: the direction in which they have to look to see each other, or an object that appears later in the sequence. In the first shot above notice how the camera has been set low, and pointing up, so that the figure of a comparatively small boy seems to loom over the viewer. Obviously we are seeing him through the eyes of the little creature in the next shot; and in that shot we are looking down at the creature through the eyes of the boy. In the next shot, showing the two boys together, notice how the camera has swung down and slightly around in the first shot, so that we look at Adrian almost over Edward's shoulder — with a definite upward tilt. Again, in the shot after that, the camera stands high and to one side looking over Adrian's shoulder. These two pictures are examples of the *two-shot*, so called

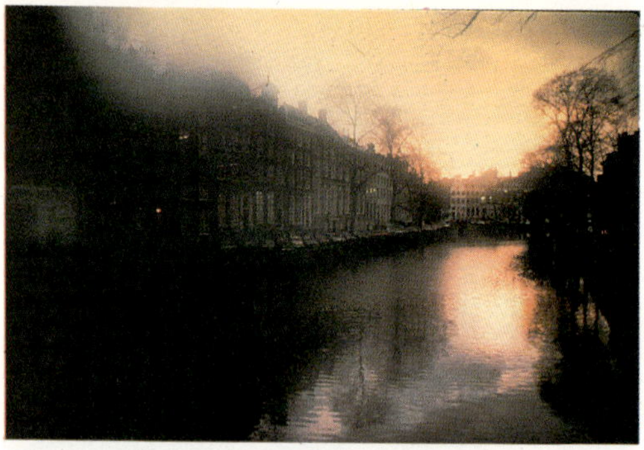

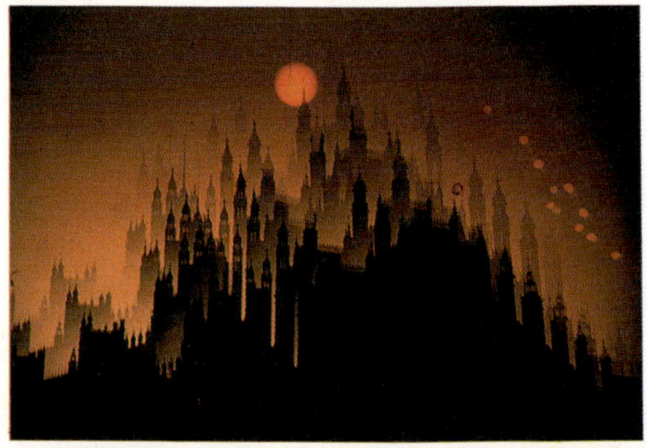

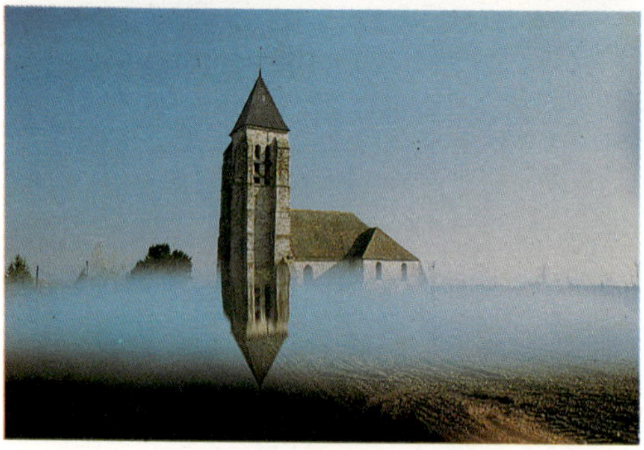

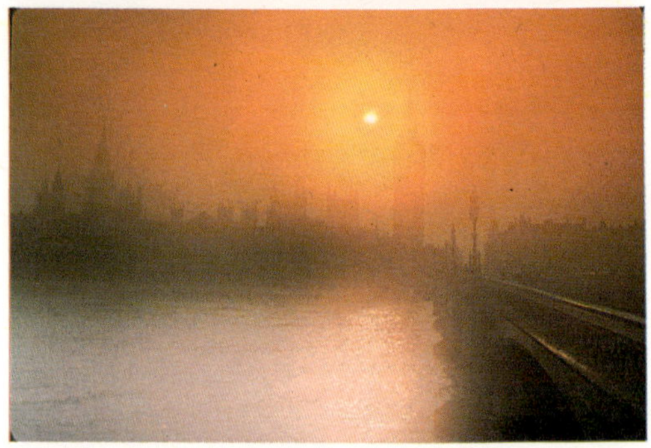

because there are two figures in it. Then comes another, this time in long shot. Notice that this time the figures are much more in profile. As you move closer, you will need to favour one figure or the other according to the demands of your script — and you will find you need to angle round towards the front of the key face more and more as you move into close-up. By the time you go into a big close-up like the final shot your subject may be looking almost straight into the camera.

Using long shots, mid shots and close-ups in this kind of work is largely a matter of following the demands of the script and your personal taste — and then using a little imagination! If you want to emphasise someone's reaction to something — like

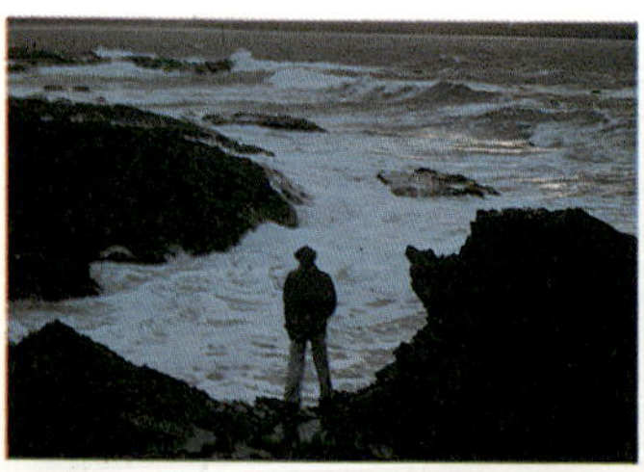

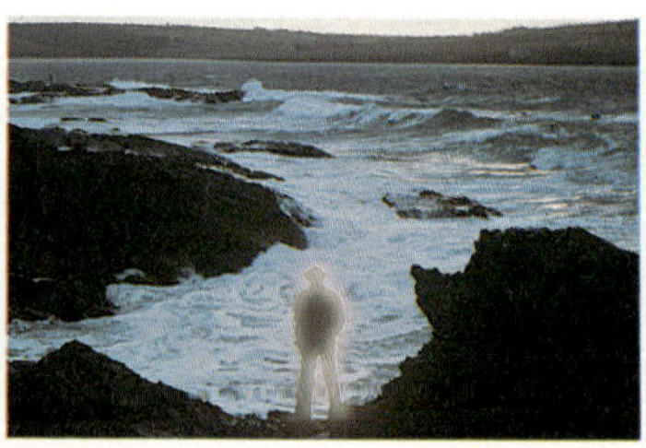

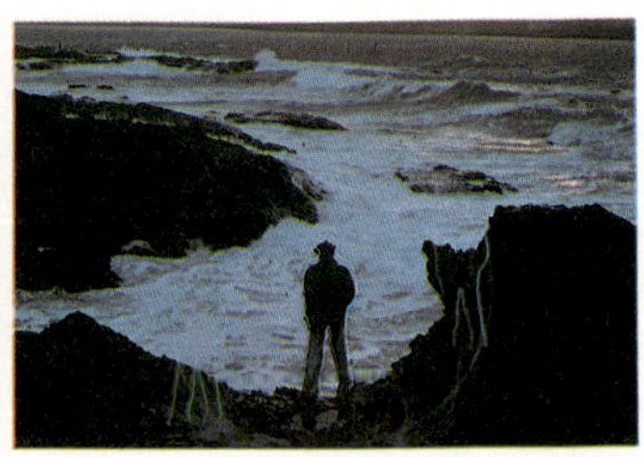

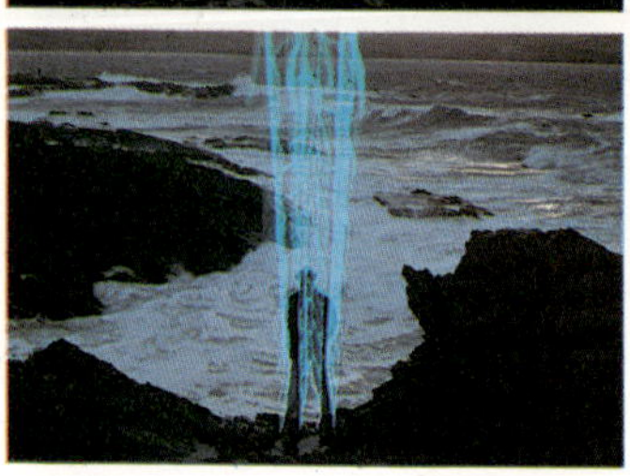

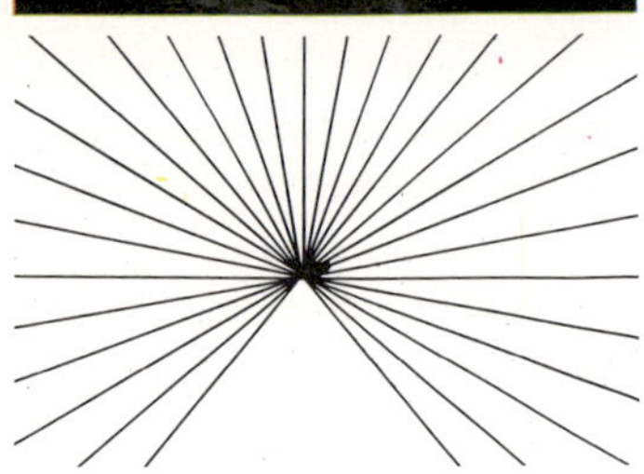

The moment of transformation from *Star of the Sea*. Below the dissolve set are the intermediate rostrum camera shots that were used by the staff at RCW to create the effect to the author's brief.

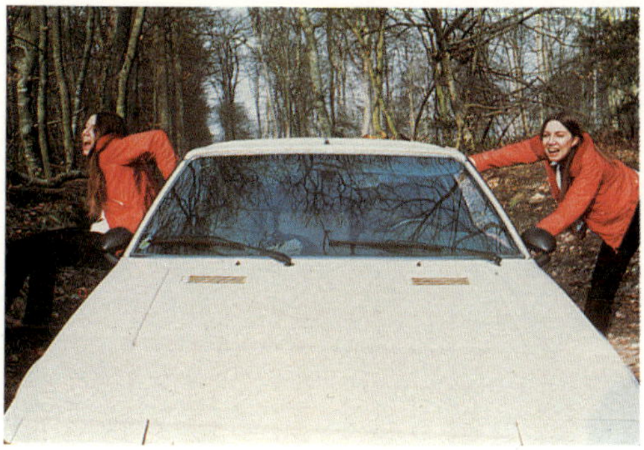

Special effects created by Jean Coquin using his Cokin filters. Shots like this could well form the turning point of an imaginative sequence, or even set the mood for a complete programme.

Adrian's look of complete surprise in that last shot — then a big close-up will do it. In fact, TV producers use it as a weapon in interviews — it tends to make even the mildest reaction of surprise look as though the victim had been hit on the head with a brick.

To study the use of these shots in action take another look at the storyboard on p. 21 and, if you like, turn back to p. 15 and look at some of the pictures I shot for *Witchwood*. That uses two projectors; of which more in a moment.

Putting your camera to work

Even the simplest camera is capable of some startling special effects that can easily — and cheaply — rival anything TV and film have to offer. Even pictures from your existing collection can be used. For instance, your camera may not allow you to take two pictures one on top of the other (double exposure), but you can still take two separate pieces of slide film and sandwich them together inside a self-assembly mount (see p. 71). Another idea is to look for specific shapes, and perhaps mount them with a slide mask (see p. 72). How about a show based on circles? Or squares? Or triangles?

Then, of course, there are the things you can do at the time the picture is taken. The oldest trick in the book is to smear petroleum jelly on the edges of the lens to create a 'soft' look — but be careful. Some lenses could be damaged when the jelly is removed. A professional soft filter is better, and there is a huge range of special effects filters now available to fit most 35mm cameras. With them you can achieve some fascinating results — take a look at the pictures above.

Finally there are specialist techniques like solarisation that are strictly for those with

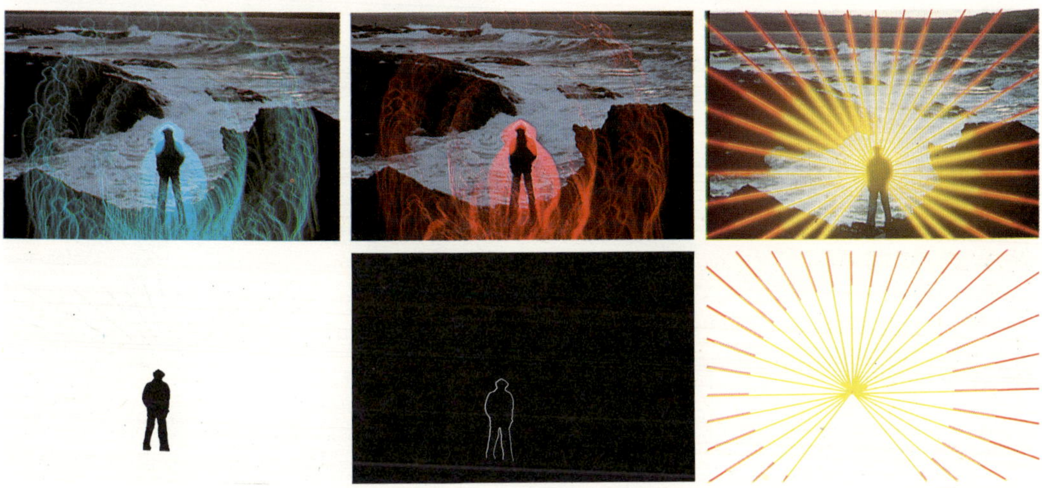

their own darkrooms and the right equipment — or for those, like me, who haven't got the foggiest idea how it's done, but know the right people to ask! At times like this the local camera club once again comes into its own — at very least you'll find someone who can tell you how to get the particular effect you need!

But if you do go in for special effects, take care how you use them. A sequence consisting entirely of special-effects shots can quickly become boring. One that builds up to a single startling shot, and uses it to take the audience by surprise, can be extremely effective. The sequence on pp. 50–51 seems to show a human figure being transformed by some enormous burst of supernatural energy. It's an experiment for a programme I am currently shooting called *Star of the Sea*. A man staying in a Cornish seaside village sees a meteorite fall onto the nearby beach. He goes to investigate. On the beach, he sees a man staggering towards him. And then suddenly the approaching figure throws up its arms, stands transfigured for a moment in a blinding corona of light — and vanishes. There is only the beach, and the gulls, and the westering sun.

Star of the Sea is another programme designed for two projectors — and the time has come to look at two-projector work and the special demands it makes on the creative photographer.

First, tear up the rule book . . .

The shots opposite were all taken for two-projector programmes. As you can see, many of them break virtually every rule in the book. What possible excuse can there be for such lopsided composition, for such singularly uninteresting subject-matter, for such inaccurate focusing?

The answer is that all of it was deliberate.

In a two-projector show, no slide ever exists in isolation for more than a few seconds. It is just one part of a continuously moving, changing sequence of images —

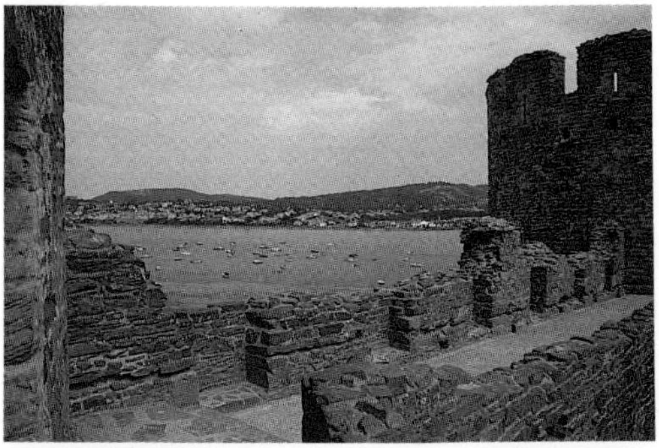
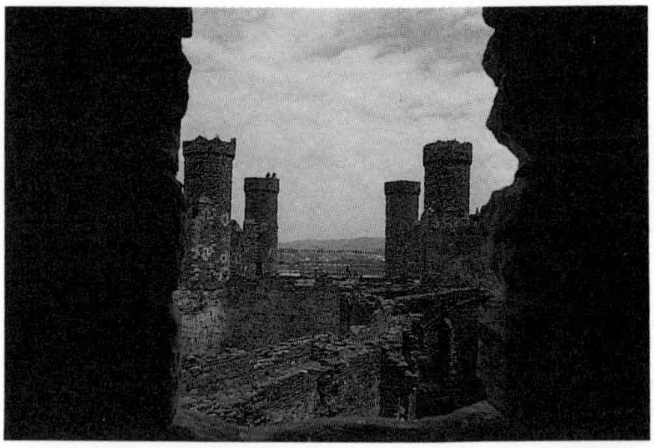
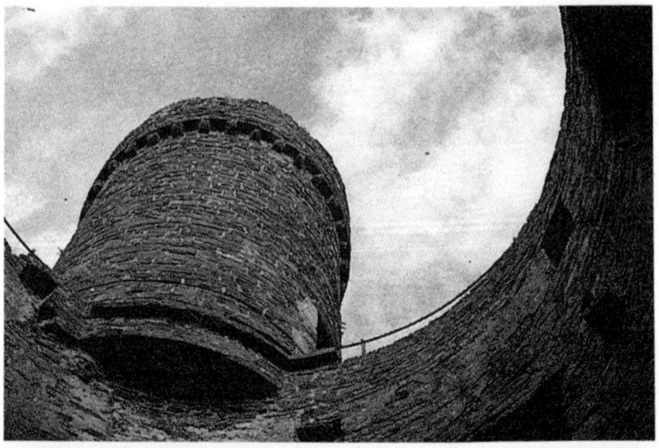
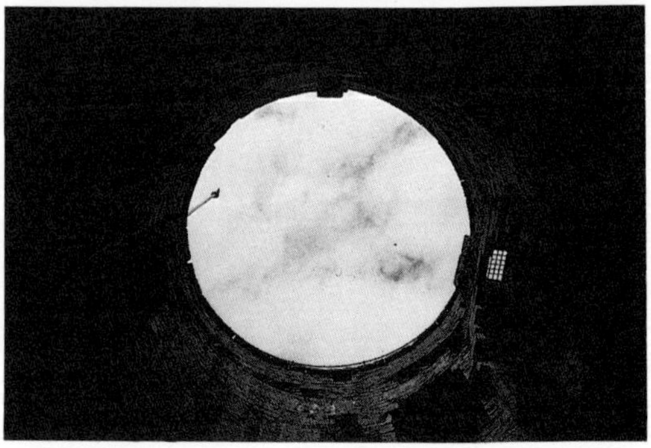

The Master of Conwy: the end of a short, light-hearted two-projector sequence with a soundtrack consisting simply of seagull cries!

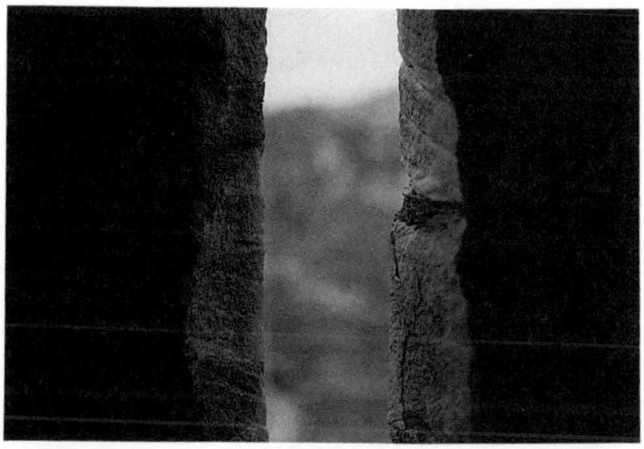
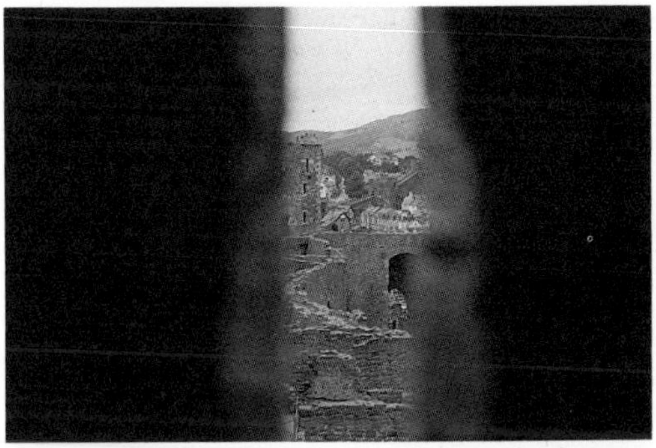
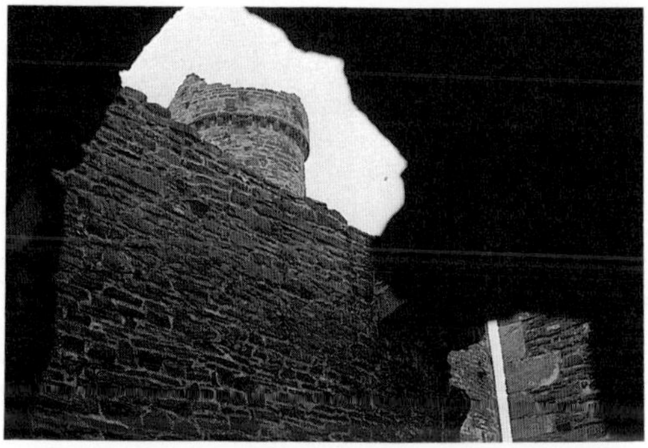
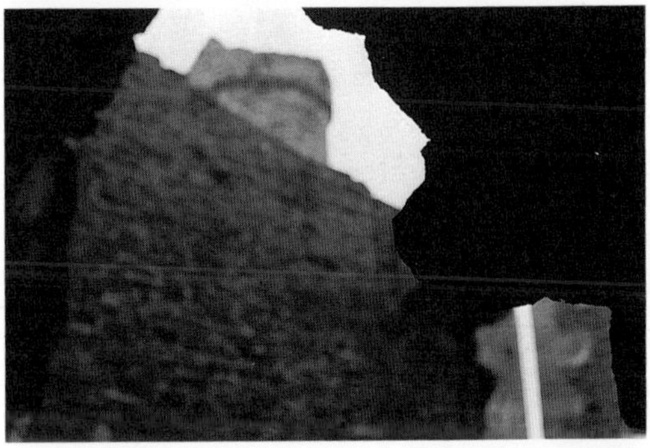
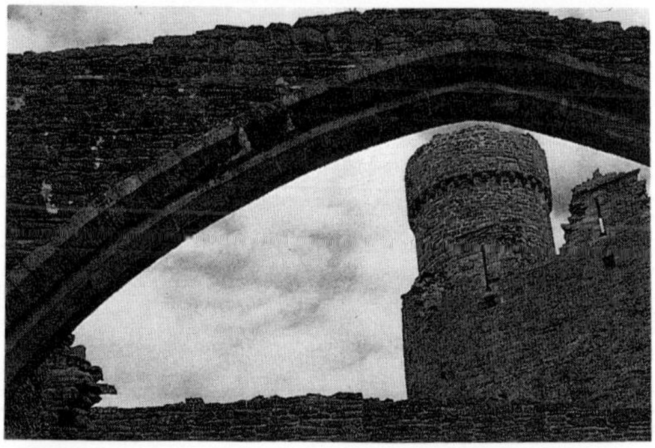
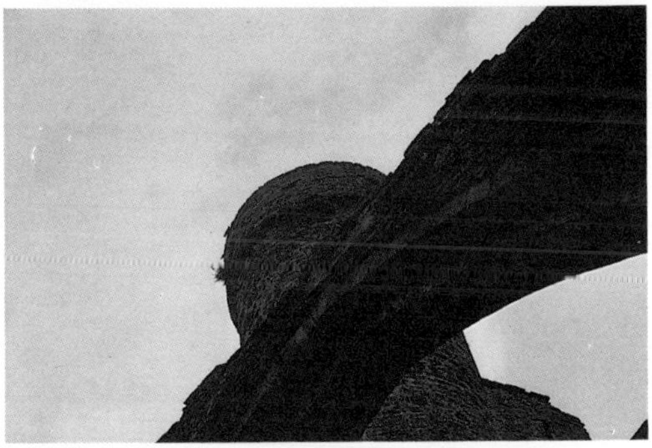
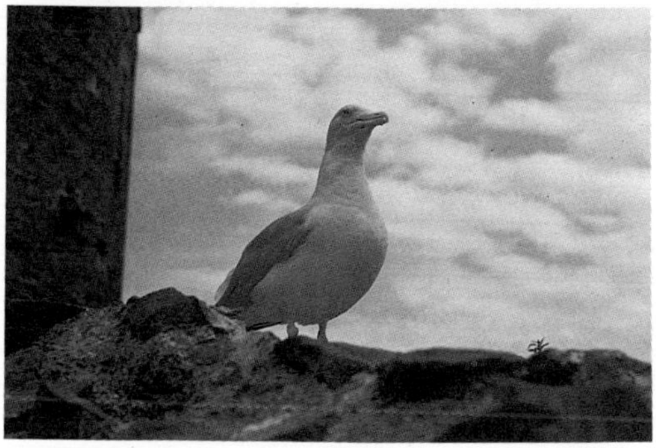
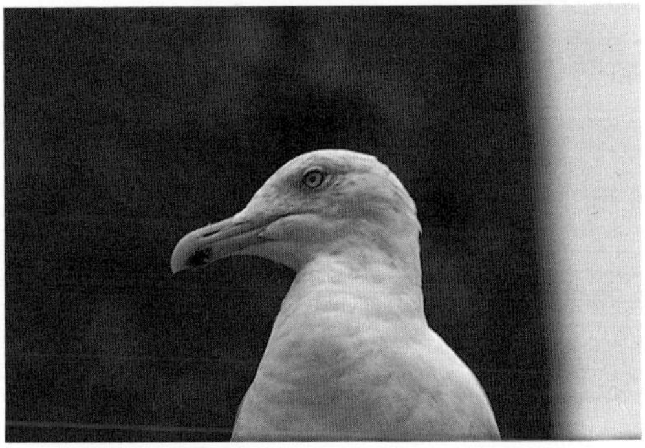

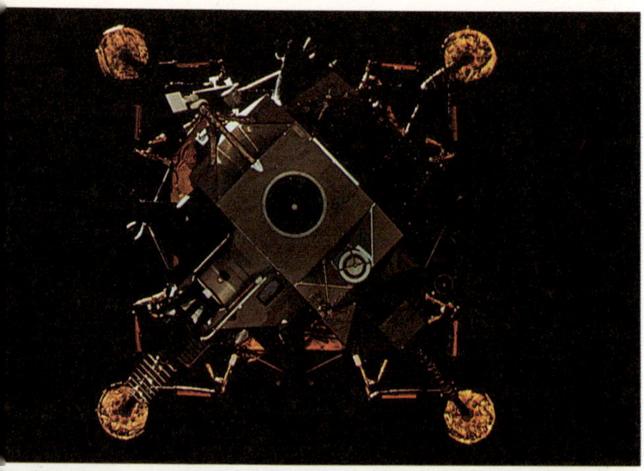

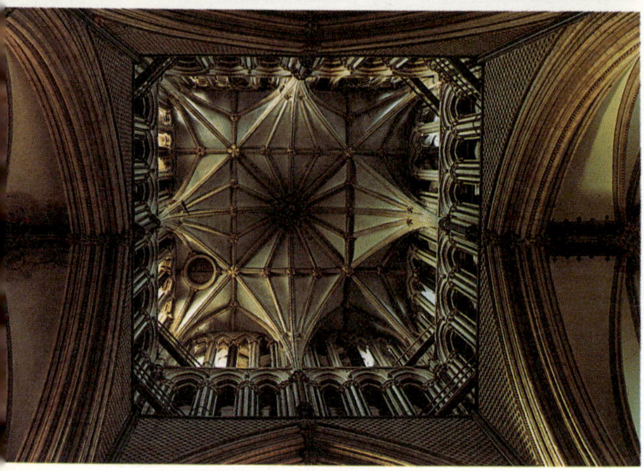

The inspiration for *Masters of Inner Space* (Woodmansterne). Space-age and medieval engineering produce strangely similar shapes . . .

and within that sequence, it relates closely to the slides immediately before and after it.

The secret added ingredient in twin projection is the way you handle the move from one image to the next.

In film and TV we are used to seeing cuts — sudden instantaneous jumps from one shot to the next. In fast action sequences, this is the norm. But in slow, lyrical sequences you may see the *dissolve*, where one image gradually fades into the next.

With two projectors, and a suitable mechanical or electronic device to control them, you can for the first time achieve something like a jump cut. More interestingly, you can also achieve a dissolve.

The shots on pp. 52–3 belong to a short, jokey sequence called *The Master of Conwy*. The pictures, taken at Conwy Castle in North Wales, lead up to a final big close-up of the Master himself — an arrogant seagull. By themselves, as you can see, many of the shots seem meaningless — but as soon as they begin to dissolve into the next shot, a new and completely different image is created as the two pictures, for just a few seconds, appear on the screen together. This is the 'third image' — and it's what makes dissolve sequences so special.

It isn't always easy to *plan* the third image. Sometimes you find it by accident, a chance juxtaposition of two totally unrelated slides. One day, for instance, I happened to pair up a shot of the Apollo moon lander, taken from above, with a view looking straight up into the vault of the central tower at Lincoln Cathedral. The two images dissolved perfectly, because their basic geometry was exactly the same. The result — *Masters of Inner Space* — was a sequence that compared modern and medieval technology, and modern and medieval ideas of the structure of the universe. The commentary was little more than an excuse for a series of spectacular dissolves. For instance, as a Saturn V launch vehicle melted gradually into the central tower of Salisbury Cathedral, the third image gave a momentary impression of the tower rising from the ground on a pillar of flame!

Taking pictures for a dissolve show becomes an exercise in creative imagination. Instead of thinking of your shots individually, you must learn to think of them in relation to each other. Basic rules of composition fly suddenly out of the window. For dissolve work, you *want* pictures that are weighted heavily to one side of the frame — because then you can cross-fade to a picture weighted on the *other* side of the frame. You might go into a wood and take a shot straight up towards the sky, with the branches of the trees forming a ring around the frame — and then take a shot of a single bird in an empty sky, so that it will appear framed in the branches.

Other, more traditional photographers may look at you very oddly when they see some of the pictures you are taking for dissolve. Ignore them. You know what you want — and sometimes even the strangest shots will find a vital place in the sequence. As a rule of thumb, you can reckon that shots you would normally throw away will turn out to be the kingpins of the programme — so don't throw *anything* out until you're sure! Even blank frames have their uses!

So who needs dissolve anyway?
If you're not yet convinced, bear with me: we've barely begun to explore the possibilities. With two projectors you're approaching a world normally reserved for *moving* pictures. It's a world where distant objects are brought by smooth degrees into ultra close-up, where focus shifts in a graceful transition from foreground to background, where day becomes night in a spectacular passage of seconds, where water ripples and twinkles under the light of a summer sun, where a bird snaps round its head in response to a noise on the soundtrack, where graphics and titles appear and disappear over pictures and diagrams with magical precision, and where frost can crystallise onto a spider's web and turn it into a mesh of scintillating jewels.

Two-projector effects are a little like sound effects. Once you have some idea of the potential, only your own imagination can really set the limits. So to start you off, let's take a look at some of those ideas in detail.

Making it move
To the beginner, the idea of making something move on screen is almost unbearably tempting. You feel you want to use it all the time, as often as you can get away with it.

Don't.

Most slide projectors take between one and two seconds to change completely from

Another dissolve pair from *Masters of Inner Space*. As the images merge, the tower of Salisbury Cathedral seems to leap upwards on a column of flame.

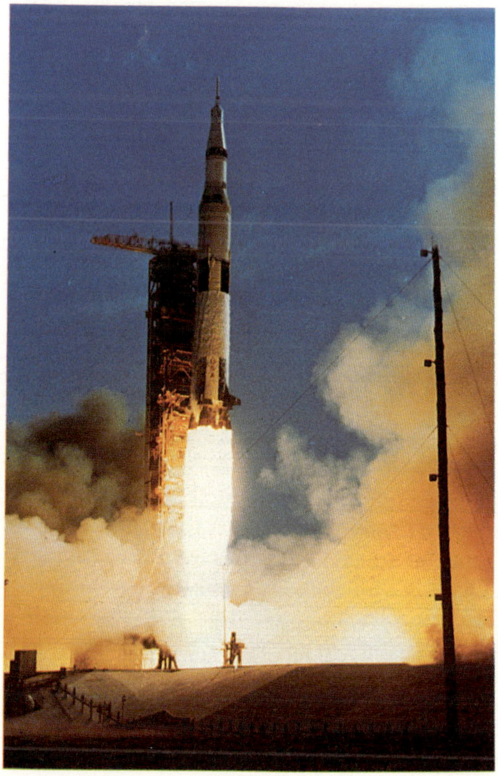

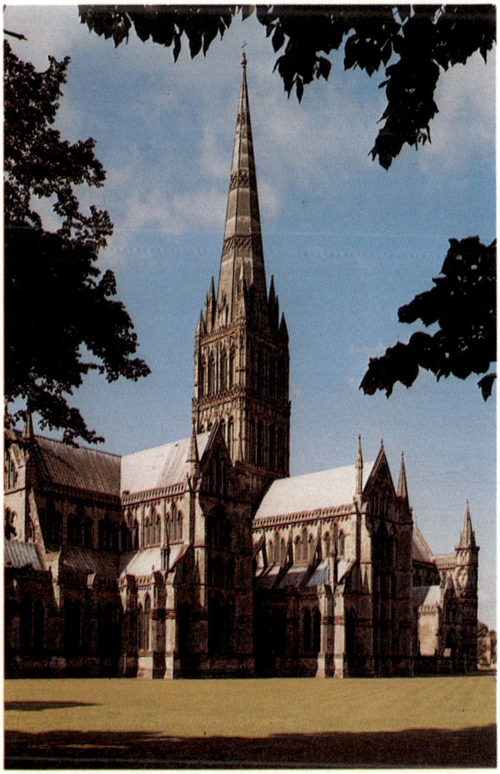

one slide to the next. Some are faster — most are not. In other words, after your first jump you will have to wait between one and two seconds for the next image. Movie film runs at 24 frames a second — that's how it creates the illusion of continuous movement. It's a speed you cannot hope to match.

Except the first time.

For one glorious, shocking moment, you *can* move an image on screen. If you can arrange for two matching images of a bird's head in different positions, you *can* jump from one to the other, and startle your audience back into attention.

But leave it at that. Once your audience becomes aware of what you are doing, they will begin to see your programme as a sort of disabled film, limping along on two rather slow crutches, instead of the superbly advanced slide show it really is. At a stroke, in fact, you will destroy their confidence in you.

True movement sequences in a slide show belong to the more advanced realms of multivision, with its massive banks of computer-controlled projectors (see p. 75). The rest of us should use it wisely, carefully, and rarely — just like any other special effect.

It's easy to remove instant lettering with adhesive tape, as long as it hasn't been burnished.

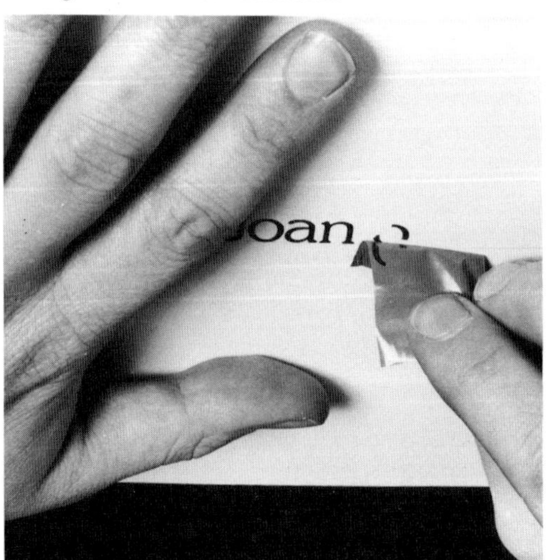

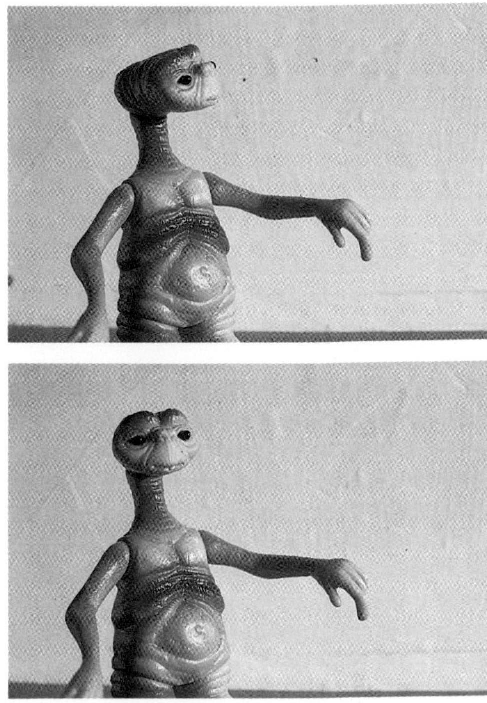

Movement. Shots like this are easy but the camera must be firmly mounted on a tripod.

Gorgeous graphics

With titling, artwork, and graphics of all kinds, two-projector shows really come into their own. For the first time you can make really professional title sequences, where captions fade gently in and out over a background picture.

Simple title slides can easily be prepared using instant lettering — but do take care with it, and do make sure you use the largest size available. Any little errors of alignment you make are going to look dreadful when they are blown up onto a big screen. Beware, too, of the automatic spacing methods offered by some manufacturers. Better to adjust lettering until it *looks* right. And don't burnish letters firmly down until you are completely satisfied with the whole caption. Good instant lettering can usually be removed with adhesive tape as long as it has not been burnished.

Experiment with differently coloured backgrounds and different lettering styles, choosing styles that suit your particular subject. Keep an eye out for the way this is done for films and TV. For adding names to maps, you can lay your lettering on clear acetate in the correct positions, and then shoot the map with and without the acetate sheet on top of it. But make sure you use the same, stable setup, and watch out for unwanted reflections. A polaroid filter can be useful here.

For coloured lettering, lay black lettering on a white ground and then shoot it on *lithographic* film (a high-contrast black-and-white film). Sandwich the developed negative in a slide-mount with a piece of coloured gel, and you will have neat coloured titles on a black ground.

If you shoot white lettering on a black card in the same way, you will finish up with a chip of clear film with black lettering that you can sandwich with any other film chip. If you took a series of *identical* shots of the original lettering, for instance, you could sandwich them all with a sequence of swiftly-dissolving pictures so that a single title appeared to stay on screen while the pictures dissolved and jump-cut behind it. For this kind of work, register mounts (see

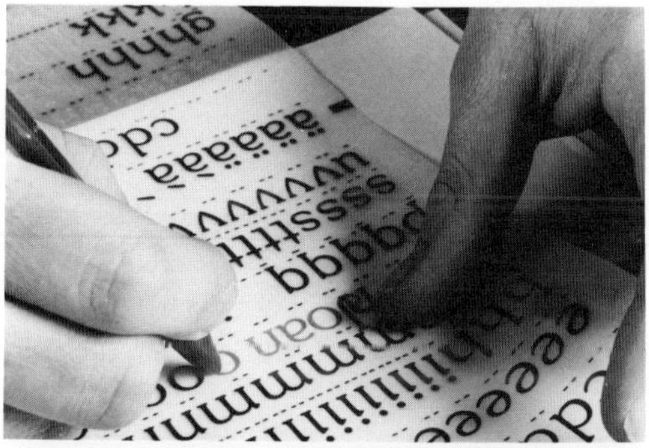

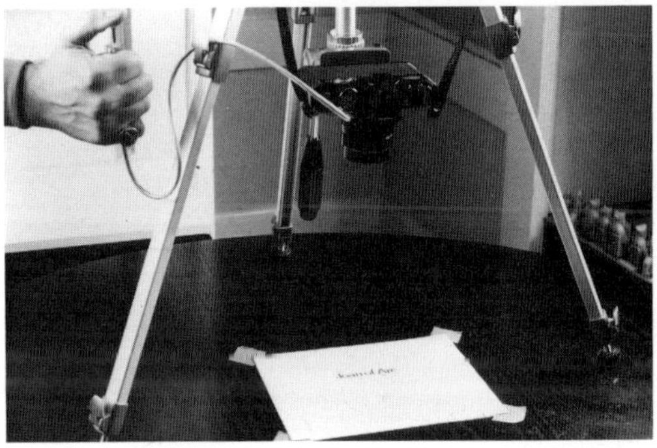

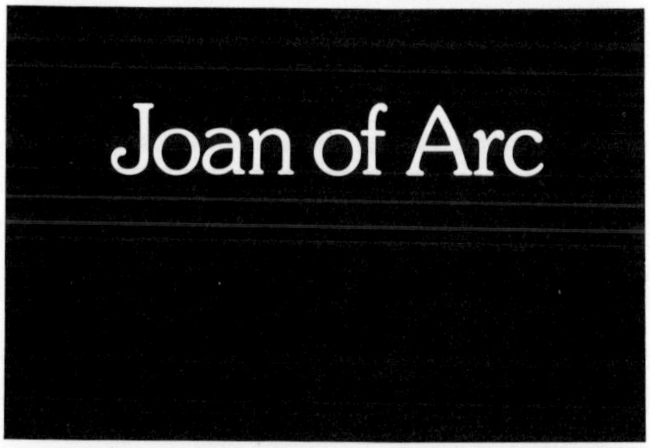

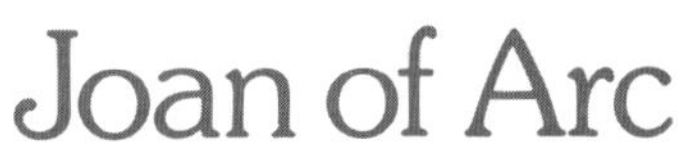

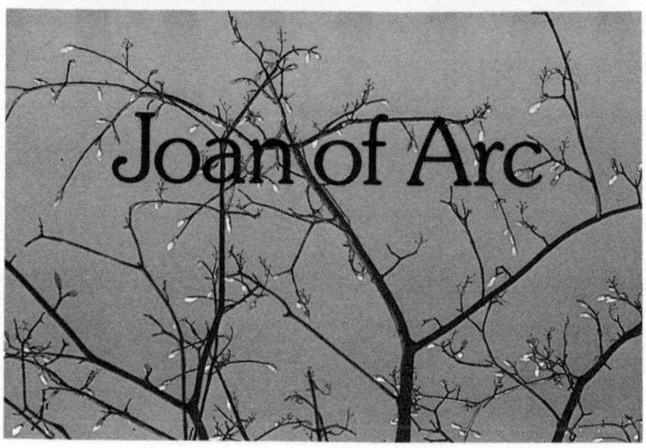

Creating a title for *Joan of Arc*. The original title is made using large commercial lettering (1) and shot on a copy stand using lithographic film (2). The negative image this produces (3) can then be mounted with coloured gel to give coloured lettering (4) or copied as a positive image and 'sandwiched' with another slide (5).

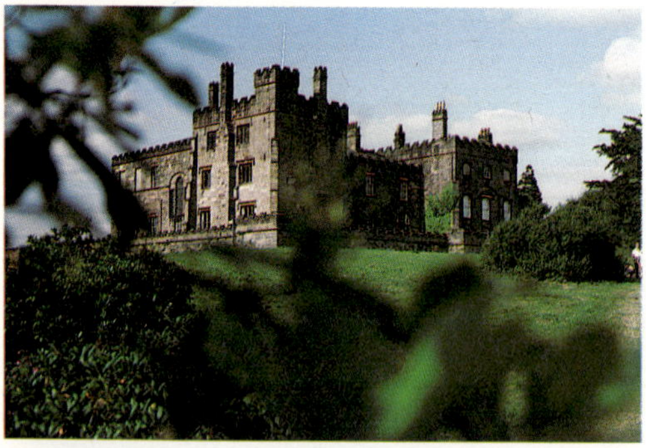

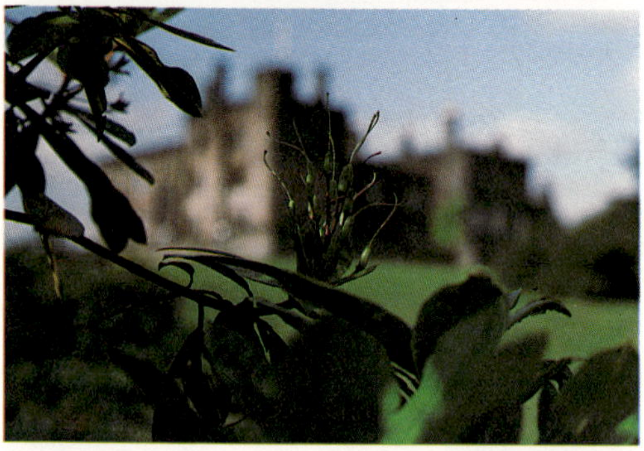

Focus shift. A gentle dissolve introduces Ripley Castle, using two shots that can both stand perfectly well on their own.

p. 72) are essential.

For successful title slides, you really need to use a tripod or a copy-stand and fire the shutter with a cable release. Titles must be positioned in the frame with extreme accuracy, lighting is critical, and if you are building up a sequence of titles you must get the relationship between adjoining slides absolutely right.

So try it — it's the only way to learn. And when you get it right, you'll also find that it's hugely enjoyable.

Transformation scenes

Both *Star of the Sea* and *Witchwood* hinge on a rather extravagant version of a standard two-projector trick — the transformation.

Like successful titling, successful transformation shots normally demand a tripod, some patience, and a good deal of planning. These pages illustrate a few common varieties. For convenience, let's call them the focus shift, the time shift, and the subject shift.

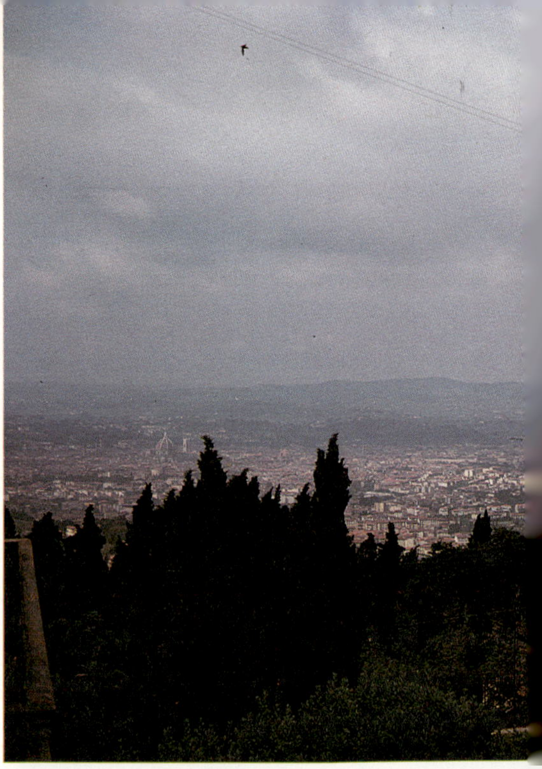

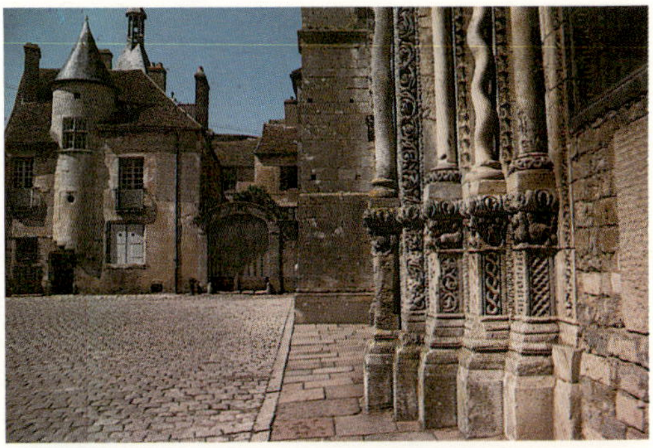

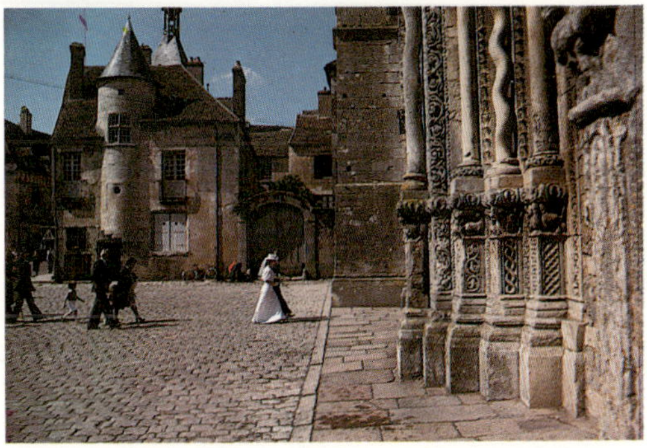

What's a church without a brido? In this time-shift pair the lack is remedied in seconds!

The focus shift is a film device that can be extraordinarily useful to the slide-show maker. With a little thought, you can set up a picture that works on two different planes of focus — one where the foreground is sharp, and another where the background is sharp. Take both pictures, keeping the composition exactly the same. At the moment of dissolve, both planes will appear to be sharp — and you have smoothly shifted your audience's attention from one subject to the other. In *Witchwood* a focus shift from a spider's web to a long shot of the walker was used to suggest danger. A shift from a windowpane streaming with water to a dark landscape might set up the idea of a storm. There are as many other applications as you can think of — multiplied by about five. So keep thinking!

The time shift involves no change in focus, but may well demand a change of

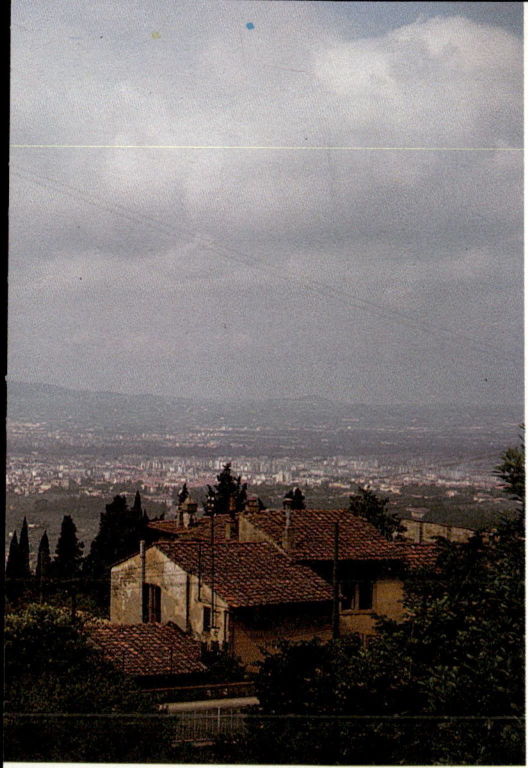

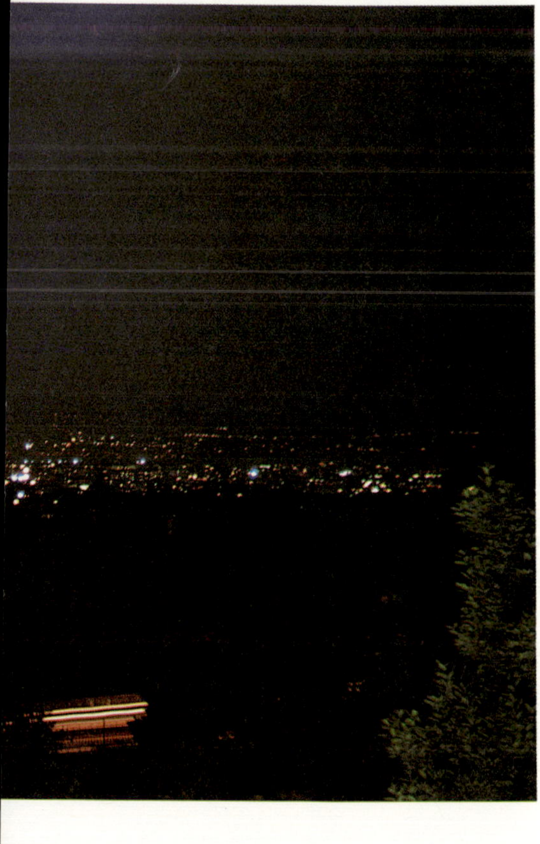

Time shift. A dissolve on these two views over Florence creates a spectacular effect of twilight shading into night.

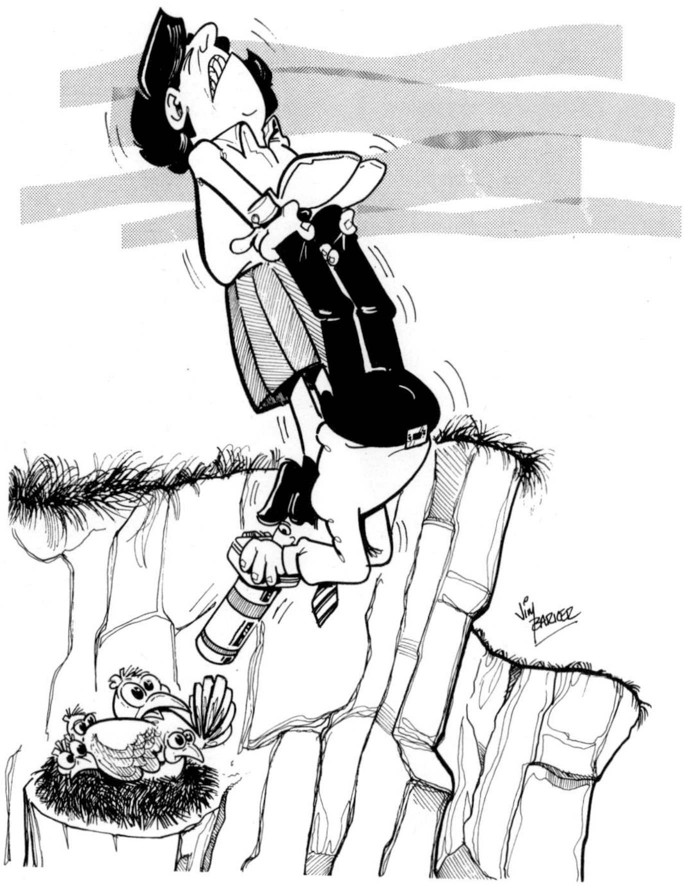

For perfect dissolves it's worth taking a little extra trouble to get the right angle . . .

exposure. The classic time-shift pair on pp. 58–9 gives the illusion of nightfall over Florence. You will be surprised at the effectiveness of a long, slow dissolve between shots like these. Another example of time shift is the spider's web trick I mentioned in the opening paragraph. For this, find a web that is coated in frost, take a picture of it with your camera on a tripod, then breathe gently on the web till the frost has melted. Take your second shot with precisely the same framing. In the programme, of course, you show the pictures in reverse order!

Subject shift depends for its success on a quick eye and a good choice of shots and angles when you are making your selection for a show. Personally, I love it, because when it's done properly it's always a show-stopper. *Witchwood* uses it (see p. 106) and so do many of my other programmes. There are no ground rules — everything depends on your own imagination. You, too, can easily turn a man into a tree, or a tree into a man. The pillars of a temple or a church can become an avenue of trees. A flowering rose can become a brilliant circle of stained glass. An old engraving can dissolve into a real view of the same place. A plant or a building can grow step by step, before your eyes. A shift of lighting can turn a demon into an angel. If you like fairy tales, you can even turn a frog into a prince; or, if you're in a radical feminist mood, a prince into a frog. Transformation, in the hands of a good slide-show maker, is almost literally a magician's wand. Use it well, and you will never lack for audiences.

Twinkle, twinkle little bat

'Twinkle' is almost impossible to illustrate in a book: the effect depends on the rapid juggling of two overlapping images on screen. Its most common use, as the name suggests, is for night shots or daytime shots showing light on a moving surface, and used carefully it can give a delightful impression of life. Two identical pictures taken with and without a starburst filter can be treated this way, but there are many other uses. Imagine, for instance, a long shot of a huge crowd in a stadium alternating at speed with another shot taken from exactly the same viewpoint a few seconds later. The result could be a wonderful impression of excitement and movement. Or how about one of those control consoles beloved of science fiction film makers, with hundreds of flickering status lights?

Fair enough, that's what *I'd* use it for. But I'm sure you have plenty of ideas of your own.

And now over to our engineering section . . .

This chapter has been little more than an introduction to the techniques of sequence photography and two-projector work. I can't pretend it's exhaustive, and I don't feel it should be — as long as it helps you think up some ideas of your own, it has done its job. Aside from the basic shot grammar, there are no real rules — I can't give you a sure-fire formula for a successful slide show. I can only point out the available tools and the ways in which they can be used.

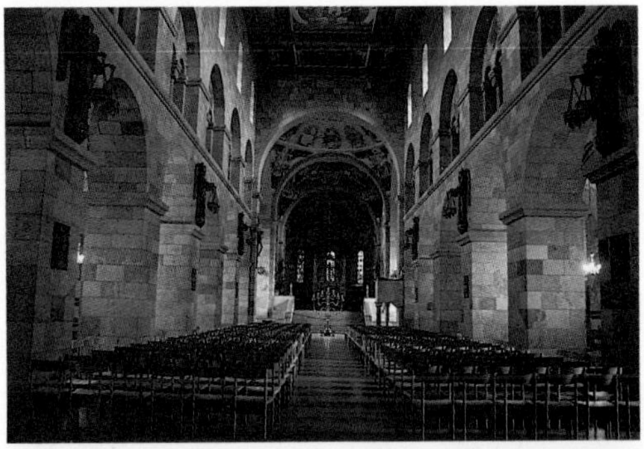

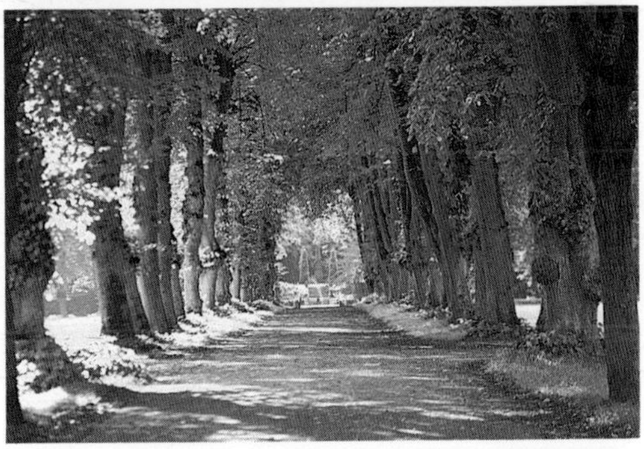

Transformation. In this pair from a show called *The New King*, the transformation from church pillars to trees recalls older, pagan days.

And talking of tools, it's time now to look at some of the hardware that goes with two-projector work — the cunning little devices that actually allow you to weave some of the magic we've been looking at. As you will see, some of them are amazingly simple — so don't let yourself be put off by self-styled experts who talk electronics at you. You can enter the world of dissolve with a few bits of wood, and two perfectly ordinary slide projectors. There's no need for complex high technology, and no need for a bank balance in five figures.

In fact, it's as simple as one plus one.

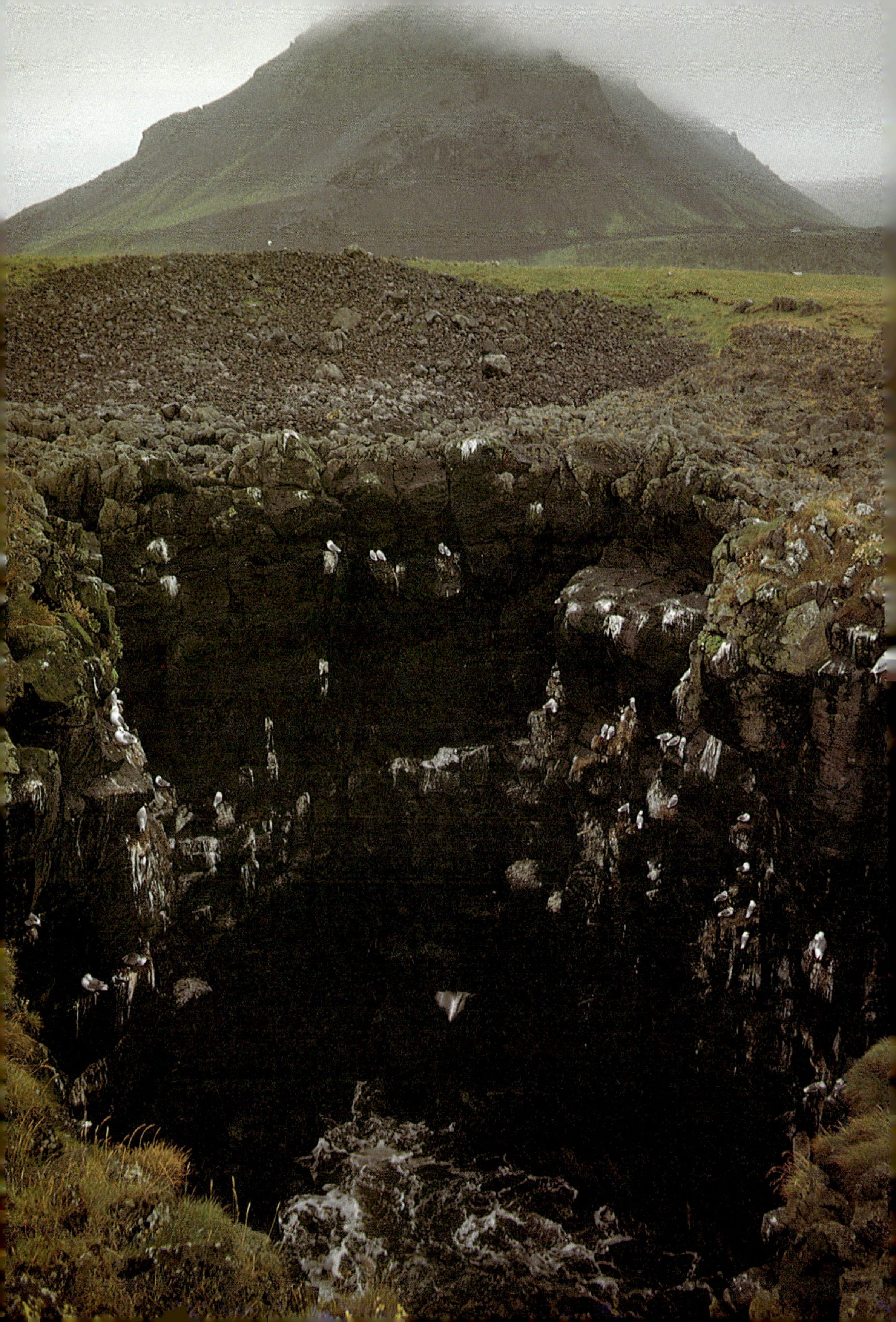

6

One projector, two projector . . .

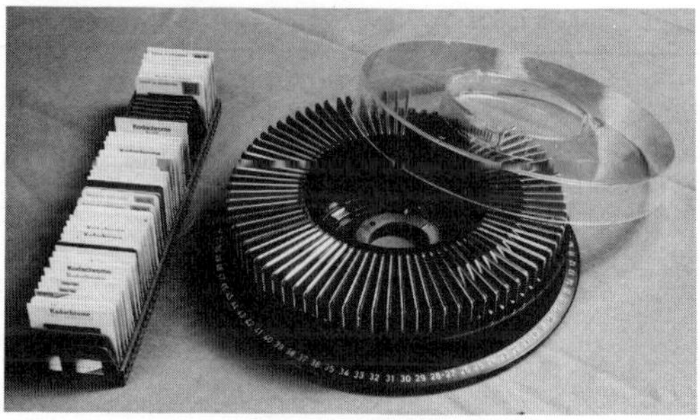

Standard DIN magazines. Most projectors use either one or the other — some can use both.

Kodak Carousel projectors, for many years the industry standard. The more sophisticated models are supplied complete with sockets for control by electronic dissolve units — other projectors may require adaptation, which could invalidate the manufacturer's guarantee.

This chapter is dedicated to a lady who once made my day. She carefully sought me out after a public show to thank me for 'the lovely film'.

And of course, it hadn't been a film. It was just that this particular lady had never seen a slide show that used two projectors.

It really does make that much difference.

I can describe what twin projection does. I can even show you some examples of it (see Chapter 5). But there is nothing to equal the impact of a two-projector dissolve programme on a large screen in a darkened room. So keep an eye open for the touring shows — there are several, and one may be local to your area. Keep an eye on the local camera club notice board, and be sure to attend any demonstration evenings. And keep an eye on other camera club members; try to persuade any that have two-projector systems to let you see them, and maybe try them out with some test shots of your own.

Getting to grips with twin projection

Once you're convinced — and I firmly believe you will be — the next step is to buy the projection equipment: either a match for your existing projector, or a new matching pair. Sadly, the battered old magic lantern from the second-hand shop won't do for this more sophisticated work. You are looking for a machine that has magazine loading (using DIN standard slide magazines like the ones opposite), remote-controlled slide change (forward and reverse) and, perhaps, remote-controlled focussing. Some more advanced projectors focus automatically, but

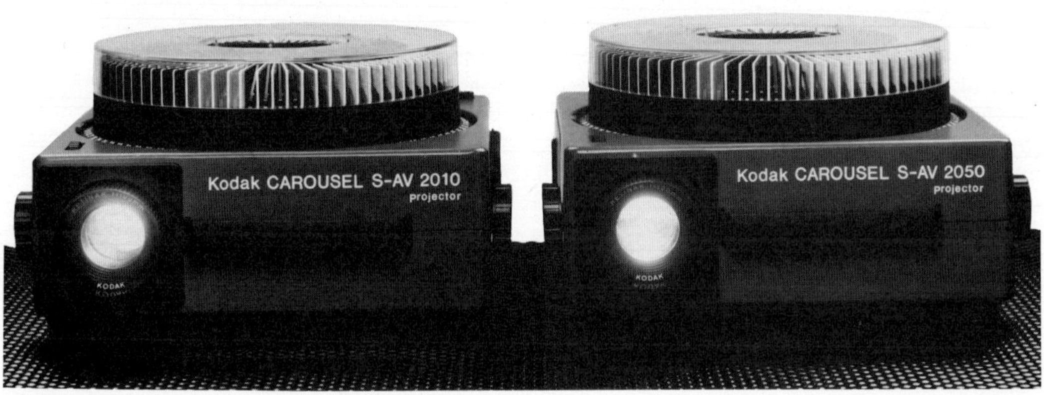

A basic (and extremely crude!) dissolve unit you can make in about ten minutes. Cut the sliding insert so that the projector lenses line up on it as indicated. You can make it of anything opaque — even thick card! To operate, slot the insert into place and move it backwards and forwards. Experiment with different-shaped slider cutouts till you find the one that works best for you.

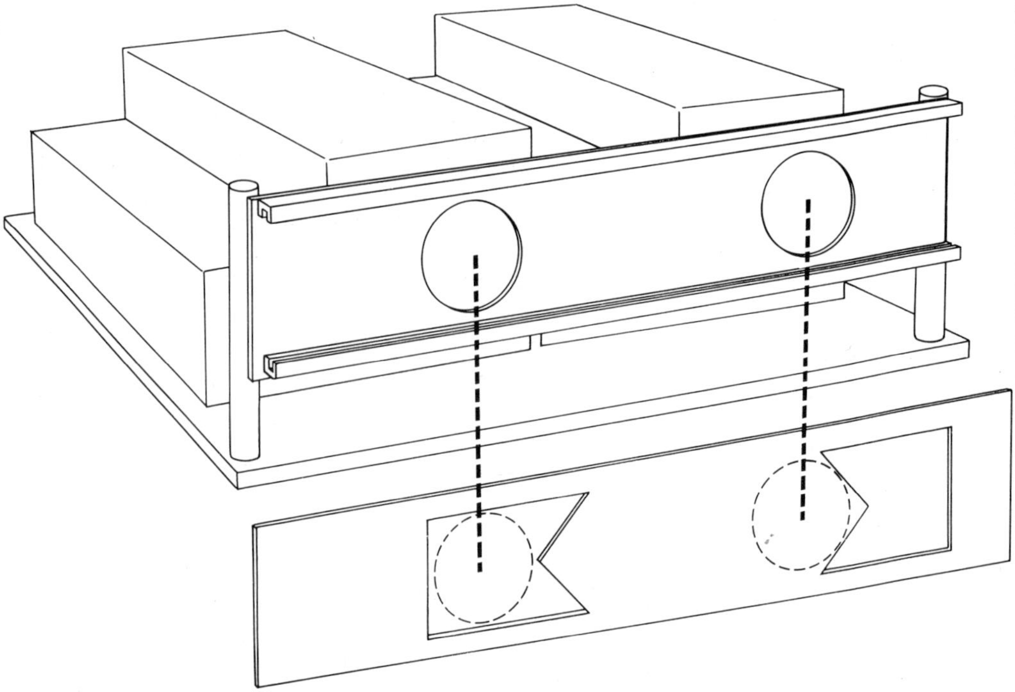

beware — some types of electronic dissolve unit can prevent this feature from operating. If you can avoid such systems, however, automatic focussing is highly desirable in two-projector work.

Beware of extremely cheap projectors. For perfect dissolves you need a projector that will place the image of each successive slide in exactly the same place on screen. It should also have firm adjustments allowing it to be tilted up and down and from side to side, so you can line up the two dissolving images precisely. Some projectors cut their price by economising on these features. It's a false economy.

And then . . . ?

Once you have two suitable projectors, you need just one more component before you're off and running — a dissolve unit. This needn't cost a king's ransom; shown above is a dissolve unit that you could probably put together in a day. Don't be put off by the term 'dissolve unit'. All it really has to do is cover up one projector lens while, at the same time, uncovering the other. Use your hands, or a friend's, if all else fails!

If you want something more professional, you have two choices. One is a ready-made manual system that does the same job as the one above, but better. The other is a more sophisticated — and usually more expensive — electronic system.

Manual systems

At the moment the best available manual system is distributed by Sir George Pollock, himself no mean exponent of the art (see p. 100). The Purlock Duofade uses two iris diaphragms and a control linkage: two cables attached to sliders that run in parallel channels. Operating both sliders together will open one diaphragm while closing the other. The diaphragms can also be opened and closed separately — a very useful feature.

The Purlock Duofade does not control slide advance in the projectors. For this, the normal remote control unit is used, taped into place next to the Duofade's control channels. The system is very easy to use, and there is little to go wrong. For a beginner, it's perfect.

Electronic systems

Most other dissolve units are electronic, and most control two separate functions: lamp brightness and slide advance. Instead of covering and uncovering the lens, electronic systems increase or decrease the power going to the projector lamps. This makes a clean, instantaneous cut from one projector to the other impossible: the lamp, especially if it is a powerful one, takes a few moments to dim completely.

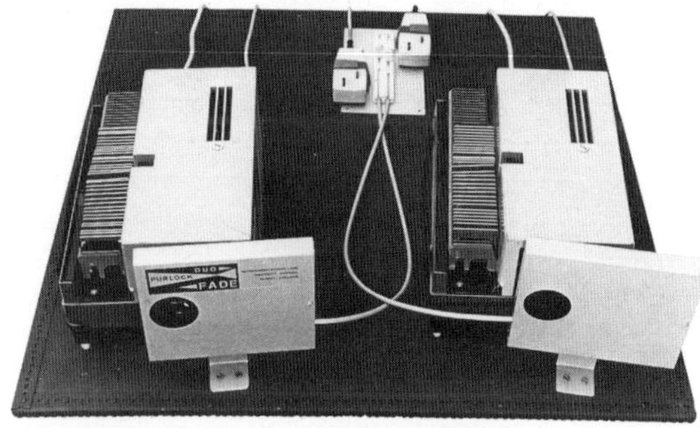

The Purlock Duofade, a simple manual dissolve unit that allows full control of each projector.

Imatronic offer one very inexpensive unit that's really an electronic Purlock Duofade: it allows independent control of each lamp, but can also advance the slide in the dark projector. The only other unit that makes this possible is the far more sophisticated — and expensive — Diafade 2. For simplicity, most electronic units are controlled either by a single slider or by push-buttons.

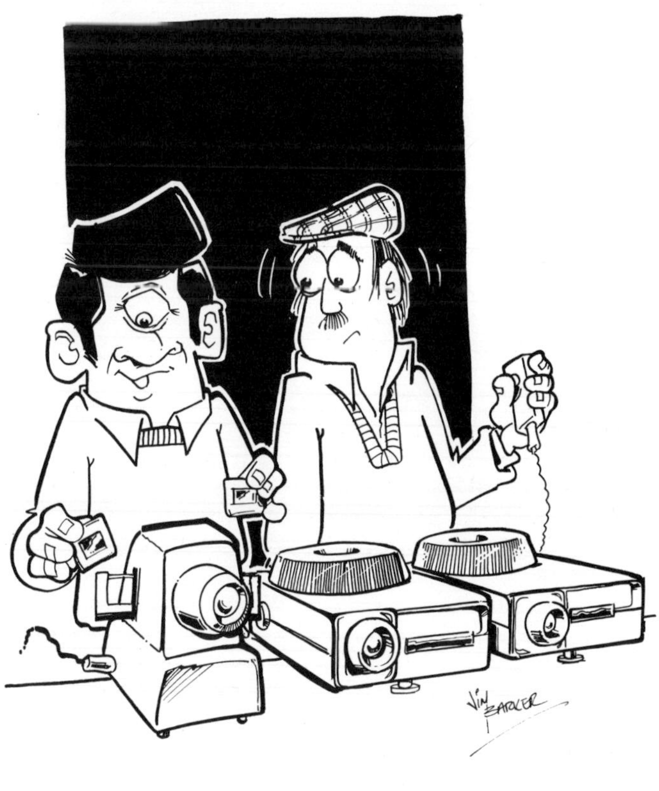

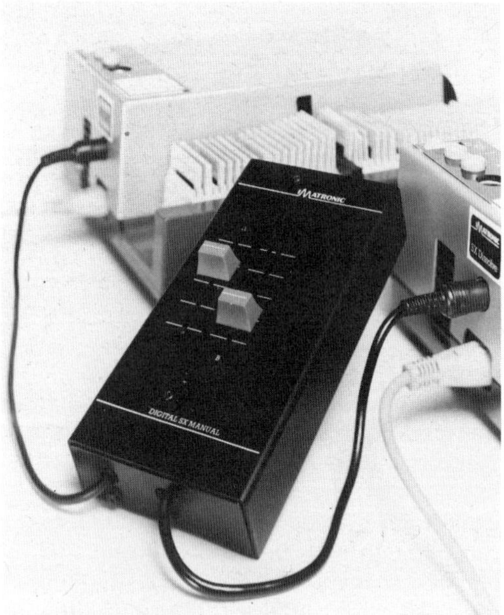

The Imatronic Digital SX Manual — just connect it to two suitably adapted projectors and you can dim each lamp individually *and* change slides in each projector. An inexpensive and useful unit — but you can't record its signals on tape.

The Imatronic IMA6 (slider) and IMA8 (push-button) handsets will both plug into the basic dissolve unit.

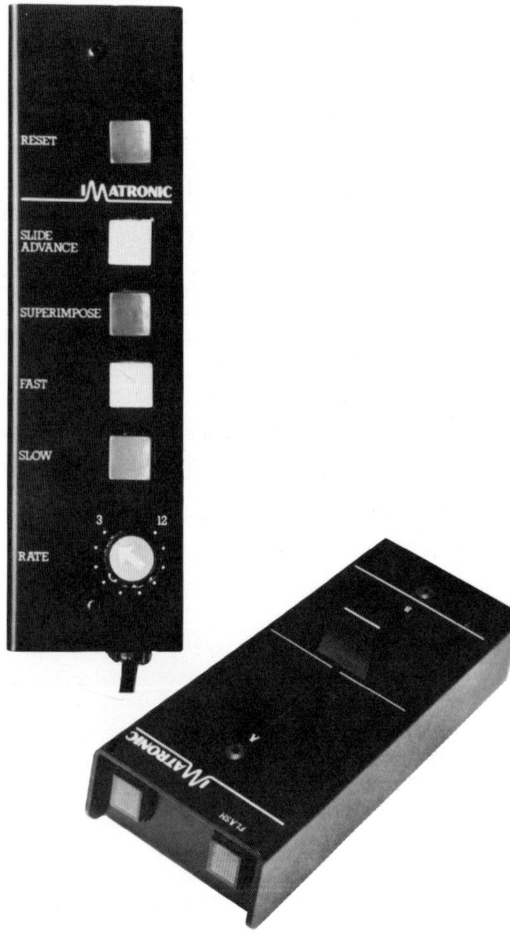

The Diafade 2, which again allows individual control of each lamp (using the slider controls) and each slide-change mechanism (using the push-buttons). Like most other electronic units, its signals can be recorded on tape — on playback they will run a complete show automatically. The Diafade is a quality unit for the serious enthusiast, and is priced accordingly.

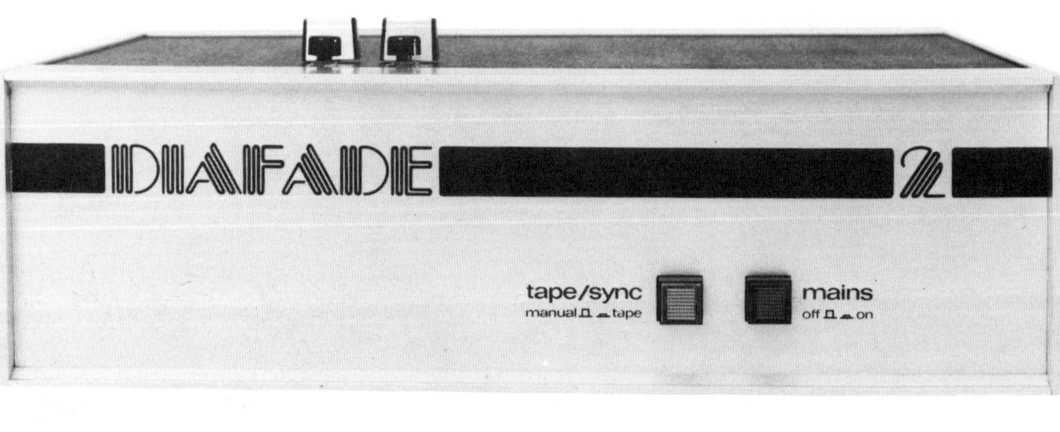

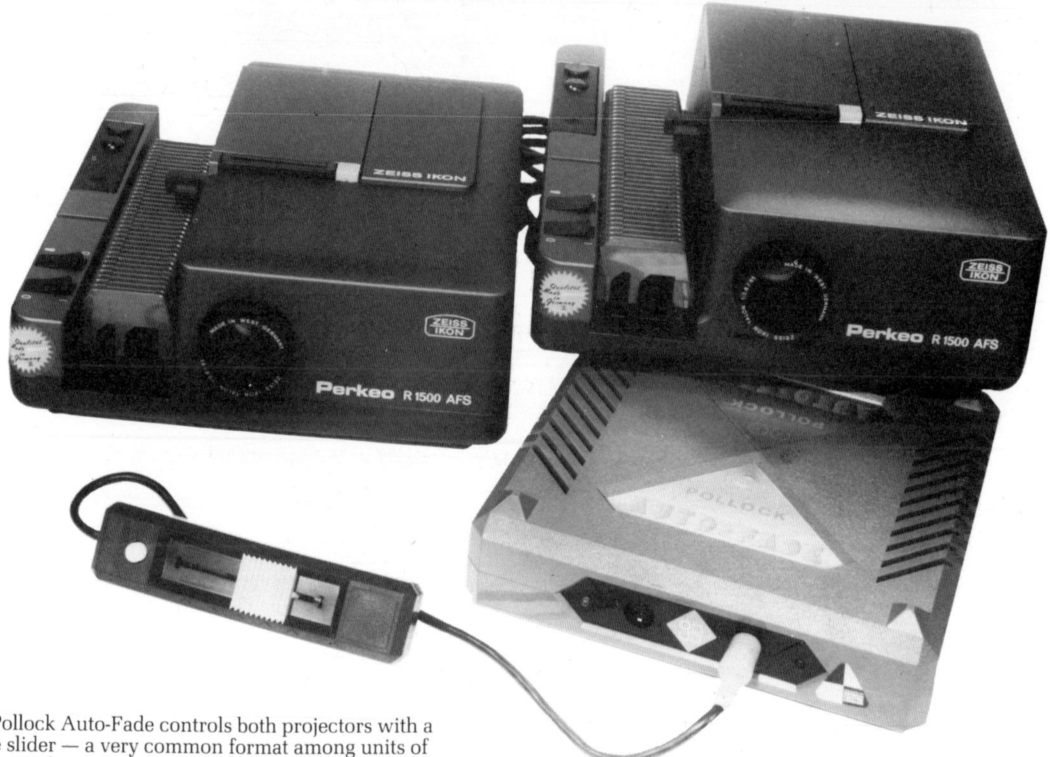

The Pollock Auto-Fade controls both projectors with a single slider — a very common format among units of this type. The Auto-Fade ensures that image brightness on screen remains constant throughout the dissolve, producing a smooth transition from one shot to the next.

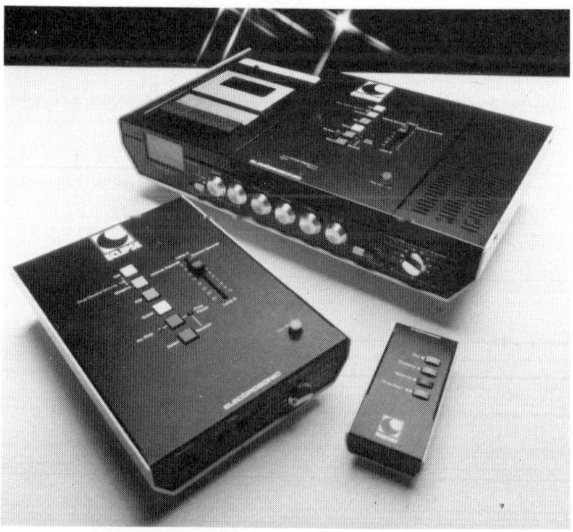

The Electrosonic Eclipse system. The Eclipse (lower left) is a self-contained unit with push-button and slider controls built in — you can use either. The Gemini (top) also has a built-in tape deck with access to a spare tape track, and a built-in amplifier — but no speaker. The Mercury remote-control unit (bottom right) allows you to make fast cuts, dissolves to a preset speed, and reverse dissolves or cuts. It will also start a tape on the Gemini unit.

The Kodak Programmable Dissolve Unit. The 12-button main keypad allows a wide range of dissolve speeds and special effects, including a reset command that automatically returns the projector magazines to their starting positions. Designed for use with Kodak Carousel projectors, this is a professional unit at a professional price — but its remarkable features (see text) make it good value for money. The unit needs a separate tape deck with full access to a spare track.

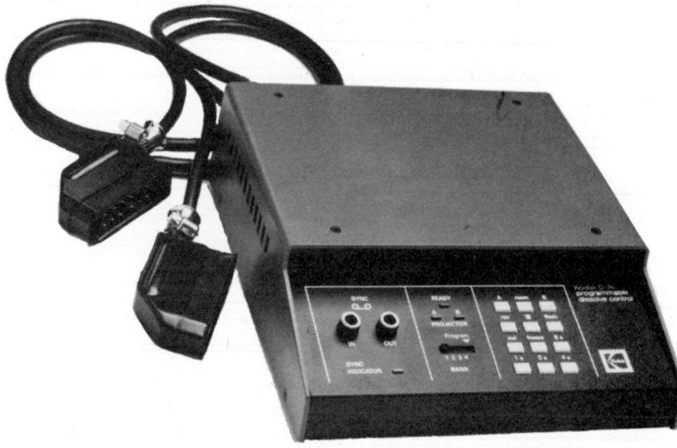

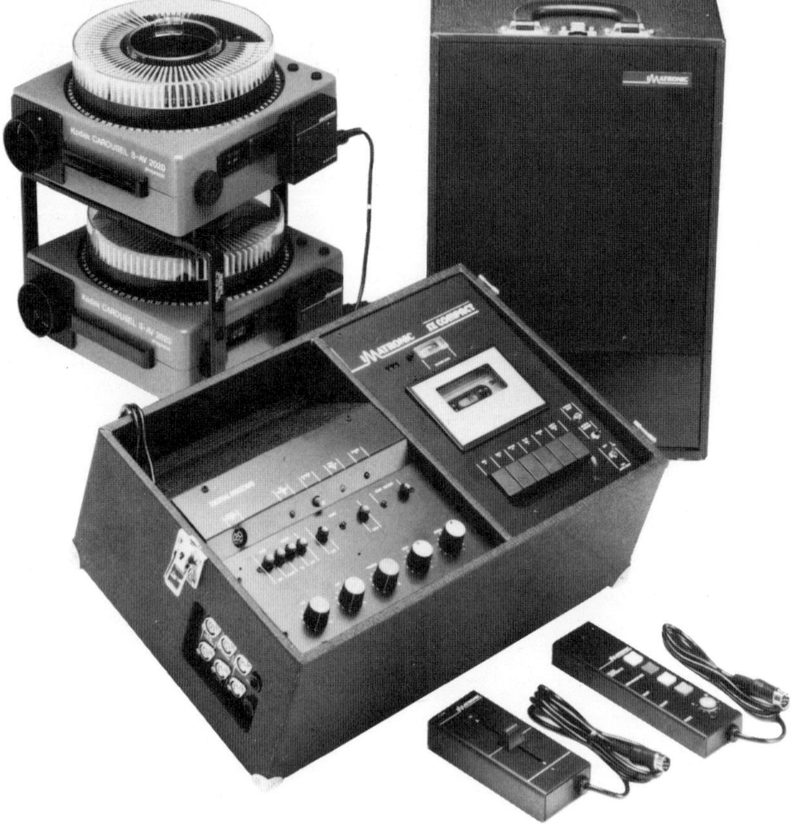

The Imatronic SX Compact system includes everything except the projectors! There's a mono cassette deck with access to a spare track, a dissolve unit that accepts either push-button or slider hand controls, an on-board amplifier, and a speaker (in the lid) that can be positioned up to 30 metres from the unit. Not cheap, but rugged and designed for heavy use.

Slider units such as the Pollock Auto-Fade or the Imatronic IMA6 are the simplest type. Moving the slider from one end of its channel to the other dims the lamp in one projector while brightening the lamp in the other. The process can be as fast or slow as you wish. At each end of the slider channel is a microswitch; an extra push on the slider operates this switch, advancing the slide magazine in the dark projector.

Push-button units such as the Imatronic IMA8 or the Electrosonic Eclipse system offer several preset functions. These might include a fast dissolve, a 'slow' dissolve at a speed that can be adjusted with a separate control, 'superimpose', which puts both images on screen together, and 'step'. 'Step' allows you to advance the slide in the dark projector independently of any other operation — more useful than it probably sounds.

Simple push-button systems are ideal for educational or business programmes, but can be frustrating for creative work. More advanced push-button units offer greater flexibility. The Kodak Programmable Dissolve Unit is excellent in this and other respects, although it's designed for use with the sturdy, reliable, but far from cheap Kodak Carousel projectors. However, control pulses recorded on tape by this system (see pp. 69–70) have an invaluable extra feature. Provided that the programme has been started with the magazines in the correct position, it is impossible for the projectors to fall 'out of step' with the soundtrack — even if you have to stop one projector to change a bulb. As soon as the projector is back in action again, it cycles through its magazine, apparently searching for the right slide, and will not put an image on screen until it has 'found' the right one — a feature worth its weight in gold!

Why do I need an electronic system?
Maybe you don't. However, if you want your programmes to run 'by themselves', only one of the better electronic systems will do.

With a manual system, every programme you present is a live performance. Unless you have rehearsed each change, each dissolve, to perfection, there is always the chance of a mistake. There are ways to avoid this problem, but in the end there is only one permanent solution: to make a record of the precise timing of every move.

Most electronic systems can do this for you — but not all, so do check! The electronic commands that control lamp brightness and slide advance on each projector can be recorded on tape, rather like the programs for home computers. This recording of the control signals can be fed back into the dissolve unit at a later date. The unit will then duplicate everything you originally did with the controls. You can even edit the tape, much as you would edit a normal soundtrack, but this can cause problems on some systems and should always be done with care.

At this stage it may be worth taking another look at the section on choosing your tape recorder (pp. 41–46). For I must emphasise that you may not need a custom-built 'audio-visual' tape deck to record dissolve programmes. Many manufacturers offer such decks either as extras or as integral parts of the dissolve system. Depending on your particular needs, such decks could be the answer to prayer, or an expensive and unnecessary white elephant.

Taping dissolve programmes
Your choice of tape-recording equipment for recording and playing back dissolve programmes will depend entirely on your own particular way of making soundtracks.

If you do not normally make stereo soundtracks for your programmes, but you do use a stereo machine for 'additive mixing' (see p. 42), then your present machine should be perfectly adequate. You can simply record the dissolve control signals onto the 'spare' track after you have finished the soundtrack. In fact, any cassette or reel-to-reel deck that allows you to record two separate tracks on the same tape on separate occasions will do, as long as it can be properly connected to the dissolve unit. The only way to find out is to try it — so don't commit yourself to buying a unit until

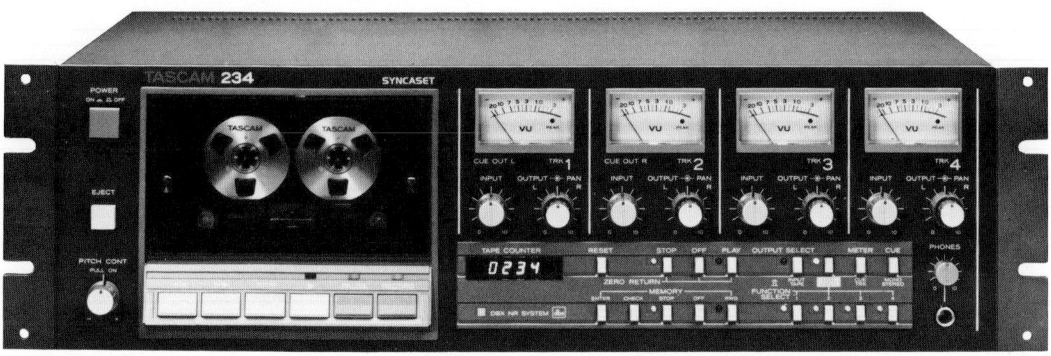

The Tascam 234 — a four-track double-speed cassette deck built to professional requirements. A deck like this will be as useful in advanced soundtrack work (see Chapter 8) as in recording and playing back dissolve unit control signals. For those with smaller ambitions, the Tascam 133 gives stereo sound plus a cue track and some attractive features, and the 124AV offers mono sound and a cue track. The cheaper machines provide standard or double-speed play at the flick of a switch.

you *have* tried it. You must also make sure that you can play back the tracks separately. The last thing your audience wants to hear is the eerie sound of dissolve control signals!

If stereo soundtracks are important to you, then you will need more elaborate equipment; in fact, you will almost certainly need a special audio-visual tape deck. As noted on p. 46, these decks allow you to record one or in some cases two control tracks completely separately from your soundtrack but on the same tape. However, do remember to use only one side of the tape — try anything else and you will lose either a soundtrack or a carefully-rehearsed and performed sequence of control signals.

Do not feel obliged to pick the machine recommended by the manufacturer of your dissolve unit. Other decks may be equally suitable — or better — and a wide choice is available. Some users may find it an advantage to buy a deck that will also control a single-projector show. This normally requires a 1kHz pulse generator built into the deck (see p. 46).

A word of warning though. Some machines of this type offer a 'free head' to record and replay the control signals. For simple 1kHz pulses, as used in single-projector shows, a free head is perfectly adequate. For more sophisticated signals, including most two-projector control signals, it may not be enough. For these, your best bet will always be a 'sync' head capable of recording and replaying even normal audio signals. Again, you should always try out the tape deck you want to use with your own dissolve unit before committing yourself to buying it.

Putting it all together

Most new slide-show makers who want to go into dissolve work will need to build their system up a little at a time. For the lucky few who can afford to buy everything in one fell

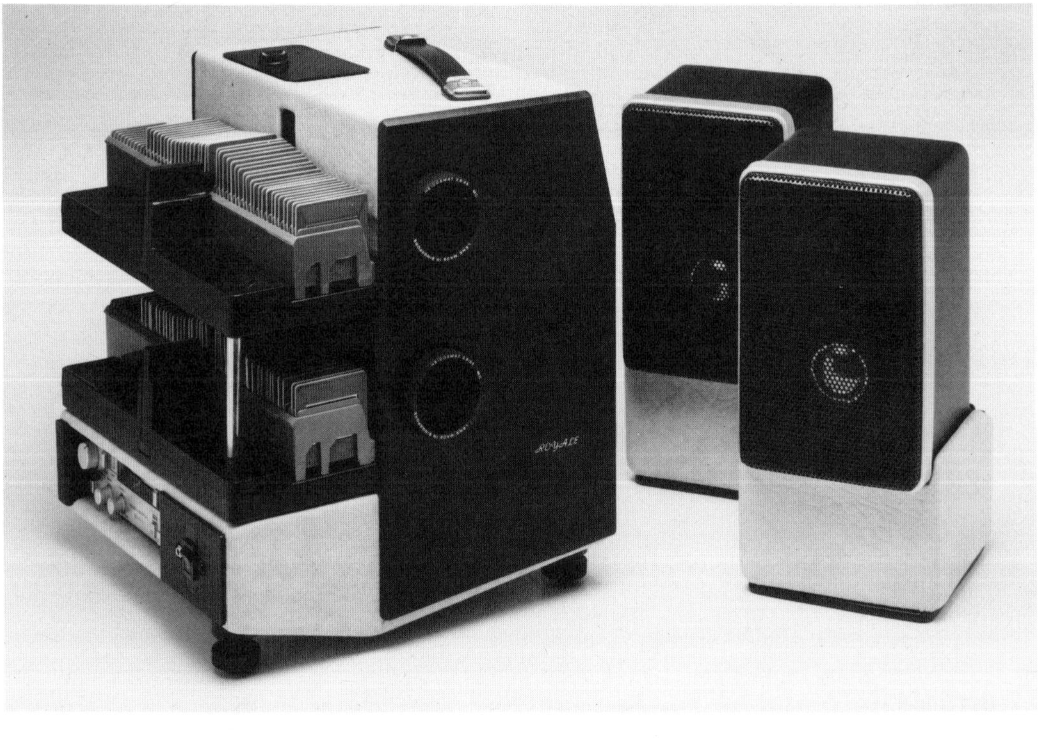

The ingenious Royale system, designed by a slide-show maker for slide-show makers. Its main advantages are its compactness, stability, and ease of adjustment. The lenses can be lined up on any screen 5 feet or more from the unit, and the built-in dissolve unit will accept control signals from the Imatronic SX 2500 or the Pollock Auto-Fade.

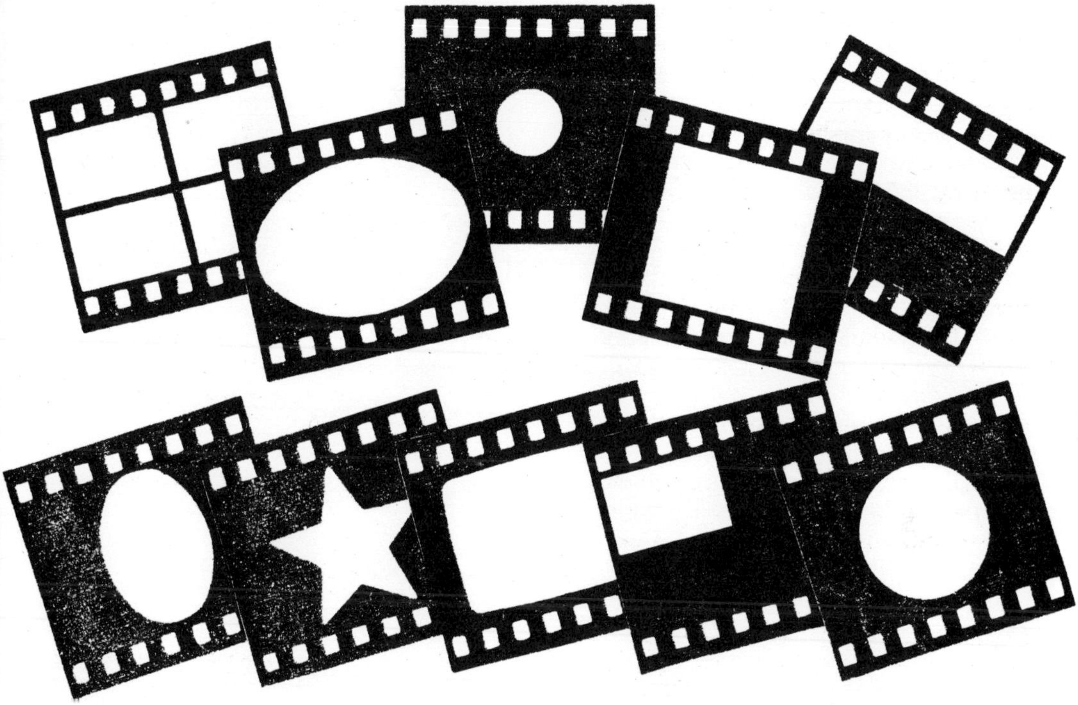

A selection of foil inserts for glass mounts, showing the large choice of shapes available.

swoop — and know that they are ready to do so — it may be well worth considering a unit such as the Royale.

The Royale has been designed by another professional slide show maker, Colin Balls. The top-of-the-line model is designed to fulfil all the average enthusiast's fondest dreams. It is a twin projection unit, a stereo sound system and a dissolve control system all rolled into one compact device. Colin has taken his basic components from a number of different manufacturers, and made a number of modifications of his own: the projector gates, for instance, have been altered in several ingenious ways to make sure that each successive slide will appear in exactly the same place on the screen.

Two things make this particular unit stand out from almost anything else on the market. First, because the projectors are both housed in a single compact casing, they are extremely simple to line up — and once they are in alignment, they stay that way. Second, it is indisputably the most portable dissolve unit on the market — and ideal for someone giving a large number of programmes to small or medium-sized audiences. For larger audiences you will probably need to use a more powerful sound system: but you can still plug the 'on-board' cassette player into it.

Even the best hardware is not enough on its own. A slide show can be made — or broken — by the work you put in *before* the performance. So the rest of this chapter is devoted to the gadgets, extras and accessories that can help make that work as easy — and as effective — as possible.

The 35mm picture frame

For an art dealer, a good frame can make the difference between selling a picture quickly and not selling it at all. The same goes for your slides. With a single-projector system you may be able to get away with leaving slides in the card or plastic mounts supplied by the processors. But as soon as another projector arrives on the scene, you're likely to be in trouble.

Slides mounted by processors leave the film surface exposed to the air — and to dirt, dust, scratches and greasy fingers. Slides mounted in this way also 'pop' when exposed to the full heat of a projector lamp. The effect on screen can be disturbing. As the film expands and moves away from the heat, the picture suddenly jumps out of focus. An autofocus projector can cope with the problem, but not completely. A 'popped' slide is not flat — so the edges will never be fully in focus.

The answer is simple, and not drastically expensive. It's called a glass mount.

The glass mount 'traps' the film chip between two thin plates of glass, holding it consistently and permanently flat, and protecting it from dirt and marks of all kinds. Various commercial firms, including GePe, Wess, and Kodak, make glass mounts — all are professional products, and your choice may well depend on circumstances. However, never mix mounts from different manufacturers within a show — and be sure to ask for 'anti-Newton' glass. Mounts using ordinary glass will sometimes produce curious rainbow-coloured 'Newton rings' when projected.

To the newcomer, the choice of mounts available may seem a bit bewildering. Most systems offer two types: a simple mount with slots or corner pieces for locating the film chip, and a *register* mount, fitted with plastic lugs that slot into the sprocket holes of the film. These are used to mount film shot in register cameras, which place each picture in a precise relationship to the sprocket holes. For instance, if you mount a register camera on a tripod, and take a series of pictures of, say, dawn over a city skyline, you can simply cut the processed film into frames, fit the frames into register mounts, and walk away with an instant series of perfect dissolves. Register cameras can also be useful for transformation effects and double images. By using a viewfinder with reference markings, it is possible to set up two different images in precisely the same place on the film frame.

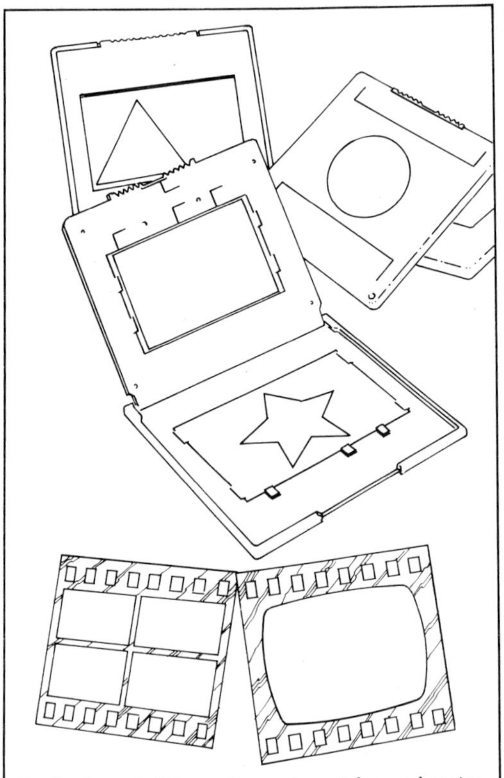

Ready-shaped slide masks can be quicker and easier to use than foils.

Unfortunately, register cameras are expensive. You *can* achieve the same effects without one — but you must be prepared to expend time, patience and maybe a few curses to line up each picture in the sequence very precisely inside its mount.

Most glass-mount systems also offer you the chance to mask off part of the film frame, either by inserting foil masks into a standard mount, or by obtaining a mount with a mask moulded into the plastic frame. You can see a few examples above. Many masks are simple shapes — circles, squares, stars, triangles and so on. Others are designed to be used as parts of a pattern in programmes involving four or more projectors (see p. 78). Used with imagination, they can transform your shows.

For instance, think of a mask that reveals only a thin horizontal strip across the centre of the frame — and then think of a bad picture shot with a wide-angle lens, where the actual area of interest is in the middle of the picture, lost amid unwanted expanses of sky area above and foreground area below. By deliberately shooting a series of such pictures, and mounting them in masked glass mounts, you can create a 'panoramic' sequence that will give your audience some genuine wide-screen entertainment!

Glass mounts are more than a means of keeping your slides clean and ensuring perfect focus. In the right hands they can be a creative tool in themselves.

Looking after glass mounts

All slides are prey to two deadly enemies — dirt and moisture. Dirt can penetrate even glass mounts, turning bright, clear pictures into a black snowstorm. Moisture can create brilliant but quite unwanted rings and markings, and provide a growing medium for fungi and moulds. All your slides — glass mounted or otherwise — need to be protected. The first rule is to clean all your slides and mounts very carefully when you are assembling them, so that dirt is excluded from the sandwich as far as possible. The second rule is to keep all your slide magazines in sealed plastic bags when they are not in use — and to keep a small packet of silica gel inside each bag. This will absorb moisture and condensation within the bag — but don't forget to renew it occasionally.

The author working at a simple lightbox. A lightbox is especially useful in the early stages of sequence-building, when you are sorting your material roughly into groups.

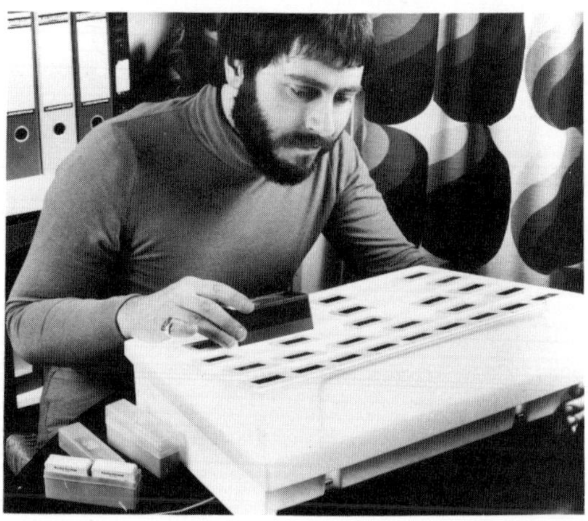

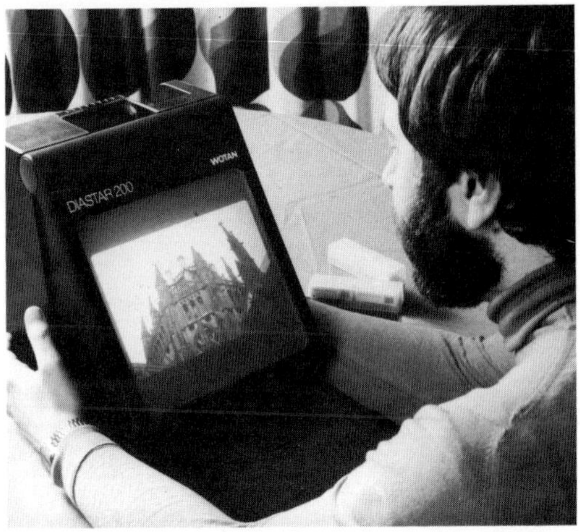

The Wotan Diastar gives bright, sharp, back-projected images even in daylight — ideal for detailed study of slides where a projector and screen are impractical.

In time it will become saturated. You can buy silica gel at any good chemist's shop.

Optional extras

There are many other tools that can simplify the slide-show maker's job or increase the creative possibilities open to him, but the most useful is probably the lightbox. This is an illuminated translucent surface where you can plan out sequences, laying slides side by side or in groups to see if they could form useful or attractive dissolves. If you're the do-it-yourself type, there's nothing to stop you building one at home. All you need is a wooden frame, a fluorescent tube or two, and a sheet of white translucent perspex — but do remember that fluorescent tubes give a slight blue colour cast. Otherwise, pick one up at your local camera shop. It may seem like a luxury, but it beats holding slides up to the light any day. Besides, *you* try holding thirty-six slides up to the light at once . . . Make sure your lightbox is reasonably large — that way you can build up even the longest sequence on it without running out of space.

Another useful gadget is a good hand viewer — you'll probably want one in any case, for that first quick look at the latest film back from the processors. Try to pick a viewer that lets you insert two slides at once — this can be useful for checking that

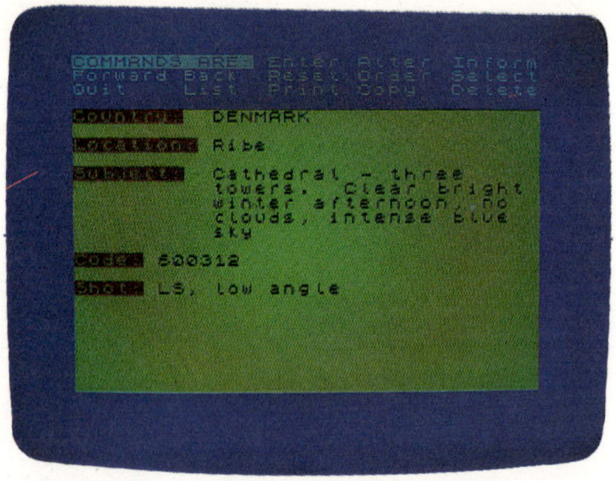

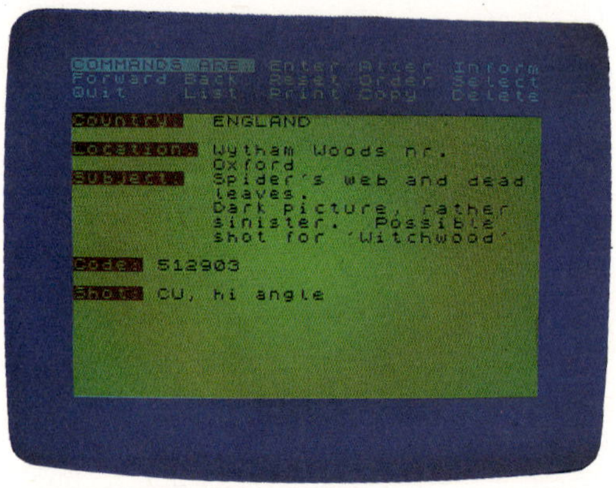

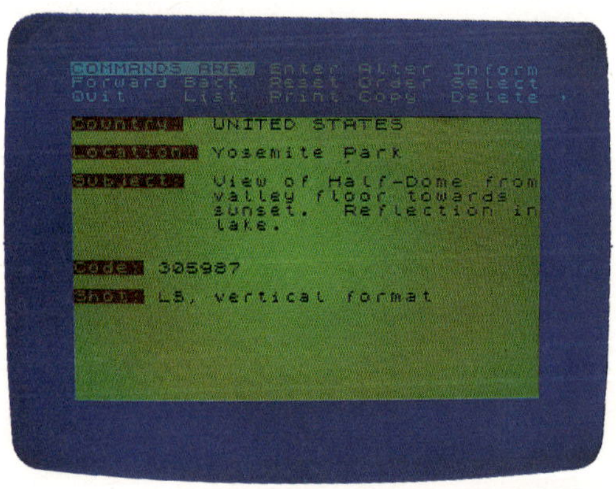

Displays from a computerised slide indexing system, in this case based on the Vu-File program for the ZX Spectrum.

'transformation' shots are in perfect alignment, or for matching up two successive shots in an ordinary dissolve sequence. But do remember that a hand viewer won't give you a clear idea of how two shots will look *on screen*; for that, you'll have to project them.

A useful alternative to the hand viewer is a back-projection unit such as the Wotan Diastar. This provides a large, bright picture without the need to set up a projector and screen. You can even use the front panel as a small lightbox.

Finally, be careful about storing your slides. As a programme-maker, you will want to keep most of your pictures in sequence, show by show — but keep the pictures you don't use in some kind of order, and keep them safe. If you can, number them and index them — you may find a card index system useful for this, or even a home computer if you have one. But wherever you keep your slides, keep them dry, keep them free of dust, and keep them out of the light. Any slide exposed to light for any length of time will eventually fade — and unless you like pictures apparently shot through a red or a green filter, you won't like the results.

Taking the next step

Using two projectors is an art that takes time to learn. But it can be learnt — and when you are familiar with it, you may start to chafe at some of its limitations. Suppose you could change slides twice as quickly? Suppose you could split the screen into thirds, or quarters, and run several dissolve sequences at once? All these things — and more — can be done. You just need one or two more projectors. And believe it or not, even advanced setups of this kind are not beyond the reach of a determined amateur group.

7

Three projector, more . . .

So what on earth is the point of using more than two projectors?

The answer is 'none at all' unless you're achieving something that can't be done with two — and many professional audio-visual producers achieve far more, in programme after programme made for prestige customers. The launch of a major new car, for instance, demands the highest possible standards of showmanship, and it's not unusual for more than twenty projectors to be used for such programmes. The results are spectacular. Images shift with dazzling speed against a coruscating, ever-changing background. A screen can be divided into a rapidly-shifting mosaic of graphics and photographs. In some shows a movie projector is used on the same screen, operated by the same electronic control unit that governs the projectors.

All of which, of course, has very little to do with a slide-show maker working from home with, if he is lucky, two projectors and a dissolve unit.

But don't give up. This kind of show, known by professionals as multivision, *is* within reach of the keen enthusiast. And, just as much to the point, the keen enthusiast may find that he needs it.

While preparing this book I paid my first ever visit to Ely in Cambridgeshire; and

Twin-screen images from *Islands in the Fens*, a portrait of the twinned medieval cathedral towns Ely and Ribe.

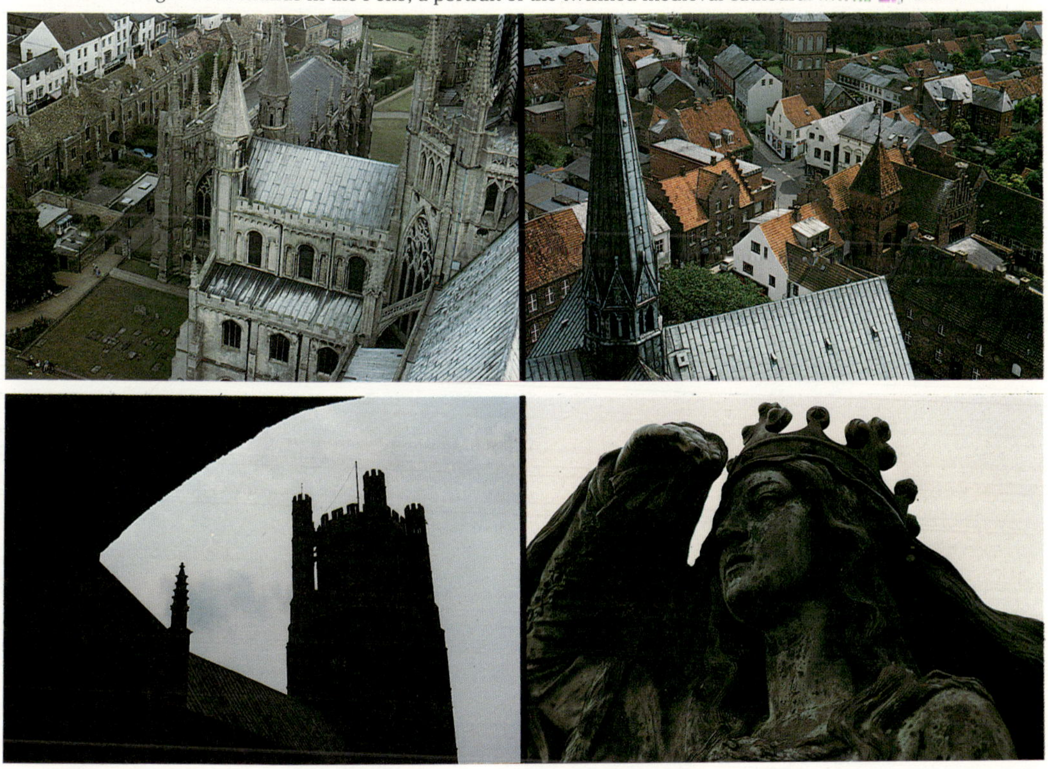

before I even got there I had the beginnings of an idea for a slide show. My inspiration was the town sign. It read 'Ely. Twin town Ribe, Denmark.' Not very interesting, you might think. Most British towns of any size have a twin somewhere on the continent. But I happen to know Ribe — intimately. Like Ely, it centres on a beautiful early-mediaeval cathedral built on an island in the fens. And the only possible way to do justice to two such marvellous subjects was with two screens — and four projectors.

Compare and contrast

Islands in the Fens uses two screens side by side. Each screen is effectively showing a two-projector programme. The difference is that the two programmes are synchronised; and with care, some very remarkable effects can be achieved in this way.

The sample screen spreads on p. 75 should give you some idea what I mean. Here multivision allows us to see the two towns side by side, and to examine the similarities — and differences — in close-up. But that's only the beginning. With four projectors, you can hold an image on, say, the left-hand screen while setting up a rapid series of changing images on the right-hand screen. Or you may decide not to split the screens up at all. It is perfectly possible to run the four projectors as two linked pairs, and produce a series of normal dissolving images that go right across both screens in a panorama format. As it happens, this technique is perfect for showing long shots of small towns in flat landscapes: it cuts out the huge areas of foreground and sky that usually bedevil such pictures (see also p. 72).

One minor problem remains — the 'line' in the middle. In an amateur show I feel this is perfectly acceptable, and relatively unimportant. Professionals have their own solutions, as we shall see.

But suppose all four projectors were trained on one screen? What could that achieve?

Pp. 78–9 offer some spectacular examples. These screen spreads are from *A Thames Calendar*, a programme I was commissioned to write by Kodak. The aim was to show high-quality picture material effectively and entertainingly in a programme lasting about ten minutes. Photography for the programme had been carried out over a period of two years by Patrick Walmsley, a producer from the Kodak audio-visual group. Each of the four seasons, on and around the Thames, was featured, showing its scenery, its people, its wildlife, and its annual events and celebrations.

Ten minutes may not seem long for a programme of this kind, but I have already pointed out that it is an ideal length for a

Simple control of three projectors. The Imatronic Triangle offers basic control functions including animation (achieved by rapidly cycling through all three projector images). A remarkably cheap unit, though it could be a little limiting for the really ambitious slide-show maker.

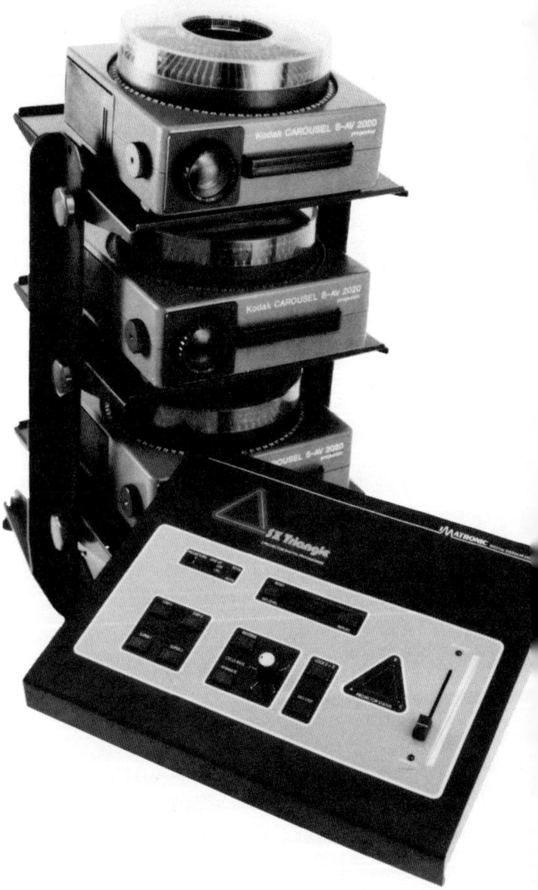

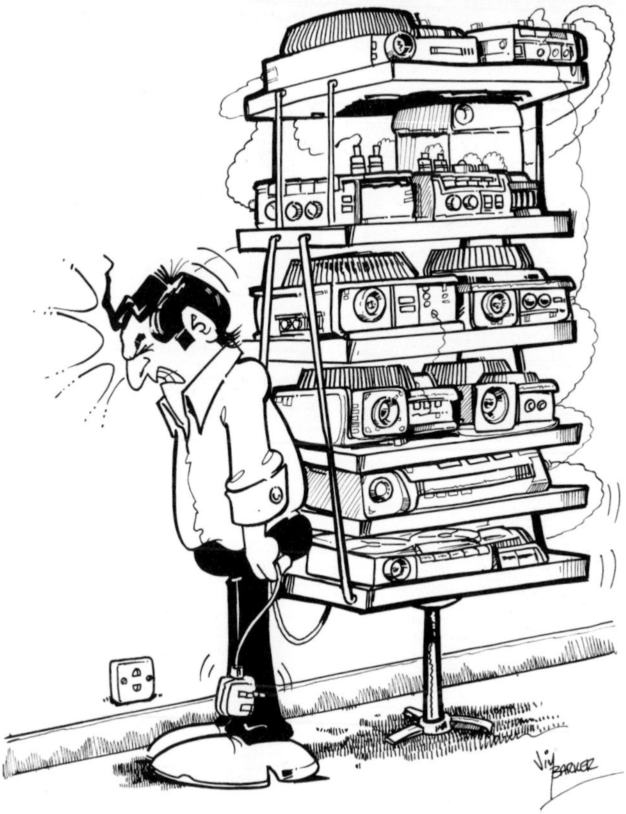

show; and within those ten minutes a great deal can be achieved, especially with four projectors. The ability to change images at speed allows you to create rapid sequences that give a vivid impression of action and excitement. We found this particularly useful in a sequence showing the races at Henley regatta. But that's not the only possibility. In slow sequences, too, images can be mingled in many different ways. *A Thames Calendar* opens with a beautiful impressionistic picture of dawn light on rippling water, followed by a dazzling set of sunrise shots. Because four projectors are being used, the first shot can remain on screen while up to three more are superimposed. The effect is surprising — and memorable.

Finally, of course, multivision allows you to divide the picture area into smaller segments, each containing its own mini-sequence. The next page shows a screen spread of this kind from *A Thames Calendar*. Professionals create these sequences with a superbly accurate copying camera known as a rostrum camera, and this is undoubtedly the best way to do it (see p. 84). But it isn't the only way — as we shall see.

You may be feeling that all these techniques are far beyond the resources of the average amateur. If so, you're quite right.

The main title from *A Thames Calendar* (Kodak). The script suggested an ornate lettering style with curlicues to give a period feel — the overall design creates the effect of a calendar page.

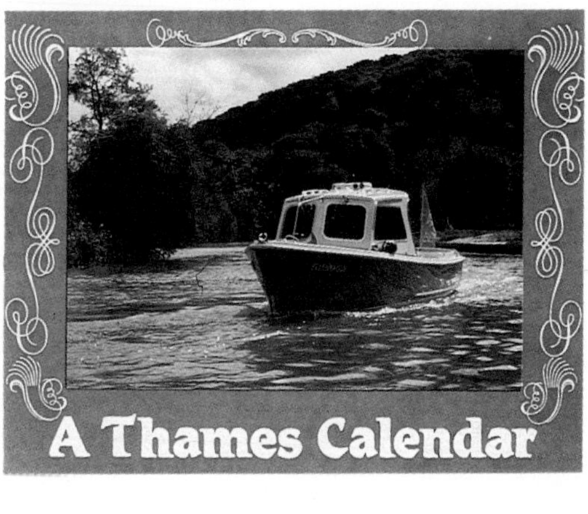

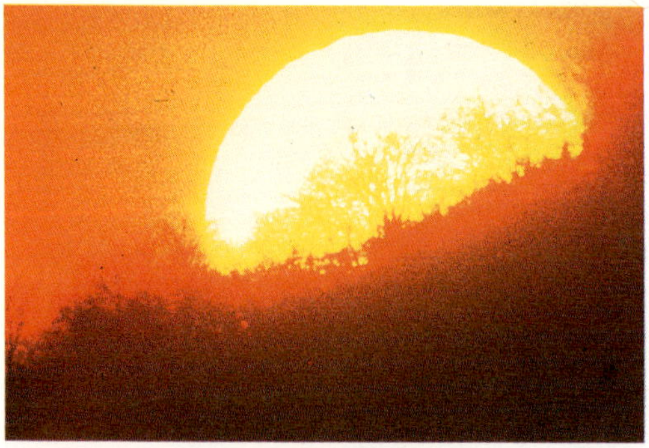

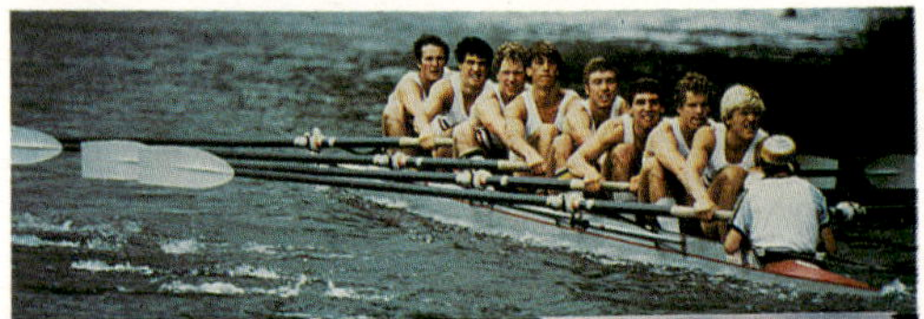

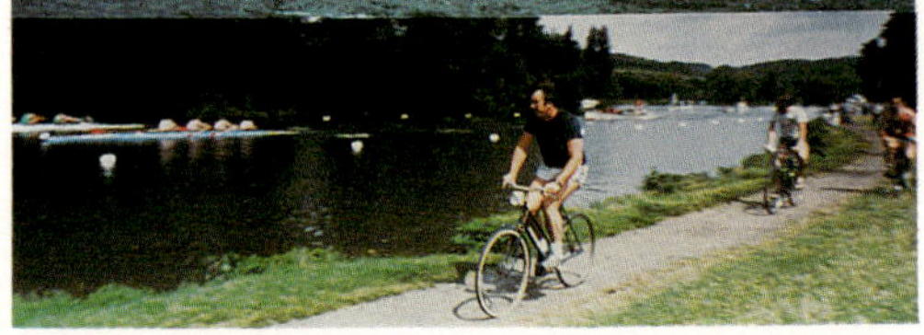

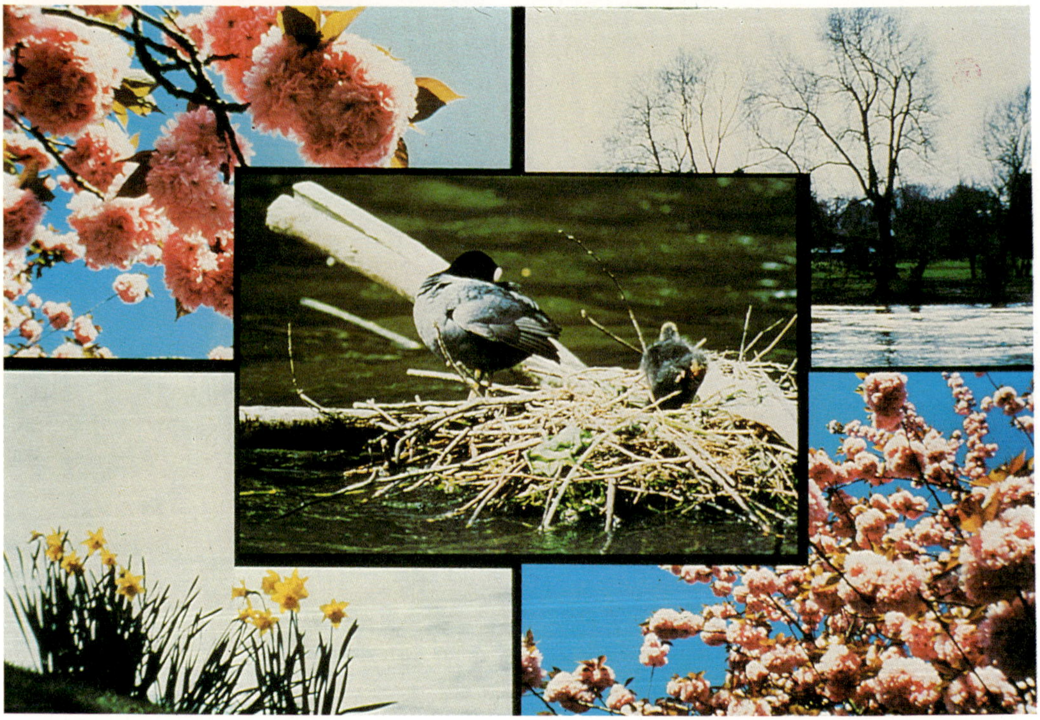

However, they're not completely beyond the resources of a *group* of amateurs; so let's take a closer look at the mechanics of multivision and see just what *can* be done on a limited budget.

Keeping control

In Chapter 6 we examined systems for controlling two projectors. Multivision systems generally start with a minimum of three. Imatronic offer a three-projector control unit, the Triangle, at a remarkably reasonable price. It certainly allows much faster sequences, and several special effects, but it does not allow complete individual control of each projector, so not every permutation available on more advanced systems is possible. For many people, though, its features may be as much as or more than they need — so if your group is interested, your best bet is to arrange to try it.

However, do also consider the only *four*-projector amateur system available at the time of writing — the Diafade 4. This offers individual control of each projector by means of a slider (for lamp brightness) and a

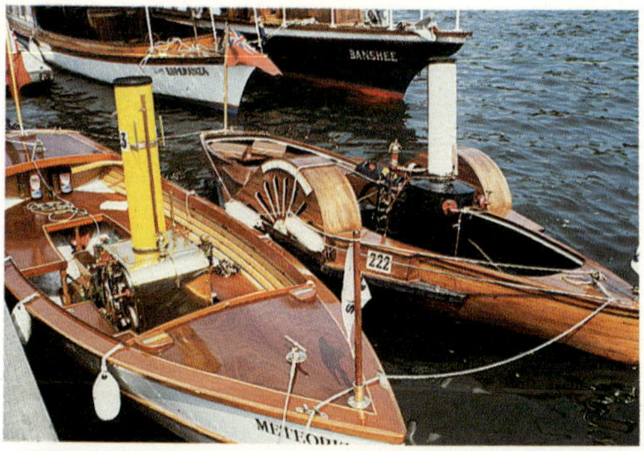

Images from *A Thames Calendar*, produced by Kodak's Audio-Visual Division, and winner of the 1983 BISFA gold award.

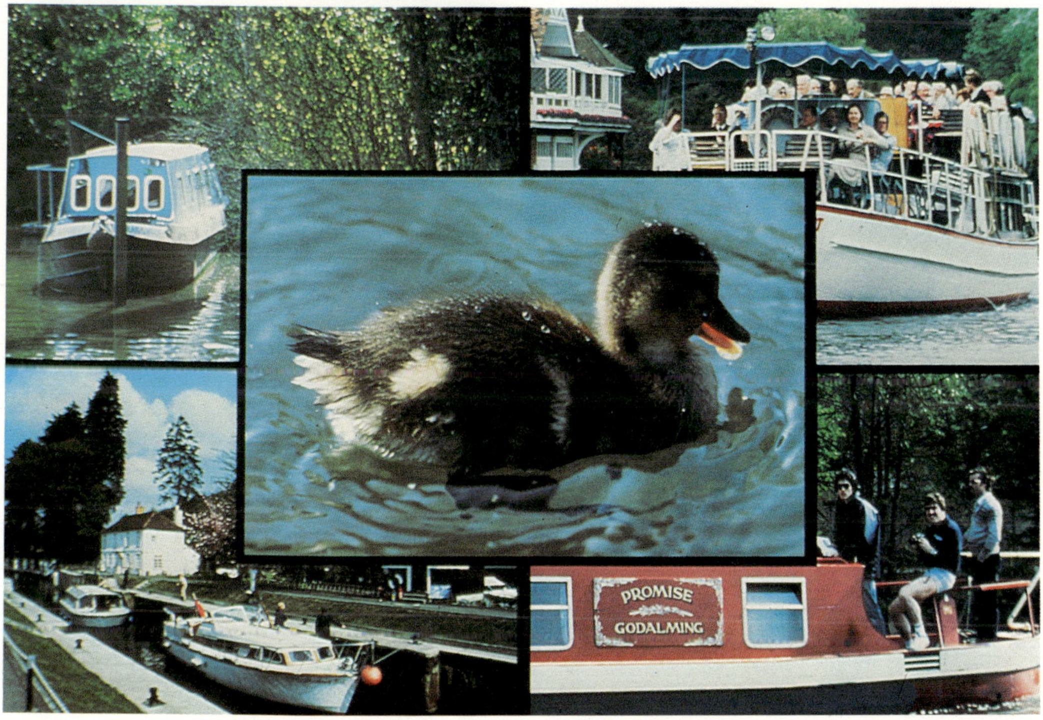

A multiple sequence from *A Thames Calendar* (Kodak). Five rapidly-changing images reinforce the narrator's description of the hive of activity on the Thames in early spring; just one more example of the scope offered by four-projector setups.

push button (for slide advance). Various additional features are available, but the basic unit simply controls the projectors directly — so the speed of your sequences is limited by your own speed on the controls. However, there is a modified version of the basic unit that allows you to record control tracks at half speed (good news for those, like me, not blessed with flashing fingers). For this, of course, you will need a tape deck with at least two speeds — and you will have to be able to recognise the cue points in your soundtrack when the tape is playing at half speed. This may need practice!

Two additional electronic control units — the Magic Box and the Dolphin — are available for the Diafade 4. They offer sophisticated push-button controls for commonly-required effects and for individual projectors. These units program in 'real time'; they do what you tell them to do, when you tell them to do it, and are not capable of 'storing' a sequence of commands. Bigger, professional units are in fact small computers: you can program in a series of commands to be executed at precise times, and the

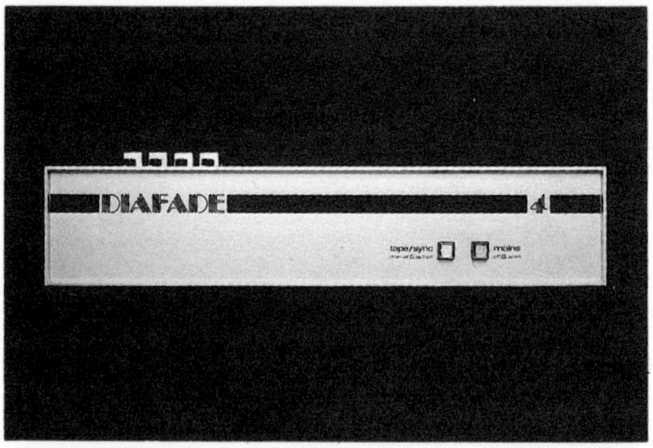

The Diafade 4 offers complete individual control of up to four projectors for the dedicated creative slide-show maker; well worth the price for those who need its facilities.

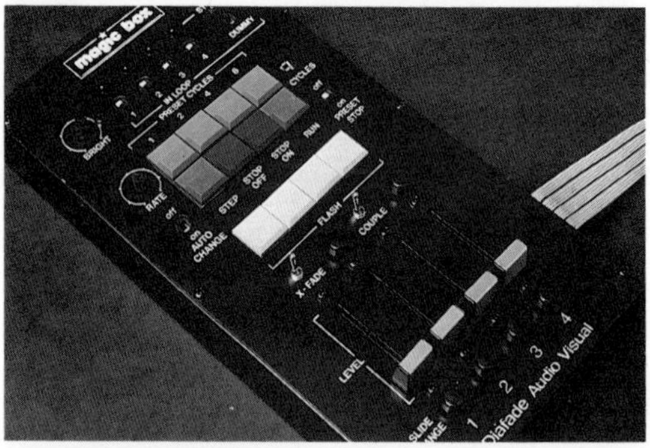

The Magic Box, a Diafade 'add-on', gives easy control of complex animation loops.

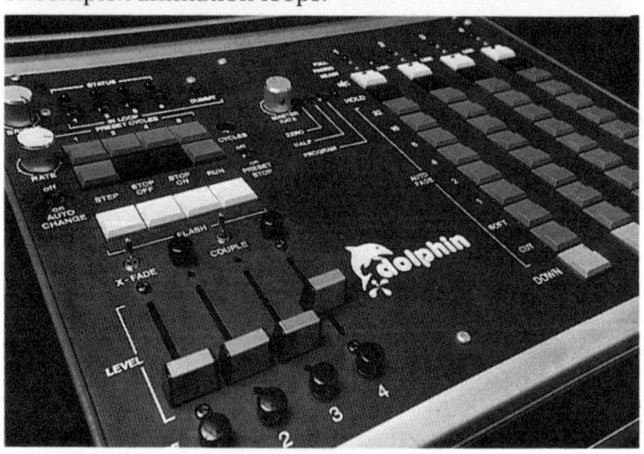

The Dolphin combines with Magic Box and the basic Diafade 4 unit to give highly sophisticated push-button control of four-projector programming.

equipment will 'remember' those commands in an internal memory system and even allow you to alter them or add to them later. Unfortunately, the price of such systems puts them far beyond the reach of amateur groups, even for hire purposes — fascinating as they are, they have no place in this book.

Of course, there is nothing to stop any amateur group chaining together two or more two-projector systems — nothing, that is, except the difficulty of controlling them.

In Chapter 8 we will be looking at quality audio equipment to see how it can make life easier for the dedicated slide-tape enthusiast. One of the most important tools at this more advanced stage is a multitrack tape deck — four tracks is the practical minimum. A multitrack tape deck is rather like a stack of mono recorders piled one on top of the other, and each using a part of the width of the tape (see p. 90). A four-track tape deck can carry two control tracks (each controlling two projectors) *and* a stereo soundtrack. If you gave up stereo sound, you could even control *three* pairs of projectors, using one track for each pair.

If a four-track is beyond your reach, then you could try teaming up with someone else who has an ordinary two-projector dissolve unit and running the show manually. It is not easy, but it is possible and I have seen it done. And at least it'll give you a chance to experiment with multivision without spending any more than absolutely necessary.

But given that you have four projectors and some means of controlling them, how can you build successful sequences for them?

The short answer is that you use exactly the same techniques you would use for two-projector shows. Only now, changes from one slide to the next can happen more quickly, and there are four basic pictures to play with instead of two.

Having a masked ball

The metal and moulded slide-masks we looked at on pp. 71–3 are not the only type available. Professional facilities houses such as RCW in London sometimes produce a range of ready-made black-and-white film chips with black areas that mask a slide just as effectively as any other type. To use them, you just sandwich them in the slide mount with the appropriate pictures.

Masks of this type are ideal for complex picture divisions like those in *A Thames Calendar* — and for making *soft-edge masks*. Soft-edge masks do not have a solid dark area with a sharply-defined boundary.

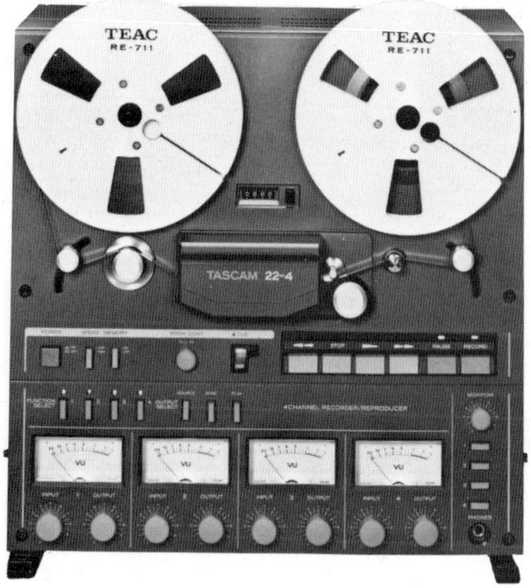

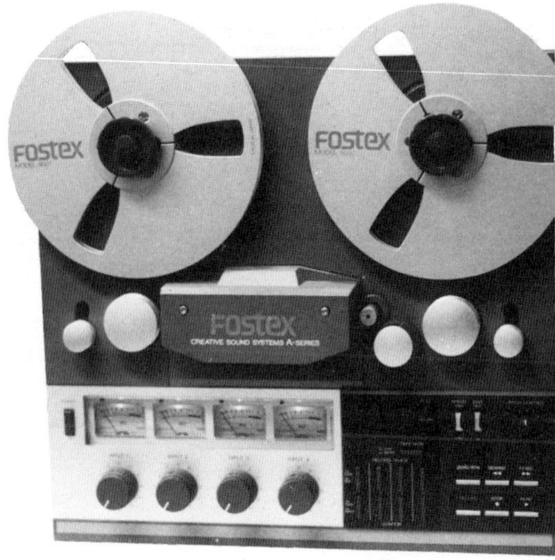

The Tascam 22-4 recorder/reproducer (left) and the Fostex A4. Tascam and Fostex are rivals in this market, so prices are comparable and the choice is up to you. Both offer quality four-track recording and reproduction with some delightful facilities. See also Chapter 8.

Instead, the black edge softens gradually to white. On screen, the masked images blend imperceptibly into one another. This can create some eerie effects (see p. 83) — or help turn any sequence into a register sequence. Near the start of *A Thames Calendar* we used a whole set of these masks for a sequence in which a patrol boat gradually approaches the camera against an unchanging landscape background. Only the central area of the shot actually changes — the soft-edge masking blends it perfectly with the unchanging landscape 'surround'.

Soft-edge masks are often used for panorama shots. In most professional programmes such shots involve three separate pictures, one to the left, one to the right, and one overlapping them both in the middle. Blending them together with soft-edge masks creates the effect of a single panoramic picture. However, if the effect is to be completely successful, then the original image needs to be split into sections with extreme accuracy.

The Wess Splitter, used to break up a single image into sections for multi-projector work.

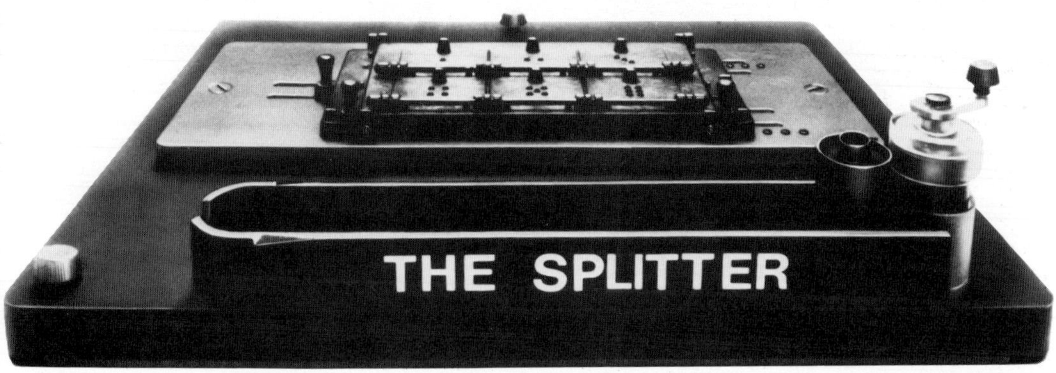

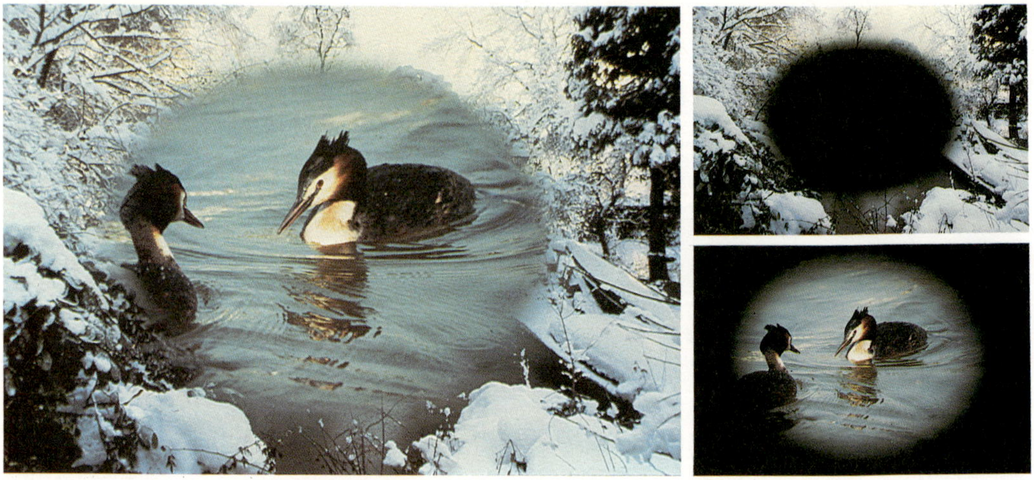

Shots illustrating the use of soft-edge masks from *A Thames Calendar* (Kodak). The wintery 'surround' reinforces a passage in the script describing the dangers to wildlife at this time of year.

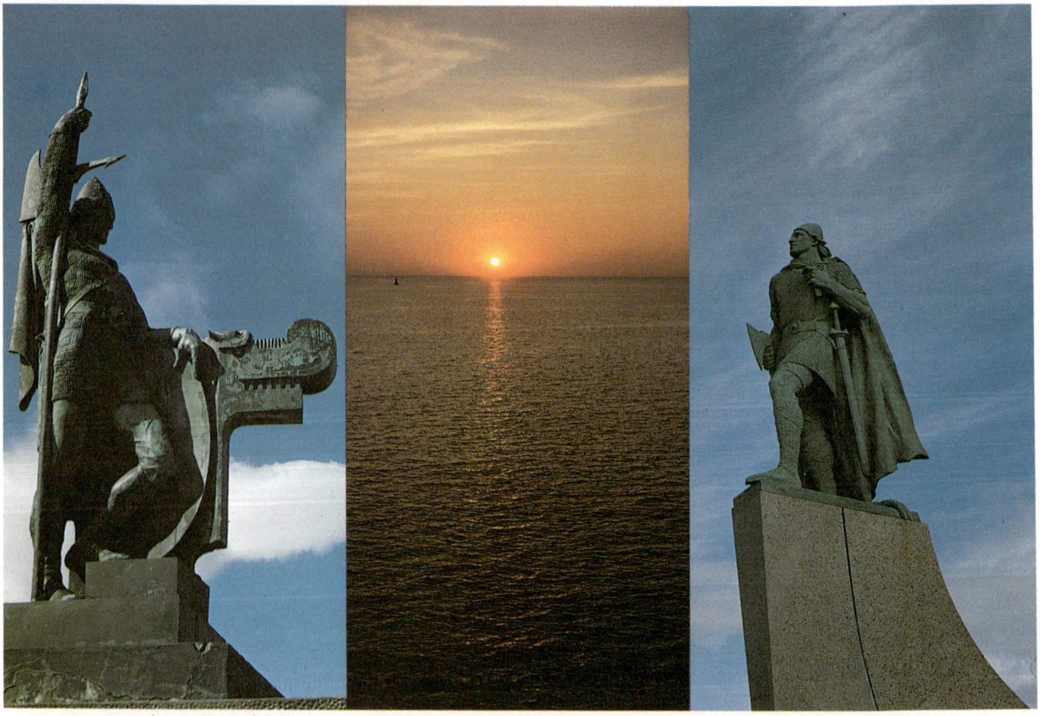

This three-way split was produced using the simple techniques described in the text.

Image-splitting for beginners

Splitting images is considerably easier than splitting the atom, especially with the help of a handy little gadget like the Wess Splitter (see p. 81). In fact there is no reason why an amateur should not be able to produce multiple images on screen, as long as he takes care and uses his head.

With the Splitter, you simply place the original slide in an enlarger above the unit, place raw film under the trapdoors, and then open the appropriate trapdoors and expose the raw film as necessary. The device is neat, simple and accurate. However, there are many occasions when you will not have a darkroom and/or an enlarger available, and in any case few amateurs will very often need to split up a single image into separate parts. They might, on the other hand, find it very interesting to split up the screen area into smaller sub-sections. Doing this can be very entertaining — but it needs careful thought at the planning stage.

The slide on the left has been split into three vertical strips, each showing a different subject. Each slide for this sequence has two-thirds of its picture area blanked out with a suitable masking device. When you go to shoot the sequence, you position each subject in the correct part of the frame, ignoring the rest of the picture, which will be masked out in any case.

However, sometimes you will need several different images to appear on a single slide.

The simplest approach is to cut out the sections of film you want with a scalpel or razor blade, and fasten them in the mount with special adhesive tabs. It's dangerous (for the film), and it must be done accurately — but even though it's a bit hand-to-mouth, it *can* work very well. However, there are alternatives.

It is possible, using commercial slide-masks and an ordinary enlarger, to copy picture material off your originals onto selected parts of a raw film frame. In this way you can slowly build up a mosaic of pictures, shot by shot, on the same frame.

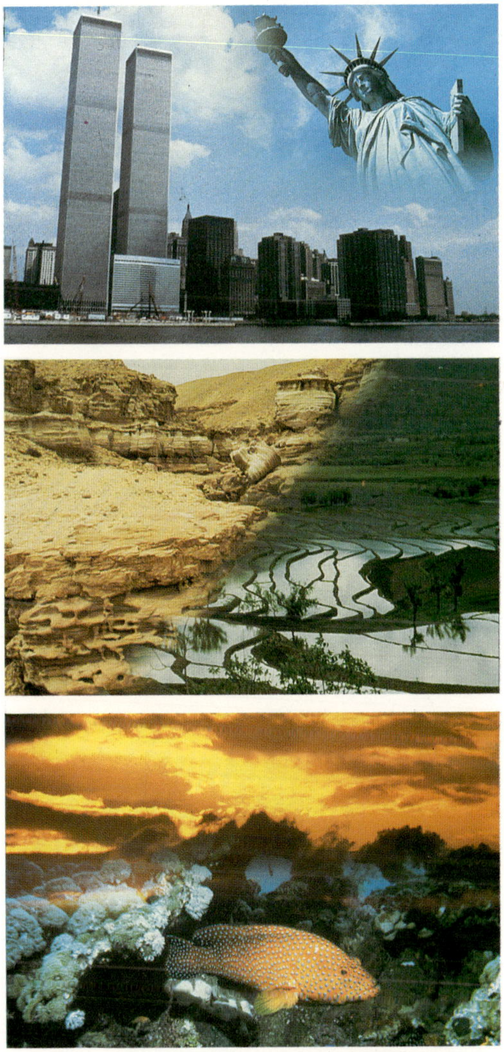

Composite shots by Richard Watson of RCW using soft-edge masks. The effect is pure magic!

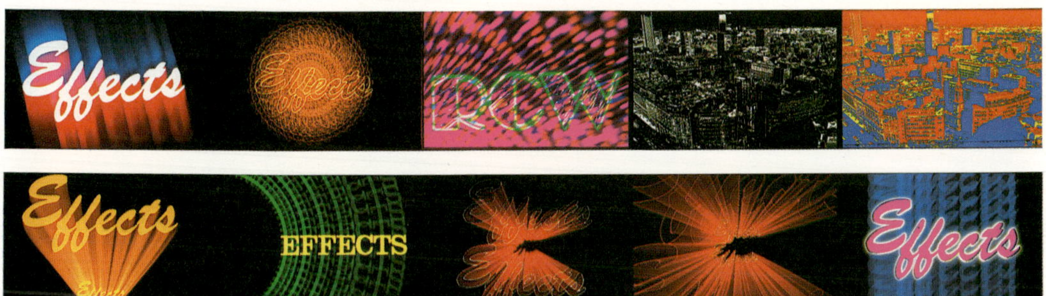

Professional fun! Special 'effects' created on RCW's rostrum camera.

Talk to people at your camera club about this — those with plenty of darkroom experience might enjoy trying it, and some very good results can be achieved in this way. But if this isn't possible for your particular group, don't worry. The process I've just described is an unsophisticated version of the job done by a rostrum cameraman.

The rostrum camera is a highly specialised copying machine that can be used, among many other things, to build up multiple images on a single piece of film — and its use is by no means restricted to professionals. If you are willing to pay for a special sequence to be made, there's no reason why you shouldn't use it, too. But don't just send the raw material — take the trouble to find out what instructions the cameraman needs, and how you can make the most efficient use of his time. When you know, deliver the material with all necessary instructions, sit back, and wait for the finished slides — and, of course, the bill.

Still, if it gives you a spectacular sequence on a plate, it may well be worth it.

Looking good, sounding good

If your group is starting to think about multivision, then it is also time you were thinking about your soundtrack. A truly professional soundtrack demands a truly professional approach — and the next chapter should give you a head start.

8

Sounds impressive

On the day you try to simulate the Great Fire of London with a combination of sixteen assorted sound effects, you may find that your domestic reel-to-reel stereo recorder is just not up to the job. In fact, all the equipment we looked at in Chapter 4 has distinct limitations. Usually this won't be a problem — but sometimes it is. Don't give up hope, though. If you are already working with a group of fellow-enthusiasts, you will almost certainly have several tape recorders between you. And if your group has ambitions towards higher things, it might well be worth considering the purchase, or hire, of a mixer.

The Audio Kitchen

A mixer has much the same effect on your recording work as a kitchen mixer does on the cooking. It allows you to work faster, more cleanly and more efficiently, and so achieve better results in less time.

A mixer is really no more than a set of tone and volume controls. You put in several different sounds at one end, use the controls to blend those sounds together into a mixture you find satisfactory, and send that mixture out to a waiting tape recorder. Most people seeing a mixer for the first time are frightened off by its serried ranks of knobs, sliders and buttons. Don't be. Even the biggest mixing desk in the largest studio is basically a row of identical control units — and if you take one unit out and study it it no longer looks so baffling. Especially when you realise that the controls on it are rather similar to those on a domestic hi-fi amplifier.

At the top, or sometimes at the back, there are sockets for plugging in tape decks, microphones, record decks, or any other sound source such as an electronic organ.

A full mixing system. The Tascam System 20 starts (centre) with a simple 'switch and fade' control unit that can handle two microphones (i.e. a stereo pair) and four line inputs. The EX20 (left) allows the use of four more microphones, while the PE20 (right) adds refined equalisation control. The MM20 meter bridge is the final touch. A system like this would be more than able to cope with the soundtrack needs of a small professional AV production company.

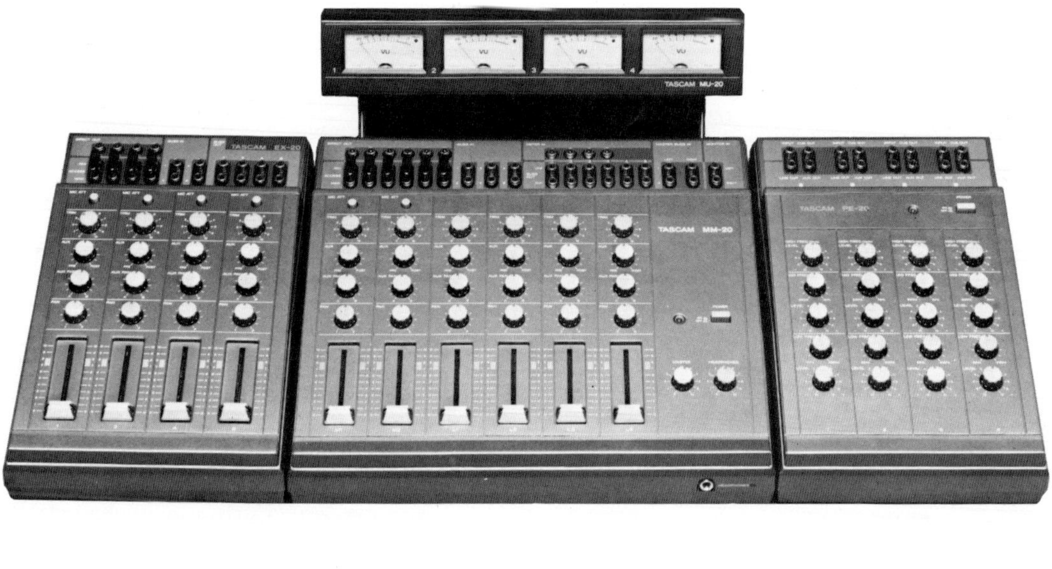

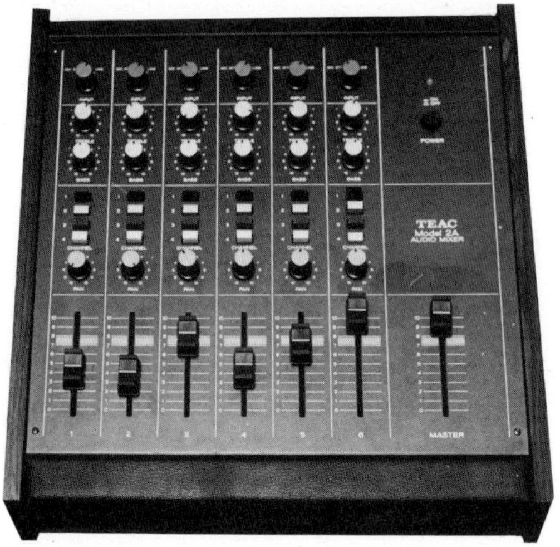

The Tascam M2A mixing system. The meters form a separate unit — you don't have to buy everything at once! The unit accepts six outside signals and routes them into as many as four output channels. The master fader on the right lets you fade all four output channels up or down together. A unit like this is the next logical step up from the 'little box with knobs on' available from many audio shops.

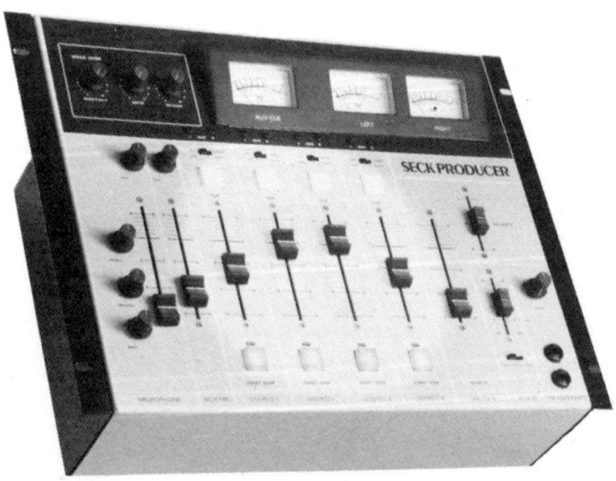

Different style, different facilities. The SECK Producer is a mixer reminiscent of the radio studio. Long-throw faders give fine control of the sound — push-buttons give instant start/stop commands to suitable tape and record decks. Each channel controls a complete stereo signal — you can adjust the balance with individual left and right presets just above each cue button.

There will also be a headphone socket, and an output socket for the tape recorder that will accept the final mix.

Then, reading from the top down, you will probably find a switch that adjusts the unit to receive signals from a chosen source (e.g. a microphone or a tape deck), and tone controls for adjusting different frequencies, rather like the treble, bass and filter controls on an amplifier. Then you may find a few switches and knobs that route the signal through to other parts of the mixer, and a 'pan' control that allows you to place a mono signal anywhere you like on the sound stage. This can be very useful. You might, for instance, have a picture showing a car on the left of the screen. Using the pan control, you can 'place' the sound of a car horn so that it appears to come from exactly the same place.

Finally, there is the most prominent control of all: the 'pot' or potentiometer. This is basically a sliding volume control. It increases or decreases the strength of the signal going out from that particular unit to the tape recorder picking up the final mix.

So each unit of the mixer accepts an external signal, allows you to adjust its volume and the way it sounds, and then feeds it out to a suitable recording machine. And that's all there is to it — like most of the best inventions, a mixer is really extremely simple. And any other way of doing the job tends to become very complicated!

Using your mixer

To begin with, you will probably use the mixer to assemble sounds from different sources onto an ordinary stereo tape deck. Page 88 shows how this can be done. Here a record deck is connected to channels 1 and 2. A tape recorder is connected to channel 3, and a microphone to channel 4. The output is going to a stereo tape deck.

The tape deck on the input side is carrying sound effects in mono. Professional effects are nearly always recorded in mono and 'placed' on the mixer, using the pan control. Speech, too, is normally recorded in mono, so only one microphone has been used in this setup. For drama, or dialogue,

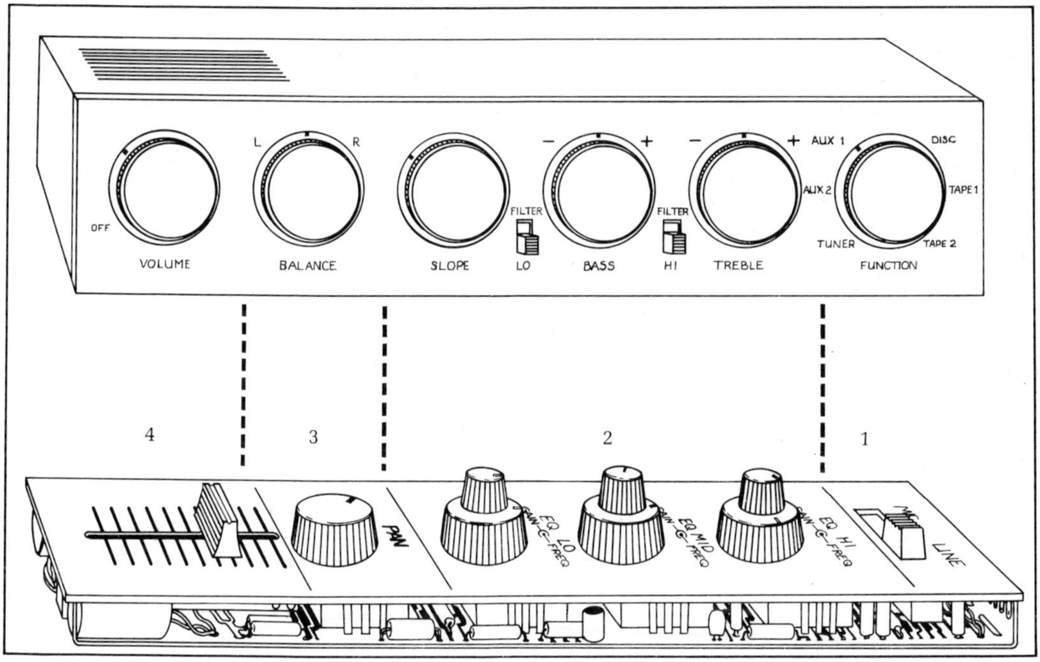

you could easily add a second microphone as long as another channel was available on the mixer. Notice that the stereo record deck is connected to channels 1 *and* 2. Channel 1 is recording the left-hand part of the stereo signal, and channel 2 is recording the right-hand part.

This setup will work, but it is rather inefficient. For one thing, you will need at least two assistants, besides your reader, to operate it. The moment anyone makes a mistake — a wrongly-cued record, a badly-aligned section of tape, or a 'fluff' in the commentary — you will have to stop everything and try again. And with four people to make mistakes, your chances of a successful first take are very slim. However, if you are using an ordinary stereo tape deck to pick up the final signal, this is your only option — so be prepared for lots of takes, and be prepared to edit the tape carefully afterwards.

One improvement you *could* make is to tape the commentary first, and run a perfectly-edited version of it through channel 4, instead of recording it 'live'. That way you, and your associates, need only worry about getting your timing right.

The knobs and switches on this unit from a professional mixer look a little less terrifying when compared with the rather more familiar controls on an ordinary hi-fi amplifier. Reading from right to left — (1) mic/line selector switch. Like the function control on the amplifier, it presets the unit to receive signals either from a microphone or from another source, such as a tape deck, a record deck, or a tuner. (2) equalisation controls. 'Equalisation' is a sophisticated form of tone control, doing the same job as the bass, treble, and filter controls on an amplifier, only better.

On this particular unit the upper knobs select frequencies in the upper, middle, and lower ranges; the lower knobs either boost or cut those frequencies. This selective control is important to cut out annoying sounds such as hissing 's's in speech recordings. (3) the pan control, like the balance control on an amplifier, allows the signal from the unit to be 'sent' anywhere between extreme left and extreme right in the final stereo mix. (4) the pot — in essence a sliding volume control.

However, the best answer is to replace the conventional deck with a multitrack deck like the ones we discussed in Chapter 7.

Mixing with a multitrack

Using a multitrack allows you to split the job of creating your master tape into two easily manageable halves. First you record all the different sounds you need down through the mixer onto the multitrack. In theory you

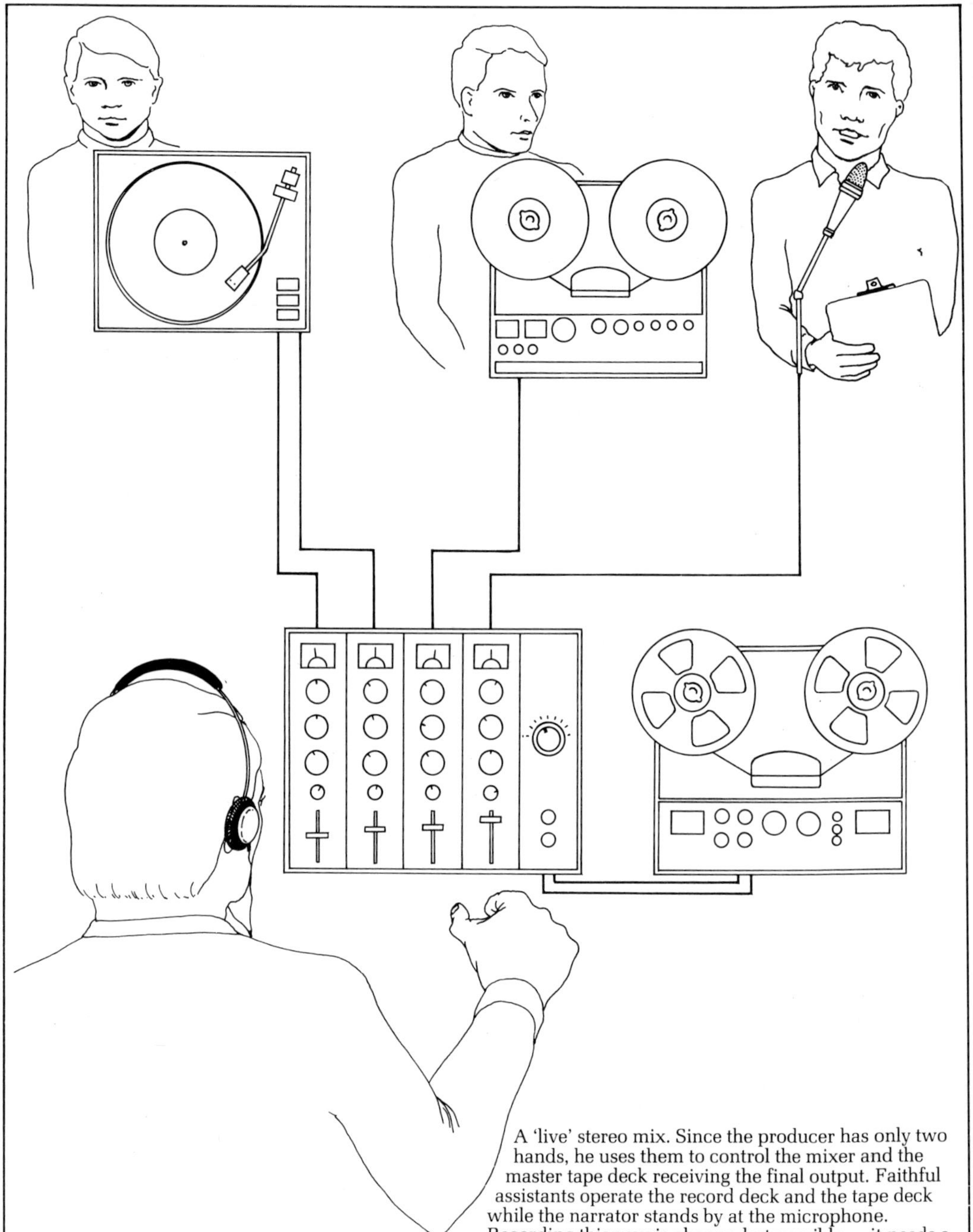

A 'live' stereo mix. Since the producer has only two hands, he uses them to control the mixer and the master tape deck receiving the final output. Faithful assistants operate the record deck and the tape deck while the narrator stands by at the microphone. Recording this way is chancy, but possible — it needs a really quiet environment, and absolute silence on the part of everyone except the narrator. If you can arrange for him to be in a separate room, perhaps with a small lamp as a signalling device, life should be rather simpler.

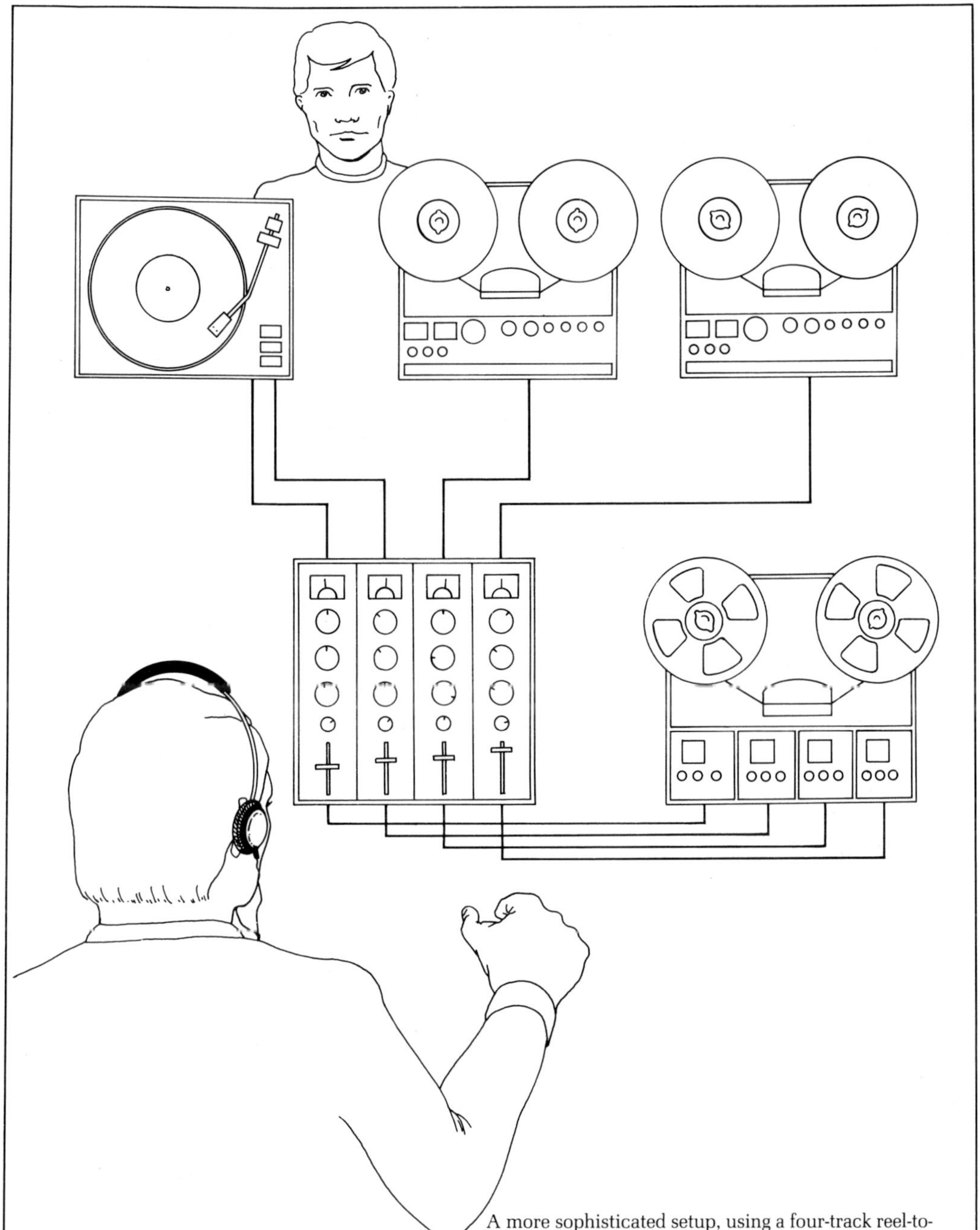

A more sophisticated setup, using a four-track reel-to-reel tape deck. This can be operated by one man (though an assistant can often be useful). Here the various source signals are being fed through onto different tracks of the four-track; later the recordings on the four-track will be fed back through the mixer to produce the final stereo mix.

could put them directly onto the multitrack, but the mixer gives you far more control. And now, instead of recording sounds from all your different sources at the same time, you can process them one or two at a time, putting each sound on a different track.

Page 89 shows a typical setup. Again, the record deck is feeding to channels 1 and 2 of the mixer, the effects tape to channel 3, and the commentary tape to channel 4. Only this time a 4-track tape recorder is connected to the output. It acts very much like four mono tape recorders operating together, and each using a quarter of the same tape. So channel 1 of the mixer is fed onto track 1 of the multitrack, channel 2 onto track 2, and so on. Because there is no need to put all the input sounds through the mixer at once, the whole setup can be controlled by one man — the sound engineer. And when all the various sections of sound are on the correct tracks and in the correct sequence on the multitrack tape, you can start phase two.

This time you connect up the multitrack to the *input* channels of the mixer, and connect an ordinary stereo tape deck to the output. Then you feed in the sounds from the multitrack, much as you might have done in the original setup. The difference is that all the sounds you need are now in precisely the right places relative to each other; in other words, you can forget your timing worries. All you have to do is adjust the pots until the speech balances perfectly with the music and sound effects. You'll need to change the settings at different times in the show, but even professionals don't get this right without a few practice runs. After a few tries you should be able to produce a perfect mix.

So in phase one, you assemble the ingredients of a perfect soundtrack. In phase two you mix them into their final form. And

Simul-sync — the secret of successful multitrack work. Each head can be either a playback or a record head (or neither) — it is either 'shouting', 'listening', or 'dormant'.

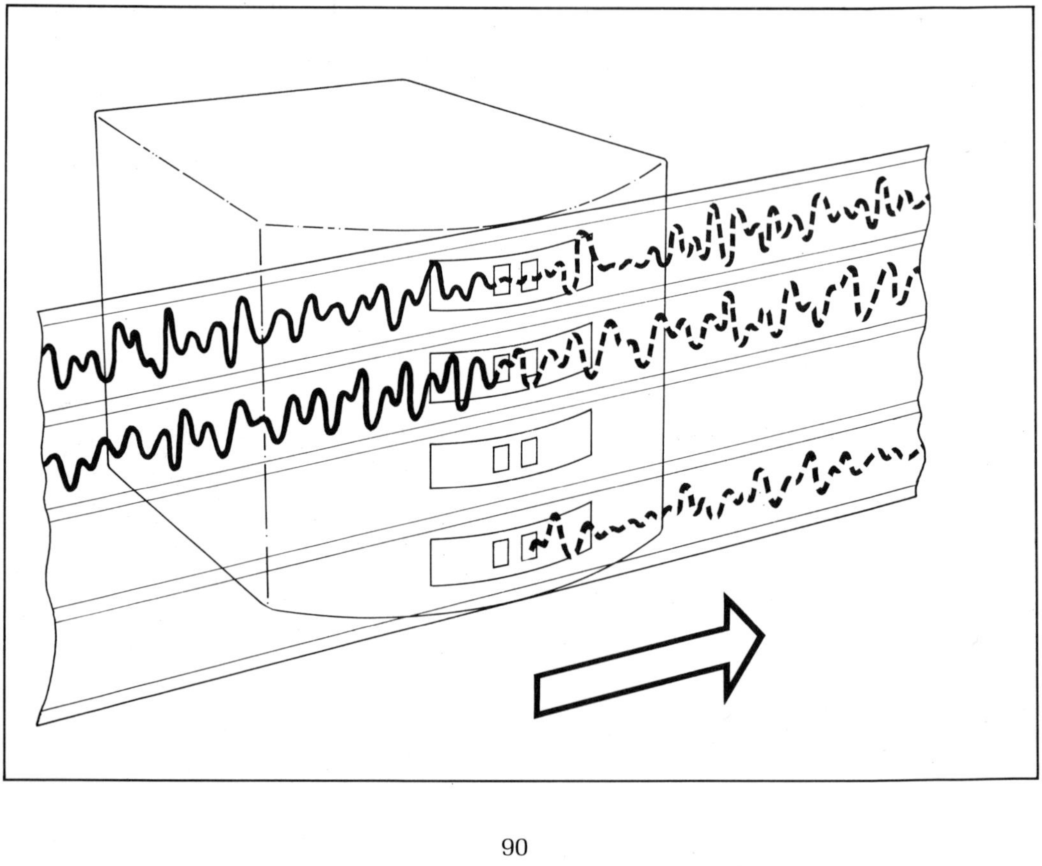

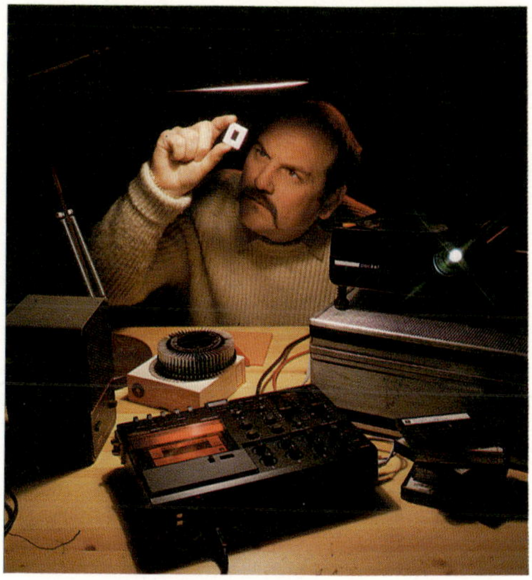

The Fostex X-15 — a complete portable studio! It even runs on batteries for location work. This four-track cassette unit is fully compatible with ordinary cassette decks or with normal-speed four-track decks from other manufacturers. It has simple volume and pan controls for mixing, built-in metering, the latest Dolby noise-reduction system, and tone controls to adjust the sounds you are recording. You can record as many as seven tracks, using a technique called 'bouncing', without serious loss of quality — the Fostex literature gives excellent and simple explanations of the different techniques and applications. The biggest surprise of all is the incredibly low price.

that's exactly how the job is done in professional studios.

Only, of course, there's a little more to it.

Introducing simul-sync

This type of multitrack recording isn't possible unless the multitrack machine has 'simul-sync' heads — and needless to say, most of them do. The reason is shown on the left. Imagine each of the four tape heads as either 'shouting', 'off', or 'listening'. For instance, tracks 1 and 2 here are shouting, track 4 is listening, and track 3 is off. If you are feeding in a new signal from the mixer onto track 4, it will record that signal while tracks 1 and 2 play back what has already been recorded — but because all the heads are in line with each other, the mixture of the two old tracks and the new one should sound exactly the same whether you are recording on track 3 *or playing back the recording.*

This is important. If, for instance, there were separate playback heads, then the timing would be fractionally different on recording and playback — and you would find it very hard to put a programme together accurately.

But that's only the beginning. Most multitrack machines have switching that enables any combination of tracks to 'shout' at an empty track — which can then record

Moving into the bigger league — two keen rivals for the cassette deck-cum-mixer market, the Tascam 244 Portastudio (top) and the Fostex 250 Multitracker. In effect, both are more professional versions of the Fostex X-15, with an improved and expanded mixer section and double-speed play as standard, to ensure the highest quality. Again, the choice is a matter of preference.

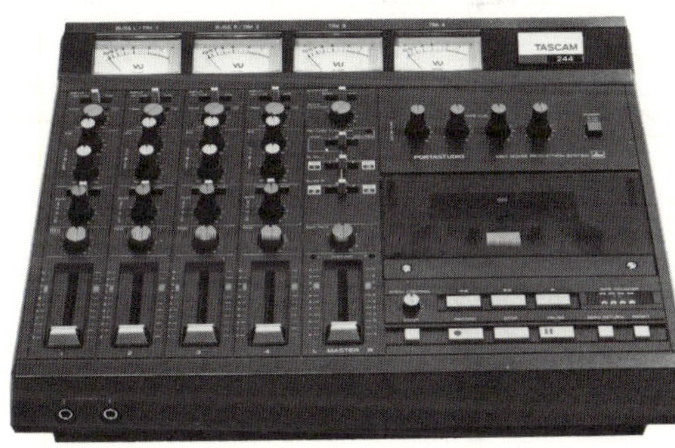

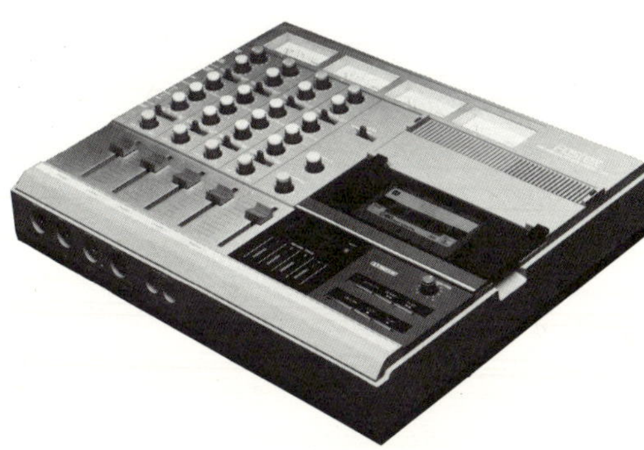

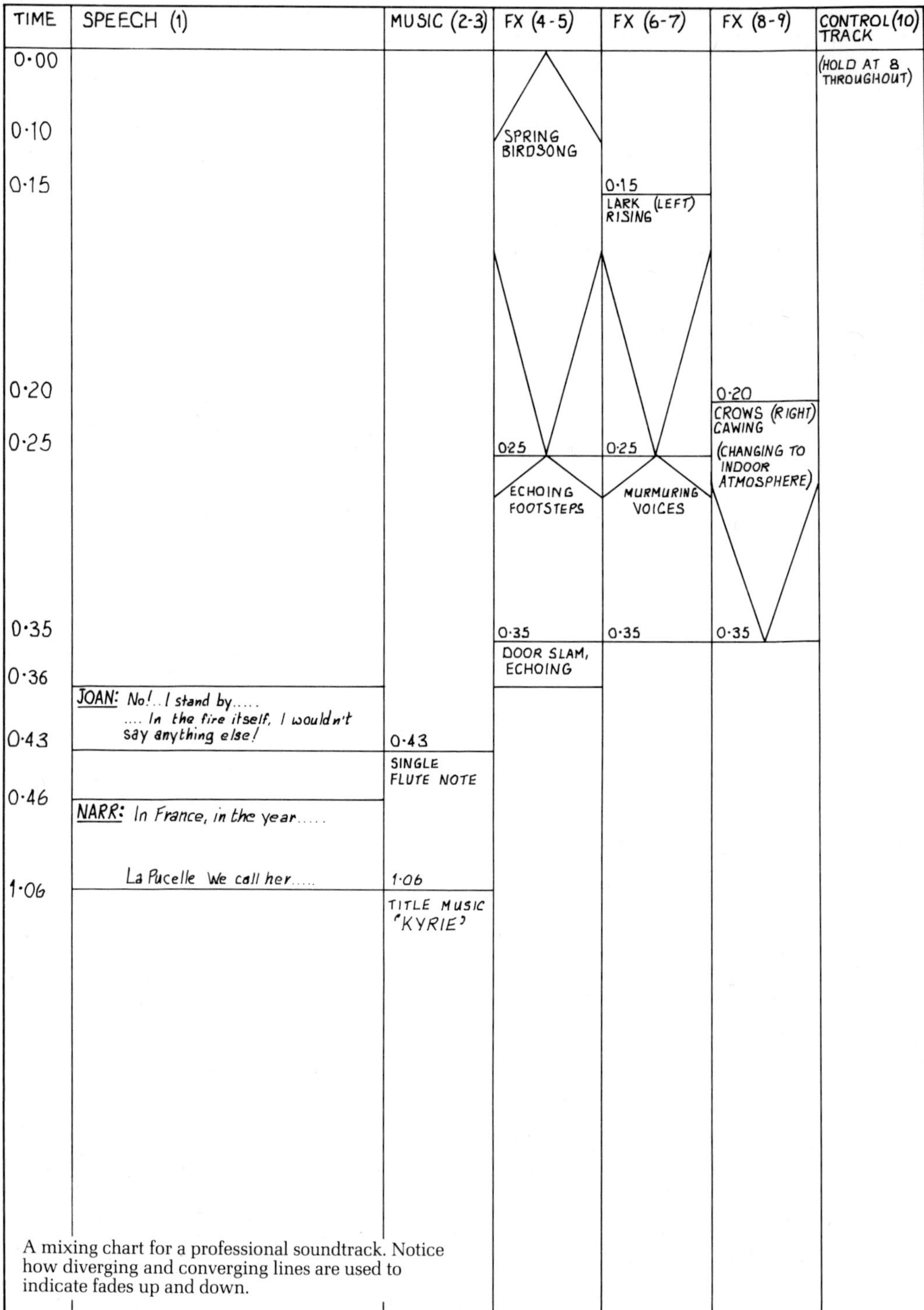

A mixing chart for a professional soundtrack. Notice how diverging and converging lines are used to indicate fades up and down.

a mix of all the other tracks. Needless to say, there is nothing to stop you routing them all through the mixer *before* they are picked up on the empty track. Using this feature you can build up a soundtrack from a dozen or so separate sources, even on a basic four-track machine. In fact, you can buy several units that actually combine a mixer and a four-track studio-quality cassette deck — perfect for the creative soundtrack maker.

Building a soundtrack

A complex soundtrack is like a building. It has to be *planned*. All the different bits and pieces of sound you want to use have to fit together exactly. And that means doing a great deal of listening. Does your chosen music fit the speech? Does it fit *well*? Just when, exactly, should that sound effect come in? How long should it go on?

You can't carry this sort of information in your head. In fact, you'll need a mixing chart like the one on the left before you even try to set up the mix.

The mixing chart is the sound engineer's cue sheet. It tells him exactly how the programme fits together, and exactly what he needs to do at each stage of the production process. In this example, precise timings are marked wherever the engineer has to do something. There are verbal cues, too: extracts from the script. These cues show how, when and where music, speech and effects recordings begin and end, and which tracks of the multitrack machine should be used for each sound. Later on, when the engineer mixes the programme from the multitrack onto the final master tape, the chart will show him when to fade each individual track up and down. The balance of the tracks — how loud or soft each of them should be — will depend on his own judgment or that of the *producer*, if the engineer is not producing the programme himself.

I don't normally prepare a mixing chart until the speech track has been recorded and edited. The business of choosing suitable music and sound effects, and working out precise timings, can be long and arduous, and if any alterations have to be made to the commentary *after* this work

The 24-track tape deck at Livingston Studios.

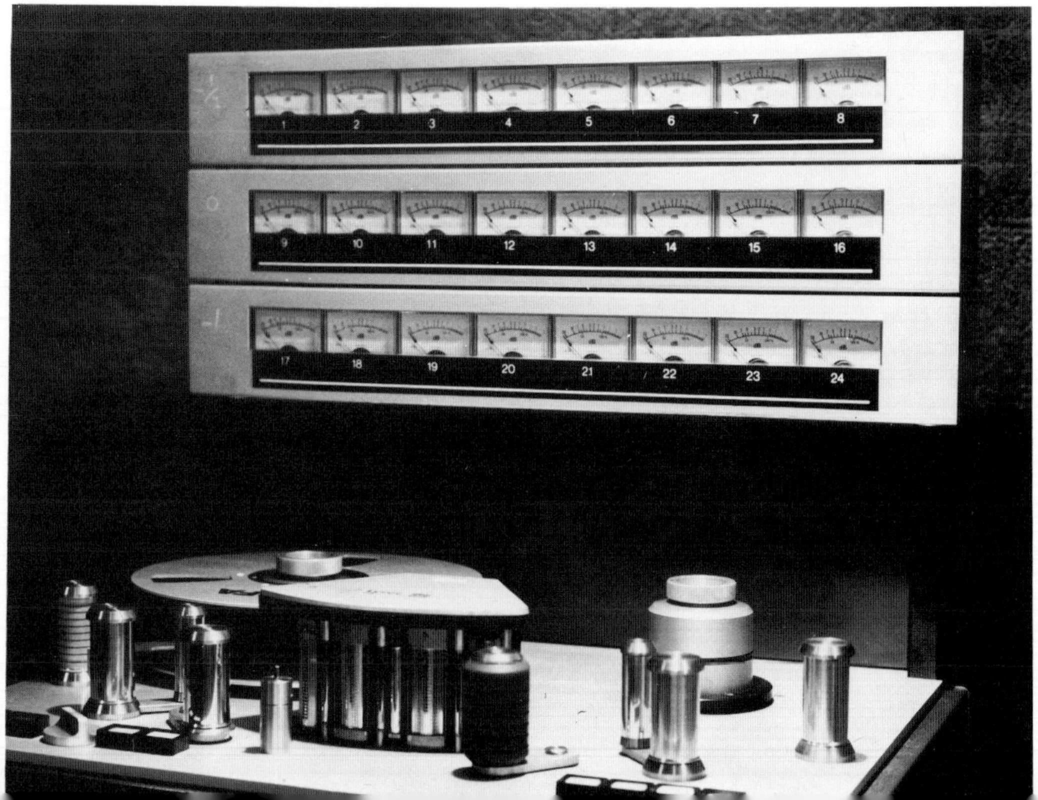

is done, much of it may have to be done again. Normally I prepare the mixing chart at home, using a copy of the speech tape and recordings of selected music and effects. Even with simple domestic equipment you can prepare a rough mono tape that will give some idea of the finished soundtrack — and the only way to make sure the elements of a soundtrack really do fit together is to listen to them.

At the end of such a 'rough cut' session I will have a workable mixing chart, similar to the one on p. 92 except that it may include up to 24 separate channels. The other preparations I make for studio may not seem relevant — but they are. Practise them from the start, and you should soon be able to produce soundtracks with the minimum of wasted effort.

A day in studio

Studio time can be expensive — that's why I've stressed the need to plan a soundtrack. But this should never blind a good producer to the need for spending time on getting things right.

The voice track first. Whenever possible, as I mentioned earlier, I record this separately, sometimes in a smaller and less expensive studio. The reader always

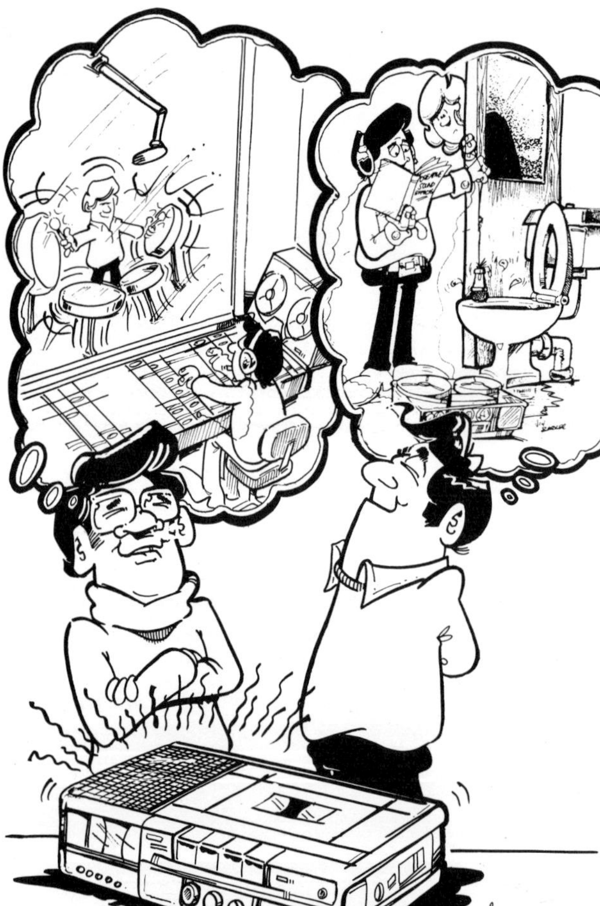

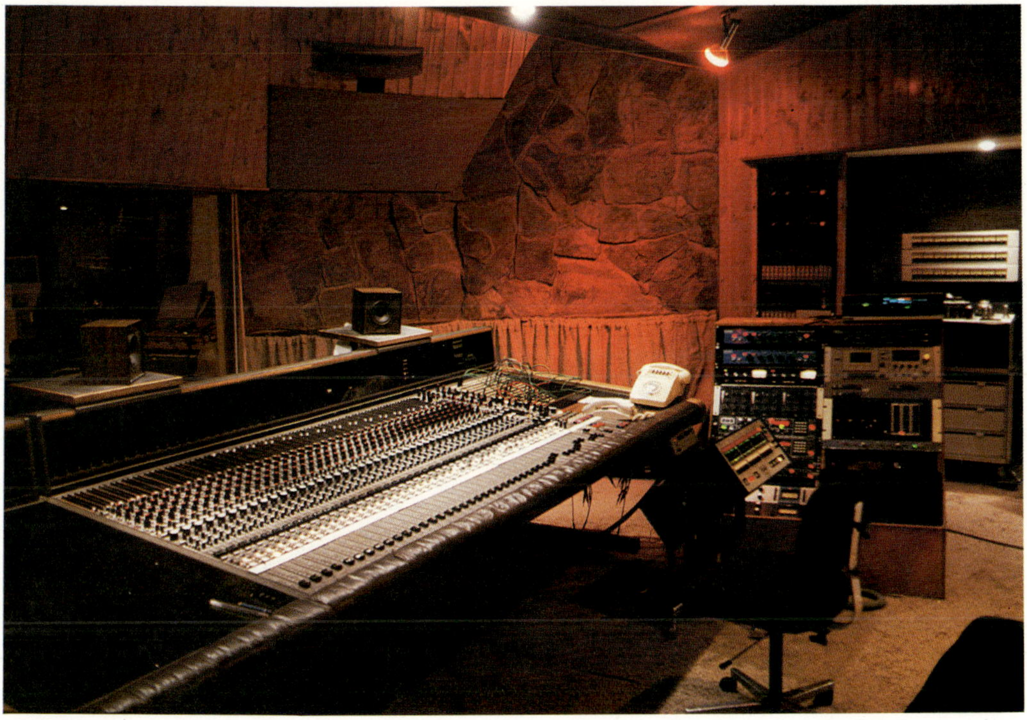

Livingston Studios, Wood Green — many of the shows mentioned in this book were created with this versatile 24-track facility.

receives a copy of the script in advance, so that any difficulties he may have can be dealt with before recording begins. Once he is comfortably settled in the recording booth, and the engineer and I feel that the mixer is correctly set for the best possible recording of his voice, I signal him to begin either over 'talkback' (a direct microphone link with the recording booth), with a cue light, or with a visual signal.

Even the best readers make mistakes, so never expect to record a whole script in one take. Mark up where each take begins on a spare copy of the script, and announce each new take via talkback *while the recording tape is running*. If these announcements are left on the master tape, editing will be much easier!

A professional reader can normally be left to deliver a script in his own way, provided he does not alter the meaning. If he does, it is the producer's job to tell him. Only the producer can decide whether or not a particular take is usable; this is not the engineer's responsibility, or the reader's! If you do spot an error, interrupt politely and ask for (and announce) another take. No one will mind.

I normally allow eight times the actual length of the commentary for recording a script (e.g. two hours for a 15-minute commentary). As long as the takes have been identified on the master tape, and you know which of them you want to use, editing should be simple. Before long you will have a complete speech tape, ready for use.

At this point I go home and plan out the mixing chart. I also try to plan out all the rest of the studio day — and that means arriving in studio with all my music and sound effects on tape, in the right order, with cueing points marked. Don't forget you can edit coloured leader tape into a spool of tape to show where each section begins and ends — and you can mark precise points on a tape with a wax marker pencil. I use tape rather than discs precisely because cues can be marked on it with such extreme accuracy. Often I set up several tape decks at once, rather as on p. 89, but in practice I rarely feed more than two through the mixer at any one time.

Laying the tracks for a programme, even under these conditions, can take a whole working day. The recording on the multitrack has to be perfect, both in sound quality and in timing. If a piece of music comes in a fraction early or a fraction late, it may not be possible to correct it later on. Better to get it right before going on to the next section. So I prefer to leave the final mix until another day.

In theory, mixing ought to be easy. In practice, it isn't. Getting a mix absolutely right demands careful judgement and a good ear — and even then you will need to practise it several times before 'going for a take'. For one 5½-minute production my partners and I spent almost all night in studio. We lost a lot of sleep — but we did get a perfect mix.

Most of these techniques are as useful in the Living Room Studio as in a professional setting. If you practise them, you will find that the step up to being a complete professional is a lot smaller than you might have expected.

9

Going Pro

If you're just starting out as a slide-show maker then the prospect of earning money from your work probably seems a bit remote. To be fair, it probably is — but it's still worth thinking about.

There are two ways of making money with slide shows. One is to perform them to paying audiences. The other is to sell them to people who need them.

The Grand Tour

Paying audiences will only part with their money if they have some idea what they're going to see. You can't just put together a few programmes and then start charging admission. First you'll have to build up a reputation — and that takes time, effort, and sometimes investment. You'll need to buy equipment — good equipment that won't let you down. Yet you'll certainly have to begin by showing your work for free. Because your most important job — and I can't stress this enough — is to know your audience. Listen to their reactions. Allow for them. Learn what people enjoy, and what they dislike about your work. You're trying to sell them entertainment — and it's your job to see that they get it. In other words, you need to find the kind of shows you enjoy making and other people enjoy watching. Until you know, you can't risk charging people money to see your work. You could knock yourself out of the circuit for good with a single, suitably-timed disaster.

Michael Tickner and Sir George Pollock at an enjoyable RPS evening celebrating the earliest audio-visual programmes of all — magic-lantern slides!

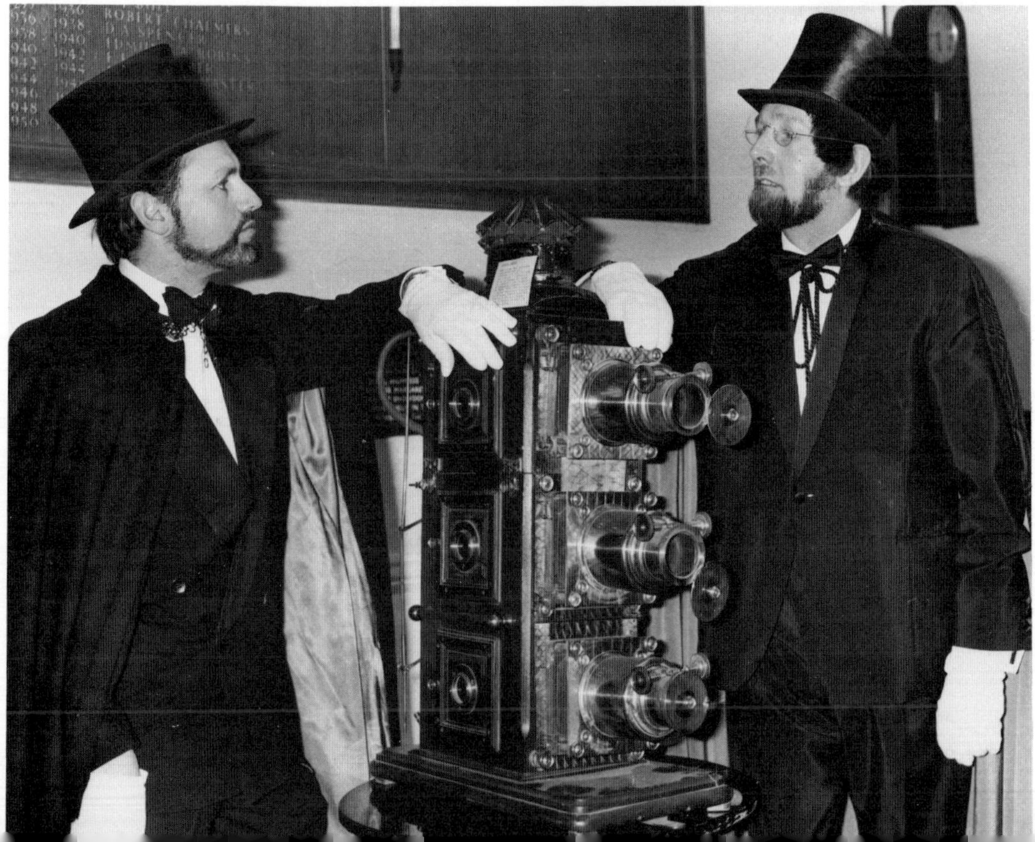

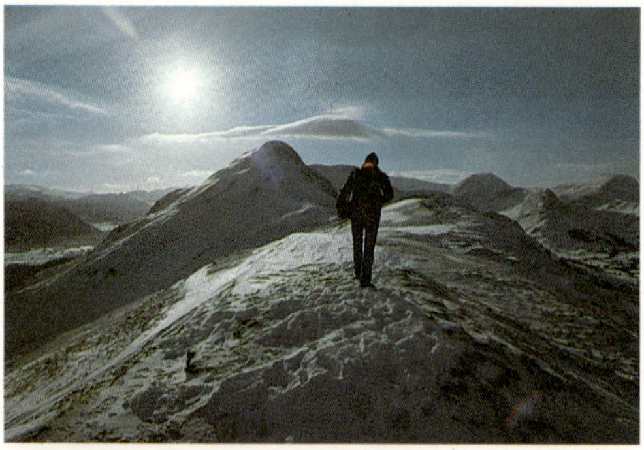

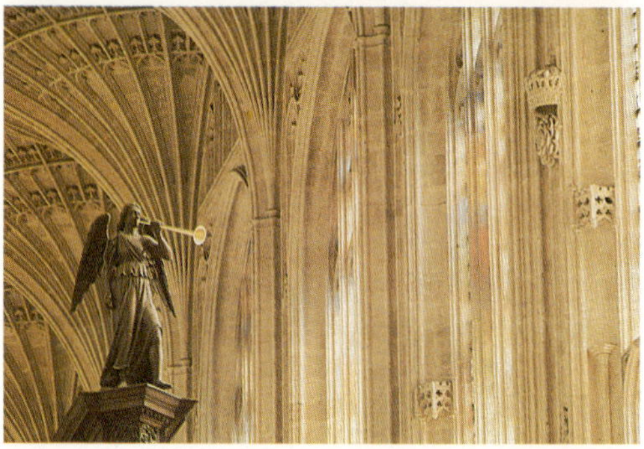

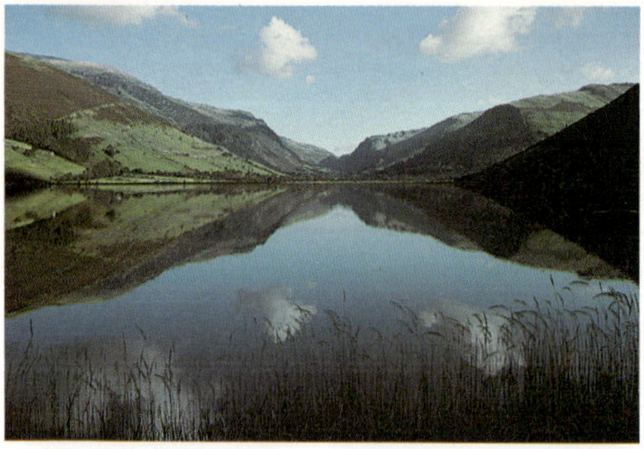

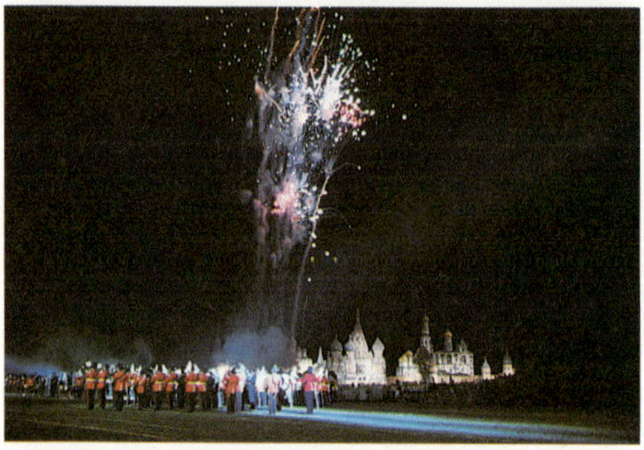

Stills from Derek Forss's touring programmes; in addition to his travelling shows, Derek also runs an active picture library and writes and illustrates his own books.

Sizing up the competition

One very good way of assessing your own ability is to enter a competition. On the local level this may be difficult, but you might try persuading your own camera club to organise one, perhaps in conjunction with other clubs in the area. On the national level there are regular competitions — and beyond that there are the big international festivals such as the one at Epinal, which is held every two years.

For details of all these competitions, you should contact the Royal Photographic Society's Audio-Visual Group — the address of the RPS, and of other useful bodies, is in Appendix 3.

Competitions, of course, are by no means the only events on offer. There are also courses, festivals, weekend workshops, and dozens of other opportunities to meet people who share your enthusiasm for the hobby. Details of most of these events are given in the RPS Audio-Visual Group newsletter — so if you are getting serious about your slide shows, I recommend joining the group. When you have a chance to see the work that others are doing, you are bound to receive new inspiration yourself. And that will make the step up to professional status just that little bit more easy.

Making the break

While researching and writing this book

Derek Forss FRPS

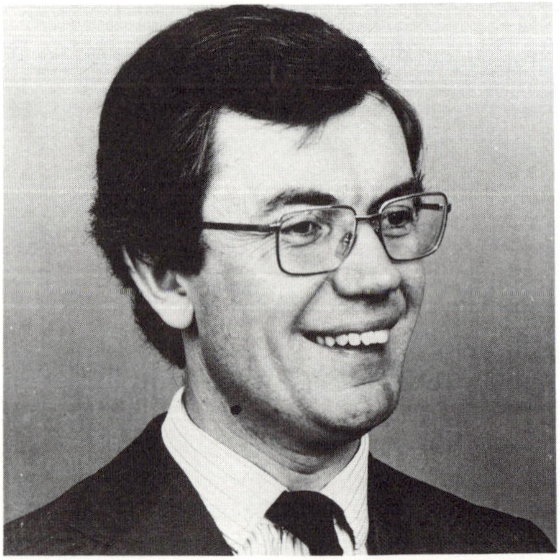

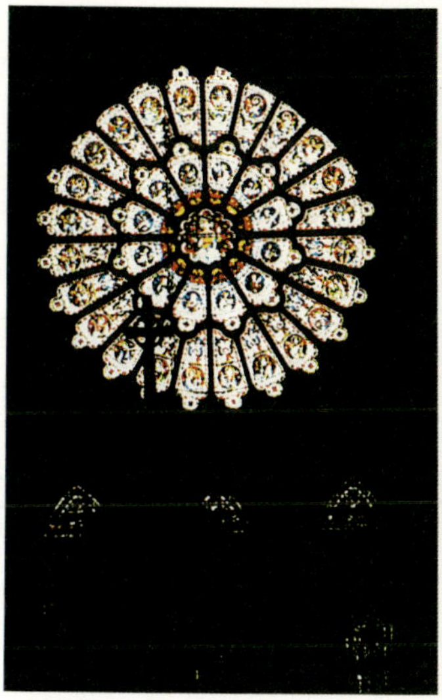
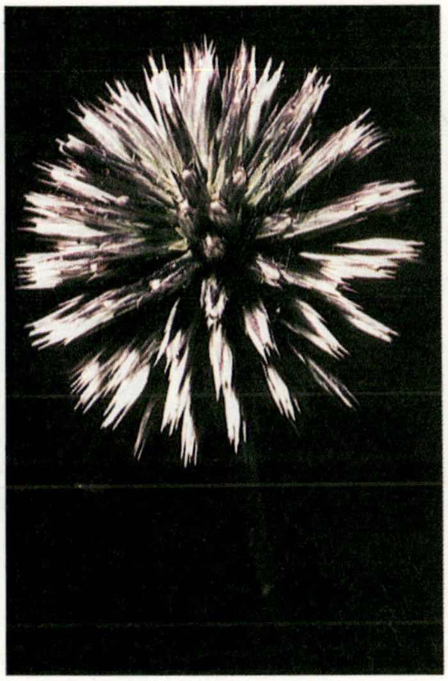
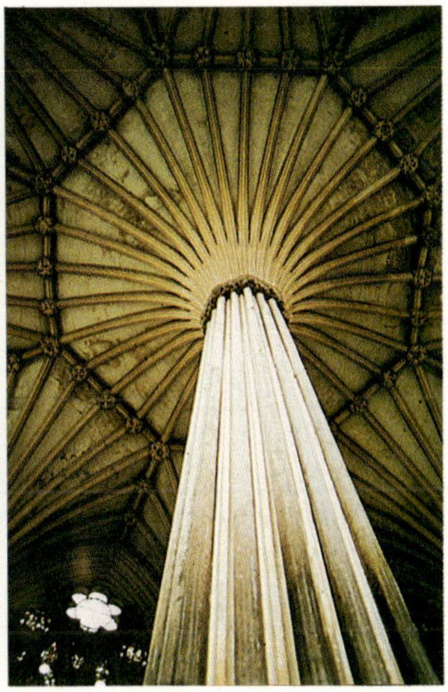

A dissolve set from *Fantasia on a Theme by Thomas Tallis* by Sir George Pollock. His 'visual concerts' have inspired many slide-show makers.

I spoke to several slide-show makers who have made the transition from amateur to professional and now spend a considerable amount of time 'on the road'. Their experiences were fascinating — especially to anyone who feels they would like to try producing a touring show.

Derek Forss FRPS now gives about thirty public shows a year using a fourteen-foot screen and the Diafade 4 dissolve unit. His background is on the audio side: for many years he worked for EMI records, and at one time hoped to become a classical record producer. He was converted to slide-tape by one of Sir George Pollock's programmes — soon after seeing it, Derek went out and bought himself two projectors and a dissolve unit. As his photographic skills developed, and his early programmes received praise and encouragement from fellow camera club members, Derek was seduced into the world of professional audio-visual. His breakthrough came in June 1978, when he gave his first major public show at the Theatre in the Forest, Grizedale, on behalf of the Friends of the Lake District. He has since been told that everyone was a little apprehensive about the venture — but by the end of the first half they were breathing deep sighs of relief!

Sir George Pollock, Bt, Hon. FRPS, FBIPP

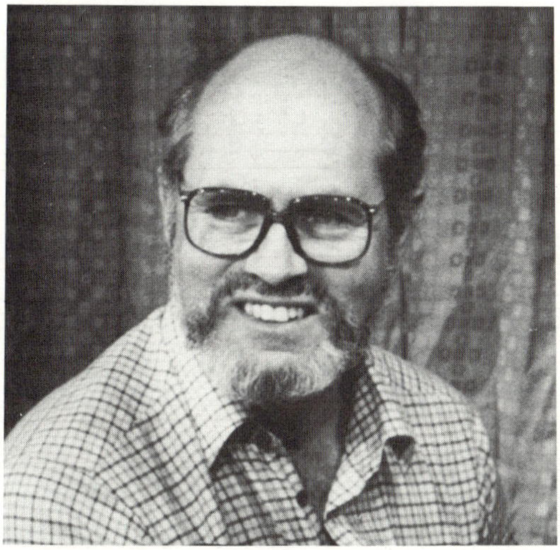

Initially with the help of an agent, Derek went on to make and perform a growing series of programmes that built up a faithful following for his work. These days he limits himself to thirty programmes a year — the sheer physical labour of transporting and setting up his equipment deters him from any larger commitment!

Derek's main interest is the British countryside, and he has found a large number of people to share it. Normally his audiences, reached through municipal authorities and the larger camera clubs, run to between 400 and 600. Derek is fortunate in being completely free of 'first night nerves': he has learned the important art of warming up an audience until they can relax and enjoy his programmes. As he is an ex-inhabitant of recording studios, Derek's soundtracks are very much home-grown — he has recorded location sounds, music, and atmosphere all across Britain, using a Uher CR340 cassette deck and AKG general-purpose microphones.

His advice to newcomers who want to 'go public' is to stick to the areas of the job they do best, and get expert help with the rest. He began with some qualms about his writing ability, and has always been willing to accept advice and assistance in that area. But even so, he now earns additional income from writing and illustrating books, as well as supplying pictures to publishers and magazines. For him, the road to success has not been easy — he needed to make considerable investments in time and equipment before he could really reap the benefit of his work, and he has found that audio-visual, like other freelance pursuits, becomes profitable only in the longer term. If you get the chance, go and see one of his shows — it will show you far better than I can tell you what can be done with four projectors and a well-prepared soundtrack.

Sir George Pollock, Bt, Hon. FRPS, FBIPP, now heads a very successful audio-visual

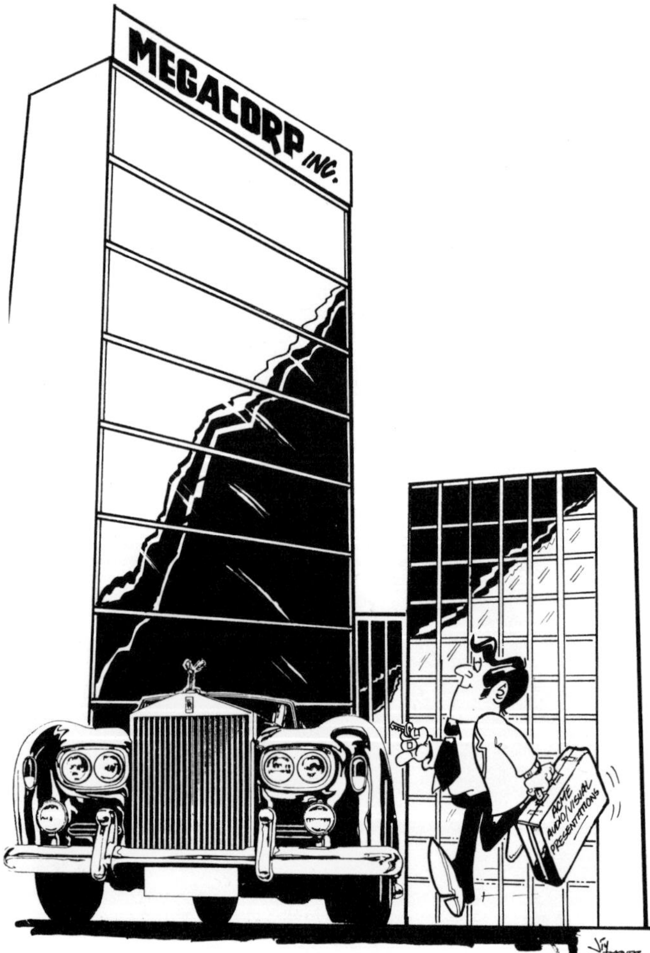

business in Dorking. In 1963 he abandoned a career as a solicitor in London to set up as an artist photographer selling original prints. He had become interested in slide-tape three years earlier, when he saw one of Ray Beaumont-Craggs' dissolve presentations. No commercial units were available at the time, so Sir George and his friend Jean Vaumoron created dissolves by fading in and out with a pair of massive triacs while changing slides manually on two Leitz Prado push-pull projectors. Programmes using this equipment were shown regularly at the Avon Tyrell meetings in Dorset, and elsewhere. As interest grew, other people began to build dissolve units. One such unit, made by David Purslow, is now marketed as the Purlock Duo-Fade (see p. 64).

One of Sir George's first public shows was an entertainment at the Dorking Halls, in which he shared the evening with classical Flamenco guitarist Pepe Martinez. The programme he showed, *Fantasia on a Theme by Thomas Tallis*, contains some of the most memorable dissolves I have ever seen, and is unusual in using only vertical format slides. Sir George's fascination with dissolves led him to make a series of eight programmes, which he performed at various venues for a number of years. The first of his major touring 'Peepshows' was put together as the result of a chance meeting with David Williams, the first importer of the Olympus OM1 camera. At Sir George's suggestion, Williams commissioned a series of programmes grouped around an advertising feature for the OM1 — but at the last minute Williams fell desperately ill, and was obliged to withdraw. However, the programmes were paid for, and with additional sponsorship from Animatic, 'Pollock's Pictorial Peepshow' was launched on a national tour. It was to be the first of many such tours, and also gave Sir George the opportunity to use twin screens for the first time. His second tour was sponsored by Agfa, Olympus, and Practical Photography magazine — and was performed fifty-five times in the course of a single winter! Today the roster includes some sixty programmes which are performed with Pollock Auto-fades, each controlling two projectors. Single-screen versions of the shows are also available, using the Purlock Duo-Fade, under the name of 'visual concerts'.

Sir George has always charged a fee for his public shows; but then his programmes were among the first to be shown in this country. Like Derek Forss, he has found that touring shows do not generate enough income on their own. To begin with, the rest came from his gallery. Later, it came from his growing audio-visual business.

His advice to beginners is to start with simple equipment. Make sure that you really enjoy working with slide-tape before you spend too much money on it. What you *must* be prepared to spend is time. Making a good slide-tape programme can take many hours, but once it is finished, it gives enormous satisfaction — almost comparable with a complete one-made exhibition. In this, Sir George certainly speaks from experience: when I spoke to him he was planning an exhibition to celebrate the twenty-first anniversary of his first one-man show!

Besides his touring shows, Sir George also runs workshops for slide-show makers. From personal experience, I can heartily recommend both.

Commercial slide-tape

There is a growing market for slide-tape in commerce and industry, too. Most programmes commissioned in this area are meant to communicate fairly basic ideas to a clearly defined audience. My own customers have included a bus company that wanted to tell its passengers about special excursion trips abroad, a major corporation that wanted to explain the full range of its activities, and a manufacturer who wanted a programme telling dealers about their cameras. Many of these programmes are produced using the simplest forms of slide-tape — one or two projectors and a mono soundtrack. But the potential market is expanding as more and more business people realise that 'audio-visual communication' is not just a

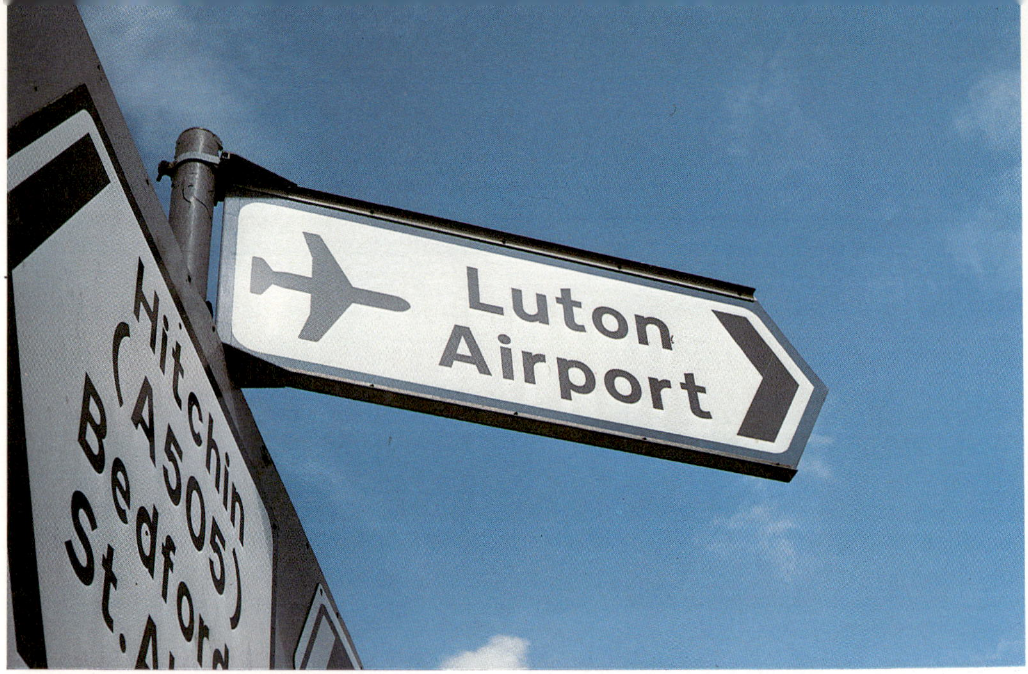

A stock shot from the ITP slide library, part of a morning's work at Luton Airport that produced pictures for four different programmes.

This shot formed part of a two-projector sequence advertising the travel services available from United Counties, a division of the National Bus Company (ITP).

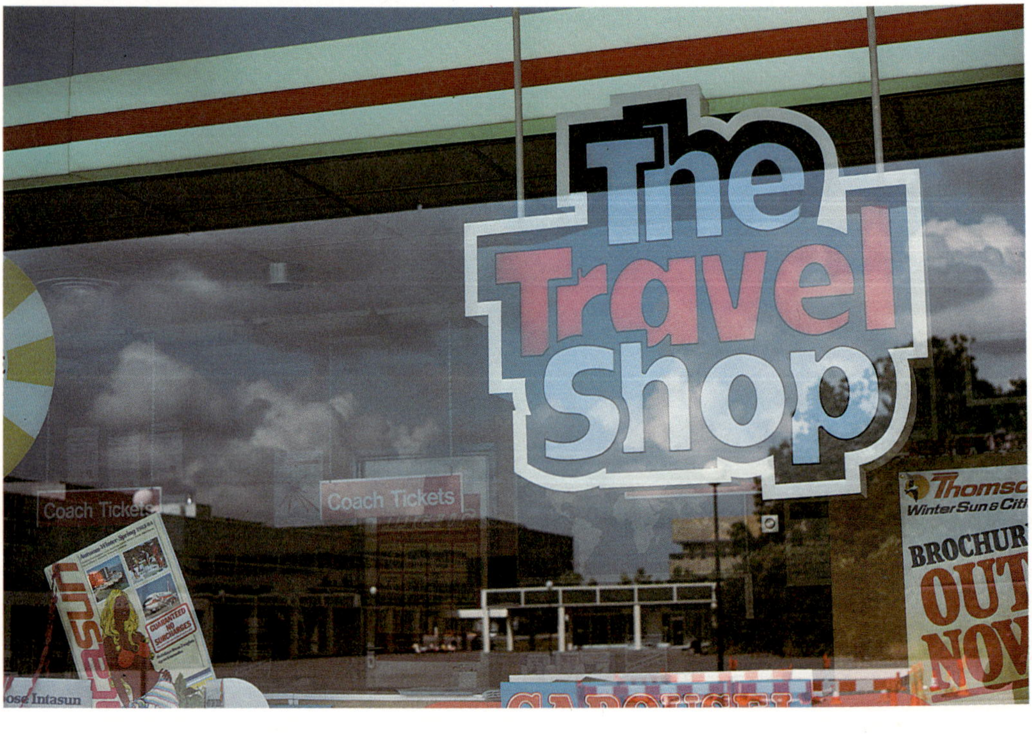

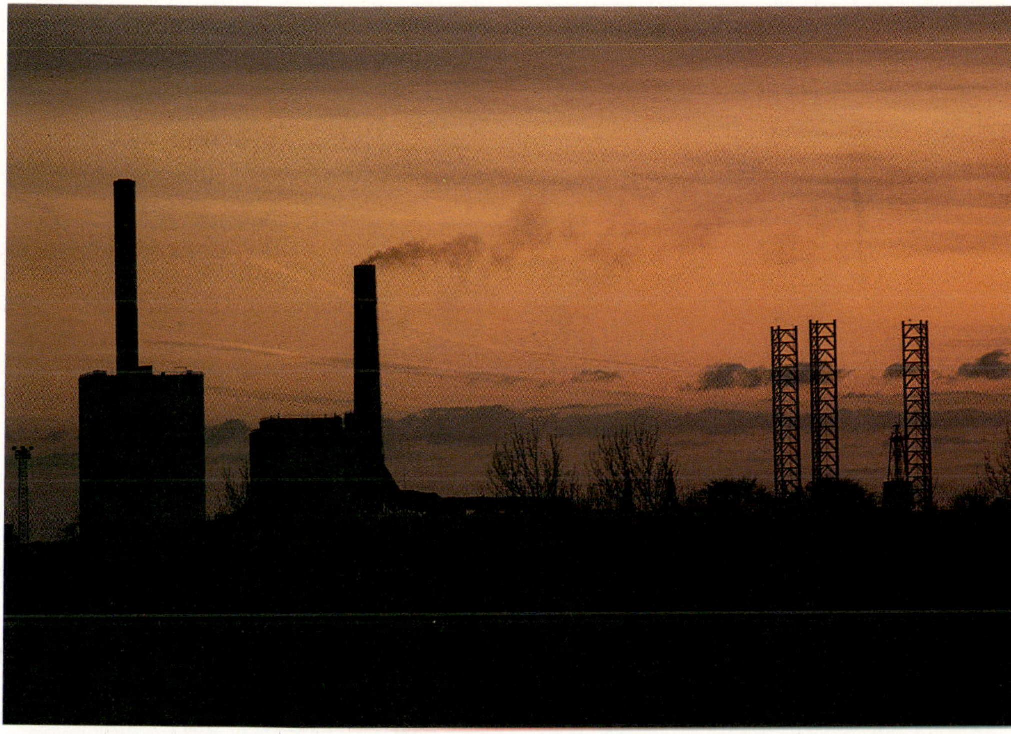

Oil town. An oil rig and a factory silhouetted against a sunset sky symbolise the arrival of a new industry in this professional presentation from ITP.

fashionable form of PR, but a genuinely effective way of putting across ideas and information.

All these programmes need photography and scripting to the highest professional standards. The soundtracks must be produced quickly, economically and effectively. And everything I have said about recognising, reaching and entertaining the audience still applies. I once thought that advertising and commercial work was sheer slog, with little or no creative content. The truth is that no one watches programmes of this kind *unless* they are entertaining. And if your job is to make the manufacture of bottle tops entertaining, then you'll need more — not less — energy and imagination to do it.

The commercial world is no place for the faint-hearted. If you can't sit still and watch a client take your carefully-conceived ideas to pieces, and then put them together again in the wrong order, try another line of work. He's paying for the job, and you must make sure he's satisfied. Of course, you don't have to make his *next* programme . . . !

Scripting a commercial show often demands journalistic skills. You must be able to take in a large amount of unfamiliar information very quickly, and process it into a simple, easily-understood audio-visual form. You must know, almost instinctively, how to structure a programme so as to present bald facts in the most immediate, memorable and entertaining way possible. And you must be able to ask the right questions, of the right people, at the right time.

Commercial experience is useful, especially if you aim to set up on your own. It will teach you how to run a business (or how not to) and it will help you understand how your clients run theirs. However, it is more likely that you will form part of a production team, in which case you can simply concentrate on your strongest area: photography, perhaps, or graphics.

Access to the profession is normally

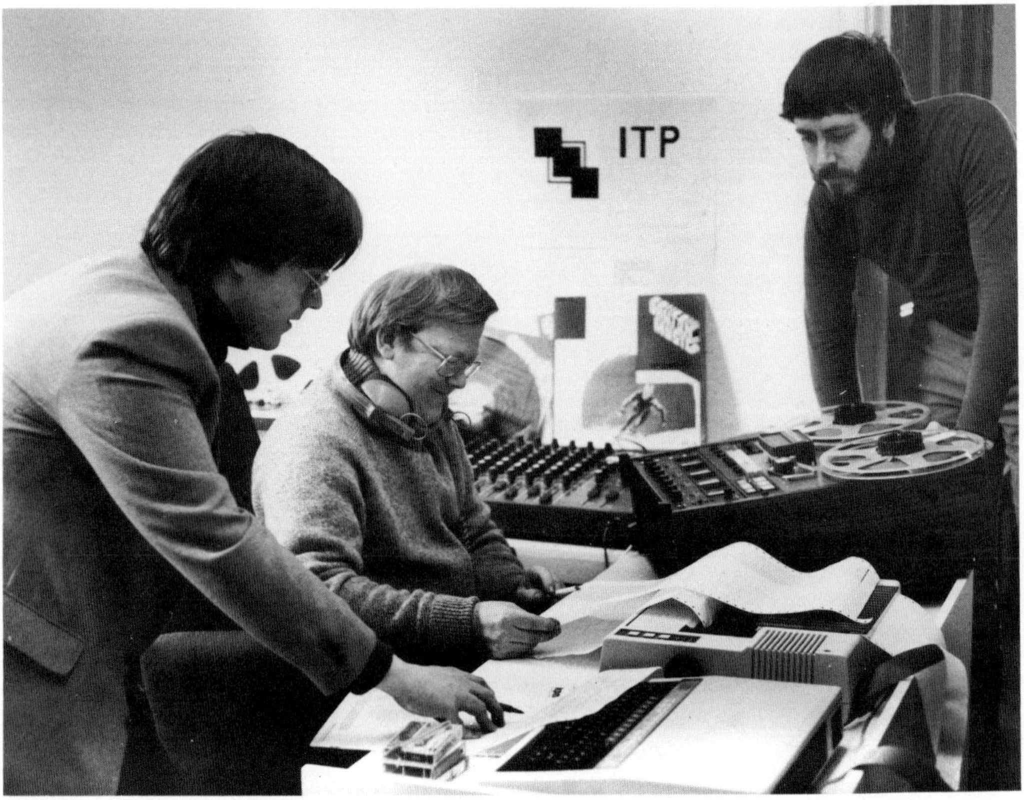

The ITP production team: the author with partners Sim Harris (standing) and Rogan Montgomery-Smith (at the mixer).

through specific courses at colleges, polytechnics and universities. Most of these courses have a strong bias towards photography and graphic design, both essential for the larger commercial shows. Even if you major in scripting, you will need to know a good deal about the visual side of the business to write really effective programmes. Some producers come from an audio background — they may have started in sound studios, or even in electronics. Others, like me, are mavericks with a background in popular writing, who come to specialise in this highly creative area. The truth is that all three disciplines — photography, sound, and creative writing — are important, and a good producer needs some knowledge of each. But success in this, as in any other creative field, demands more than mere training. It demands a certain flair — a certain creative ability. Only you can find out whether or not you have that ability.

There is one more important quality that most professional audio-visual people share. It's the ability to work in a team: the ability to use their own particular skills to the full while appreciating and relying on the particular skills of others. A good team member knows something about *all* the different aspects of the job, but chooses to specialise in one particular area where he can be of the greatest value.

That can be a very useful attitude to get you started in the business of making slide shows — even if you're only doing it for fun.

10

Getting started

If you've just read all the way through this book, you may be feeling a little punch-drunk by now. How, after all, can I possibly expect anyone to be good at so many different things? I seem to be looking for someone with the combined skills of Lord Snowdon, Tom Stoppard, Robert Redford, André Previn, a sound studio manager, and a graphic designer. The answer, of course, is that no one is likely to have *all* these skills. And it doesn't matter a bit.

Slide-tape for fun

The main reason for starting this hobby is to enjoy yourself. And as long as you *are* enjoying yourself, your skills will develop with time. What I'd like to do in this chapter is to suggest a few ways in which you can *help* them develop, to an extent where you'll feel confident enough to put your work in front of a wider public. This isn't going to happen overnight — it will take time and effort. But it'll be effort of the most enjoyable kind — and before long you may find you've become more of a perfectionist than many hardened professional producers.

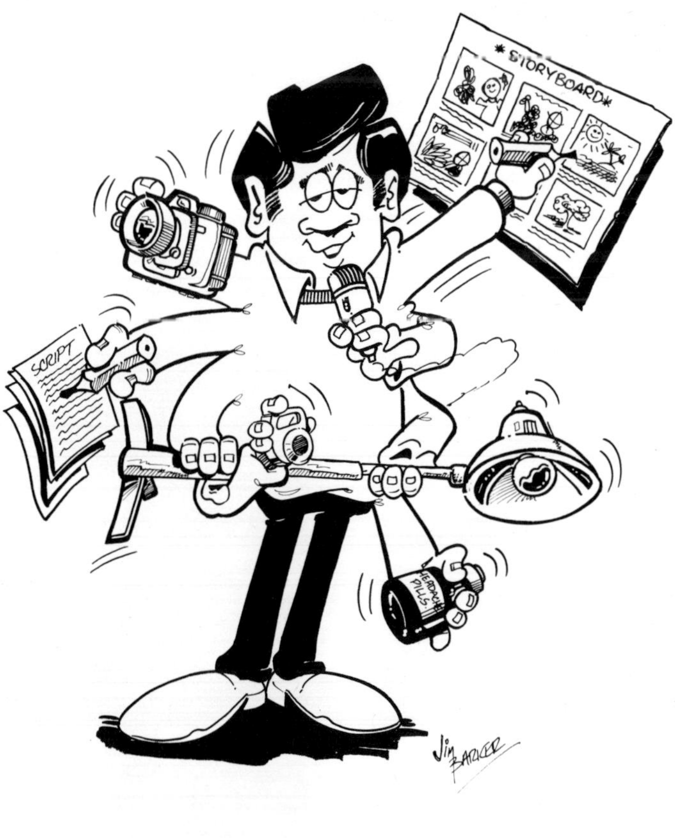

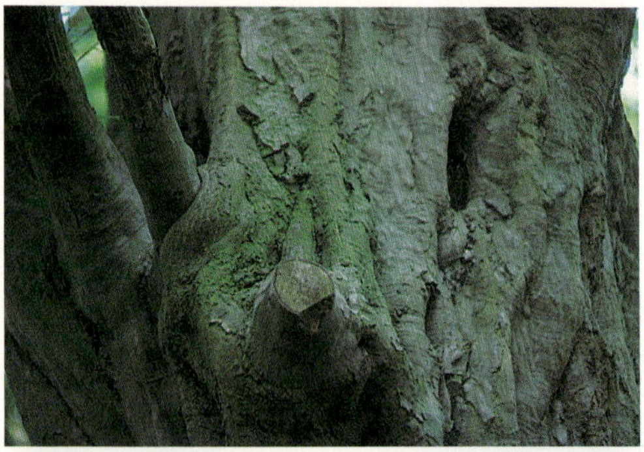

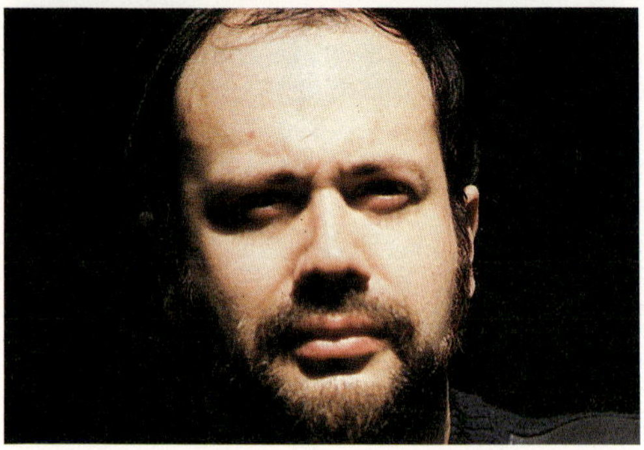

Visual imagination at work — or spot the similarity. Science-fiction writer Mike Scott Rohan submits to the comparison with his customary stoicism in this extract from *Witchwood*.

Thinking visually

The first skill to work on is your own visual imagination. Like the editor of a popular newspaper, for you a good story will not be enough. You have to decide whether it makes good *pictures*.

Many people who go to see the film of their favourite book come away disappointed. How often have you heard them say 'It wasn't a bit like the story'? And there's a reason why it very rarely can be. A book exists as several hundred pages of closely-packed print. Even the longest screenplay couldn't afford to be *that* long. Most books are written as long stretches of narrative broken up with dialogue. A film consists of dialogue and pictures — and even the most skilful director can't bring out every nuance of a written description with a series of pictures. Finally, a film is a form of drama — and plays and novels are as different as chalk and cheese.

Most directors and/or screenwriters solve the problem by making a 'play of the book'. They take the main plot thread of the original book, ditch any sub-plots and minor characters that are no longer needed, and work what is left into dialogue. Unless the author had a very special ear for dialogue (as, for instance, Raymond Chandler did) much of the original dialogue will need to be rewritten, too. Sometimes it is even necessary to change the plot. In fairness, this can sometimes be an improvement. The result is a piece of drama with a strong visual bias — the film of the book.

Again, look at television adaptations of children's stories. You will see the same simplifications, the same need to make the original ideas *visual*. The BBC programme *Jackanory*, for instance, comes closer than most to a slide-tape show. The reader (usually a well-known actor) simply reads the story aloud, while the screen shows a series of stills — usually coloured illustrations. By a careful use of selective close-ups and camera movements, the number of original illustrations needed for any one programme is kept to a minimum, but even in this very simple form of visual adaptation, most of the stories are heavily edited, and for the same reason. Whatever is

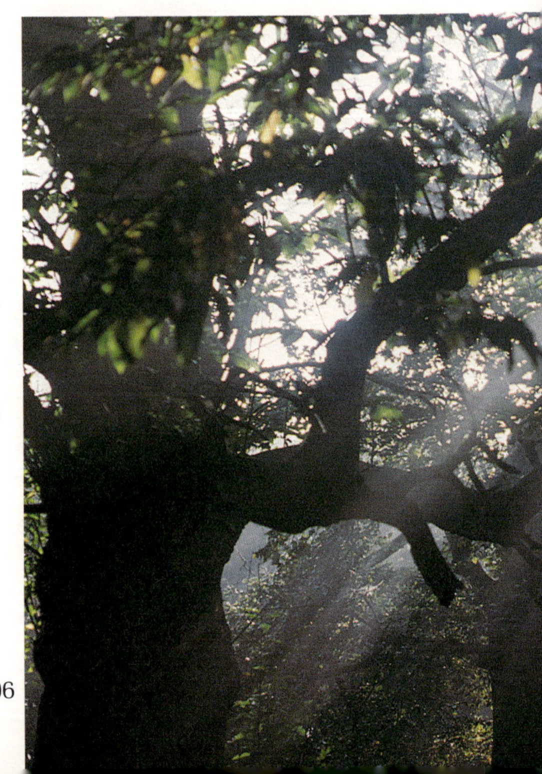

going on in the story must be visual, too.

So how can you learn this skill?

The simplest way is to think like a camera! When you're putting together a storyline, don't do it in terms of words. Imagine you're a camera, and try to think about what you're seeing. How far away are you? Are you looking up? Looking down? Are there figures in sight? Where? Which one(s) are you interested in?

Before long you'll find yourself drawing up a storyboard.

Telling the story

In Chapters 3 and 4 we looked at ways of putting together a programme, and at one particular storyboard. Until now you may have been used to working the other way round — for instance, by getting out your holiday pictures and writing a commentary to go with them. By now I hope you can see that it's far easier to take pictures to fit your commentary. The camera must do what *you* want! Again, it's worth studying films and TV to see how the professionals do it. Clint Eastwood might not look nearly such a tough guy if it weren't for his choice of lighting and camera angles. Bo Derek might only manage 9 out of 10 in a badly-directed

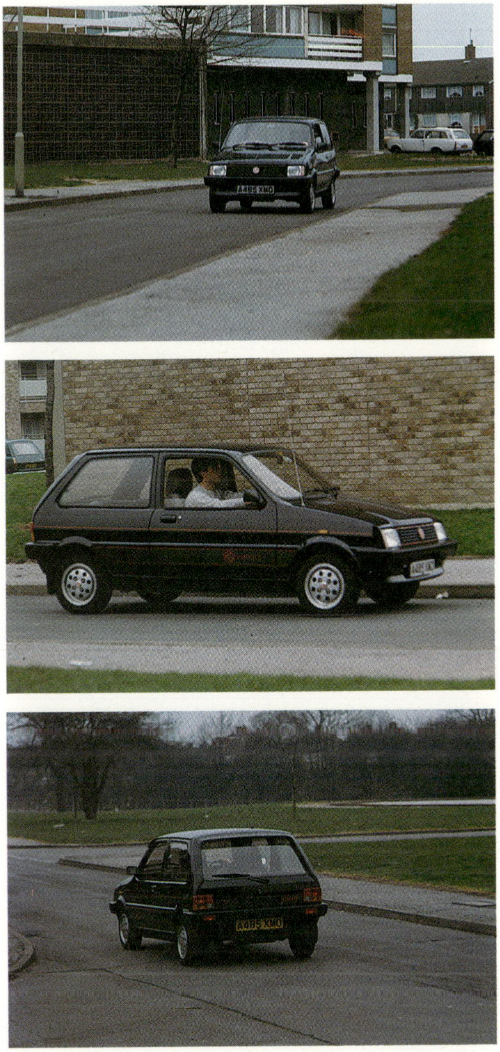

Some mistake here, surely? Shooting from the wrong side of the street in the middle of this sequence appears to turn the car around!

film. And even the most spectacular action stunt looks like nothing at all if it's been shot from the wrong angle.

In Chapter 5 I talked about 'shot grammar' — but I haven't been able to give you much more than an introduction to the subject. Much shot grammar depends on simple common sense. For example, imagine a shot of a car on the left-hand side of the screen,

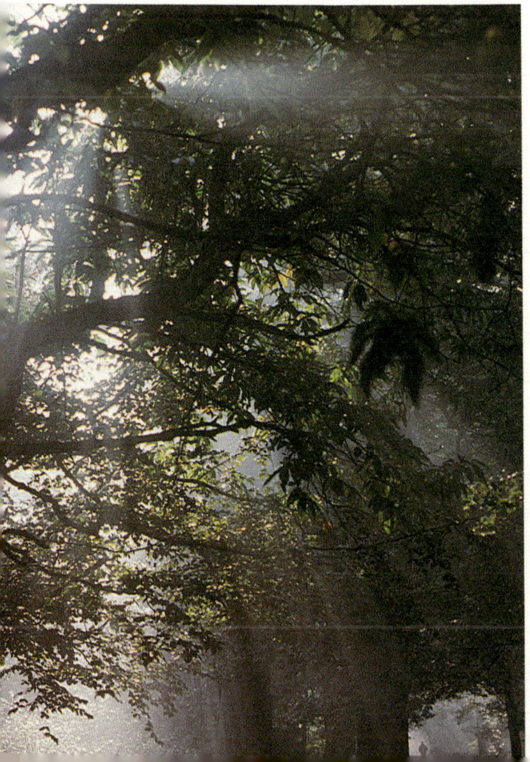

Thinking like a camera. Trees in a wood create a ready-made starburst filter — but to get this kind of shot you have to be looking for it.

driving towards the right. The next shot might show the same car at the centre of the screen, but still pointing to the right, and the final shot might show it disappearing off the right-hand side of the screen. Fine. But suppose you had taken those shots in three different streets, to give an impression of the car travelling some distance? And suppose, by accident, you had taken one of those shots from the other side of the car? To your audience, it would look as though the car had suddenly turned round and was now going the other way! Put like this, it sounds obvious — but it's just the kind of mistake that is very easy to make when you are actually out taking pictures.

The same rule applies to people, too. Once you have established that they're running, say, from right to left, then all the subsequent shots in that sequence must show them running in the same direction (though you could cheat by inserting a short sequence showing something different, so that your audience had time to forget where your runners were going). And when your runners sit down to catch their breath, keep on one side of them — don't suddenly take a picture from a position behind their backs if every other shot has been taken from the front.

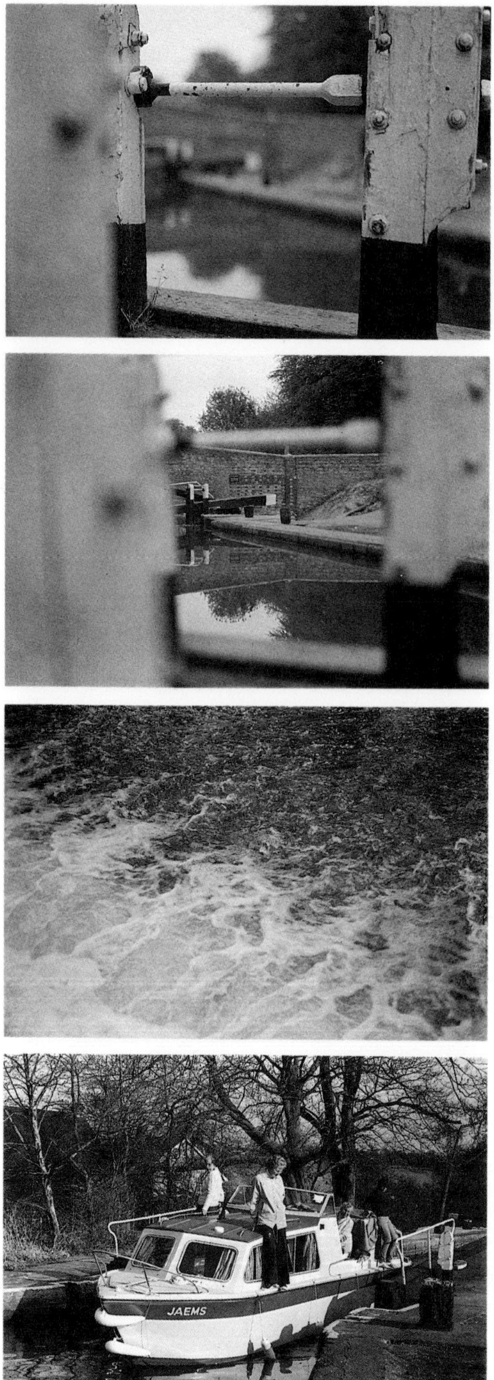

A simple sequence using some of the techniques described in this book.

Taking control of your pictures

If all this still sounds very theoretical, then the best way to put it into practice is to take out your camera to an interesting location and start shooting. Only this time don't just take every interesting picture that presents itself: *look* for pictures. If you've taken a good shot, think of other shots you could take that might lead up to it or develop from it.

For example, while I was shooting *Down at the Zoo* at Whipsnade I caught a one-off shot of a hippo staring disgustedly into my camera and making a noise like a giant cistern. The shot on its own is fun, but it needs to be part of a sequence — so I shot a close-up of the sign saying 'Hippos', and some selective close-ups and mid-shots of the people watching them, as well as a few more tranquil shots of the hippos themselves. The completed sequence would start with the sign, dissolve to a shot of the hippos, and then to a shot of the people watching them. A cut would take us into a close-up of a small girl looking startled, and the next shot would be our disgusted hippo. (If you can't make a small girl look startled without the aid of hippos, then you should stick to landscape photography.)

On holiday, too, make the most of your opportunities. If you're not sure what to take, take too much rather than too little. If you've paid out large sums of money to reach some exotic location, don't grudge the price of a few rolls of film when you've got there. Professional photographers, especially in audio-visual, always take many more shots than they will finally need — the shots in *A Thames Calendar*, for instance, were selected from some 3,000 pictures of the Thames, its wildlife, and its annual events shot over several years by the show's producer, Patrick Walmsley. Practise on your home ground, and teach yourself how to put sequences together. That way, when you finally get to that lost Inca temple, you'll know what to do. (Aside from finding the treasure, of course.)

You control your camera. It doesn't control you. And once you've made up your mind who's boss, you'll find it can do almost anything you need it to do.

Starting at the bottom

Unless you're very confident of your own abilities, now is too soon to go out and buy two projectors and a dissolve unit. Take a little time to become familiar with the medium. Put together a few single-projector programmes and see how well you can cope with their limitations. Many professional programmes are still made for single-projector presentation, so it's a skill well worth learning. Besides, after making a few single-projector programmes you'll probably be itching to try it with two.

Keep your first programmes short, and stick to things you can photograph in or near your own area. If you like, put together a family story like *Guess Who's Coming to Dinner* or a programme about your home town. Or try out some of the ideas in Chapter 2. After a few of these 'trial runs' you should begin to get the idea, and some of the sections in this book will begin to make a lot more sense.

Whatever subject you choose, look for an 'angle': a unique slant. You don't need to make it funny, and to start with it may be better not to try. Unless you're a natural comic, writing funny programmes is the most difficult art of all. But you might decide that there's a song, or a tune, that sums up your town or your street — and then take the camera out to prove your point.

If you have a home computer, why not use it to help you make a programme? You could put together a whole sequence using computer graphics you'd programmed and designed yourself. At very least, you could use them for titles within the sequence. Or you could have a 'computer character' to

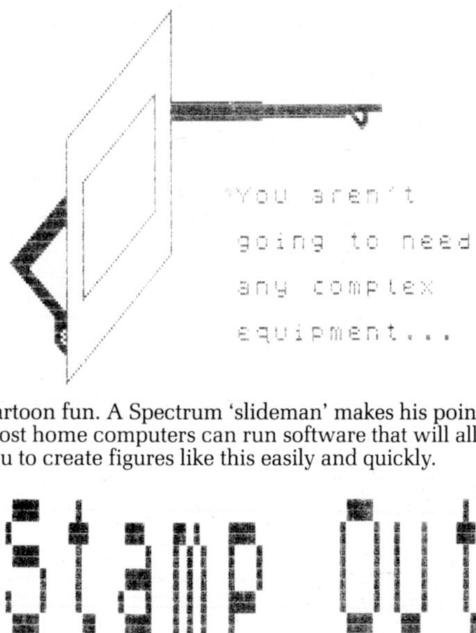

Cartoon fun. A Spectrum 'slideman' makes his point. Most home computers can run software that will allow you to create figures like this easily and quickly.

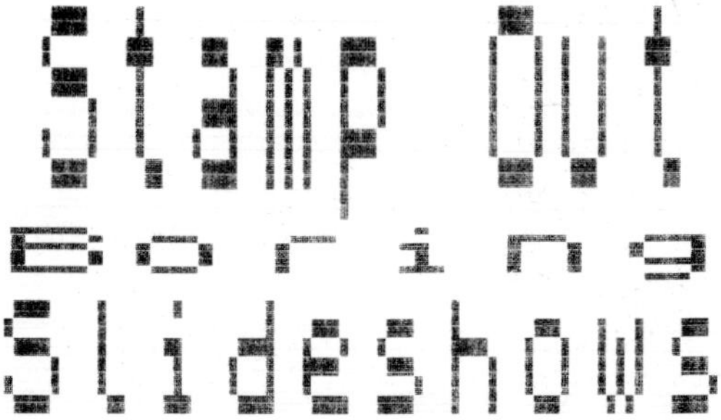

Computer power. A Sinclair ZX Spectrum delivers the message of this book using a simple program written by the author.

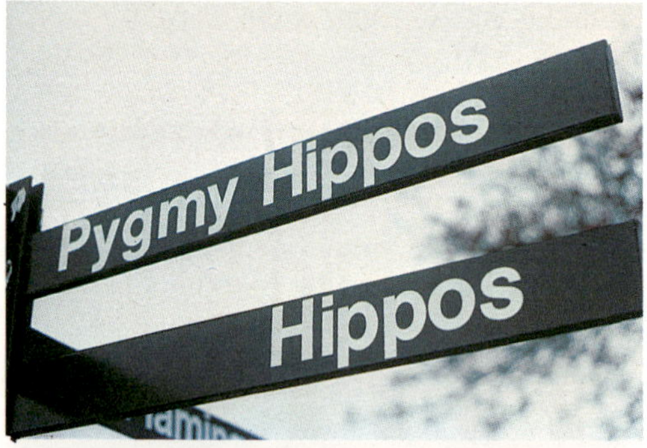

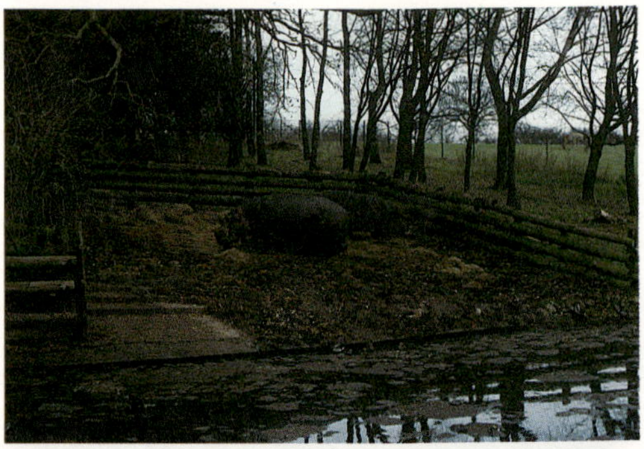

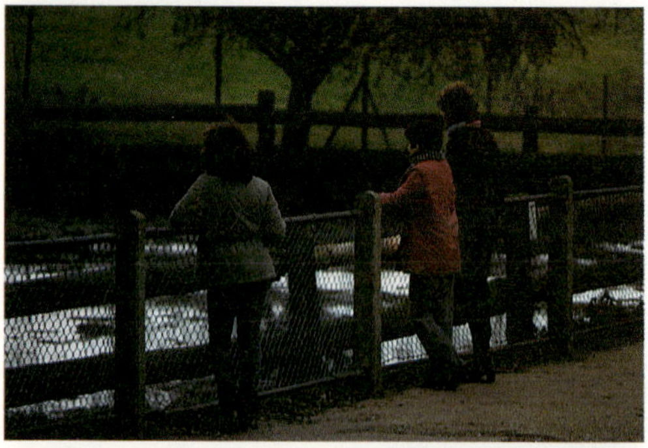

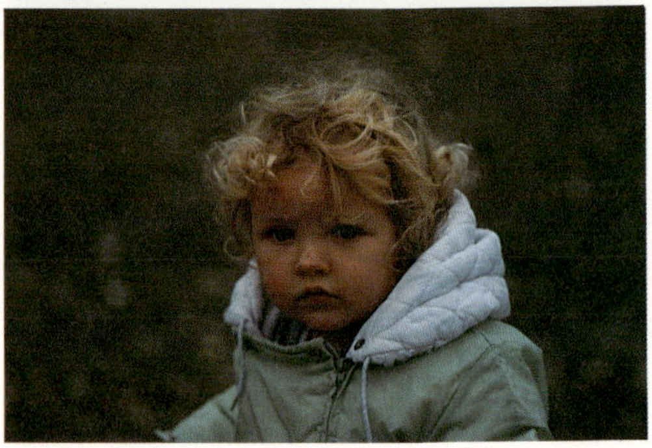

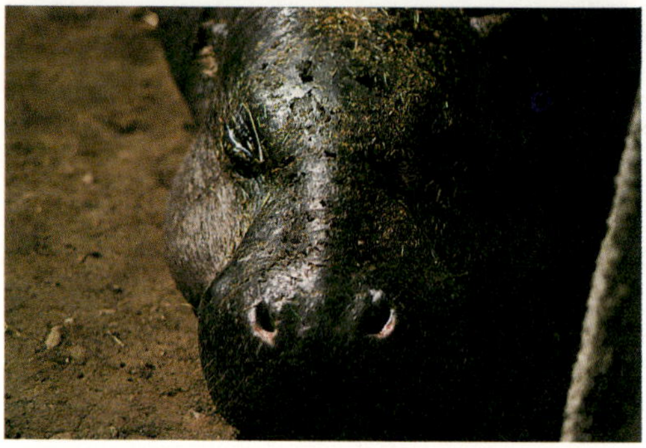

Animals and children at Whipsnade Zoo. This sequence from *Down at the Zoo* shows how careful sequence-building and candid telephoto shots can combine to tell a purely visual story.

comment on the action. I'm working on a short instructional piece called *How to Make Slide Shows* in which a computer character tries to teach a slow learner how to put a programme together. The computer character is useful because, with a simple twist of the programming, he can turn into something that looks like a projector, a camera, a tape recorder — or a mixing desk!

Taking the next step

If you enjoy these early programmes, and find you're getting more and more interested, now is the time to start thinking about where your real interest lies. Are you more of a photographer? A writer? A sound-track maker? You don't have to be all three — no one could expect you to be equally good in every branch of the hobby. Very occasionally a slide-show maker will combine a complete set of production skills, but such people are very much the exception. Generally speaking, successful slide-show makers are specialists in one particular field. The secret of their success is that they know their own limitations.

The programme about Joan of Arc (right) is a good example. Although I'm producing the show myself, the script has been researched and outlined by my father, who is an expert on the period and on Joan herself. He has also supplied most of the photography from a collection acquired over many years of travel and study. Since the bulk of the programme relies on Joan's own words, I'm obviously disqualified for the voice part, too — instead, I'm using the voice of a young actress called Adrienne Bunn, who has a much better chance of sounding like a 17-year-old girl. And the music is being supplied by an old friend, Colin Prior, who has a special interest in French popular music of the fifteenth century. (Admittedly I shall be playing some of it myself, but without Colin's research — and the support of his instrumental consort — there would be no music score.)

By the time *Joan of Arc* goes into full production, many people will have been involved, either directly or indirectly, in its creation. Nor is there anything wrong with this, if the result is a better programme.

Witchwood, too, is the result of a collaboration with Colin Michaels, an accomplished guitarist and photographer, and Tim Phillips, composer extraordinary.

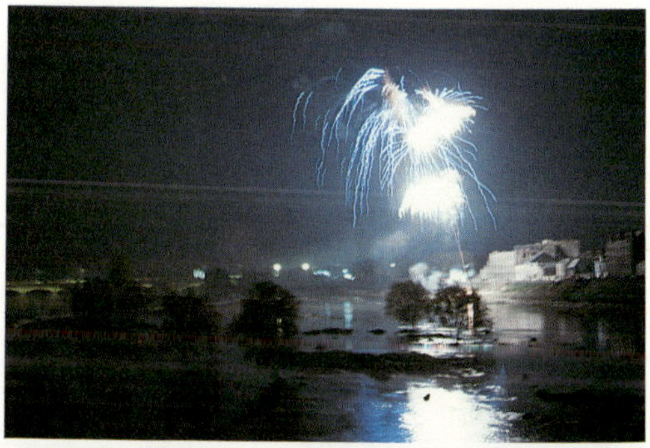

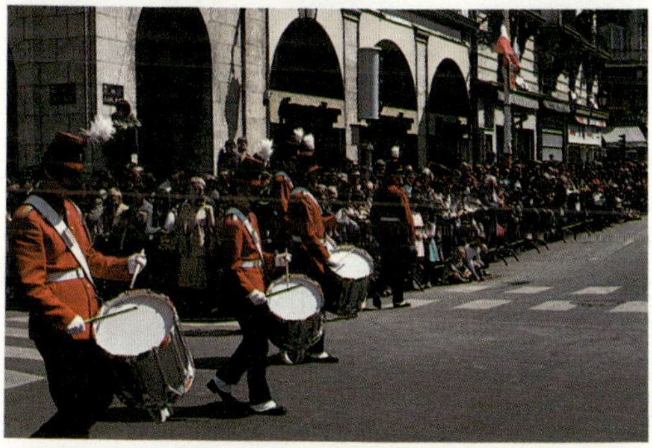

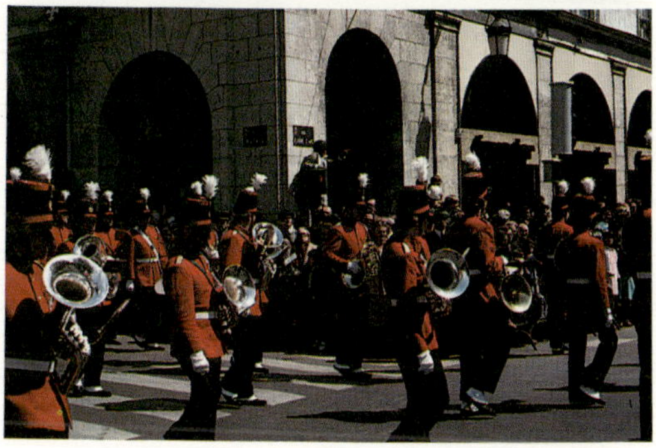

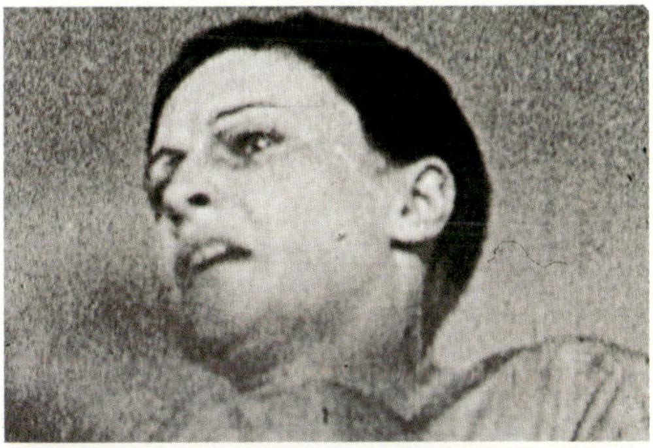

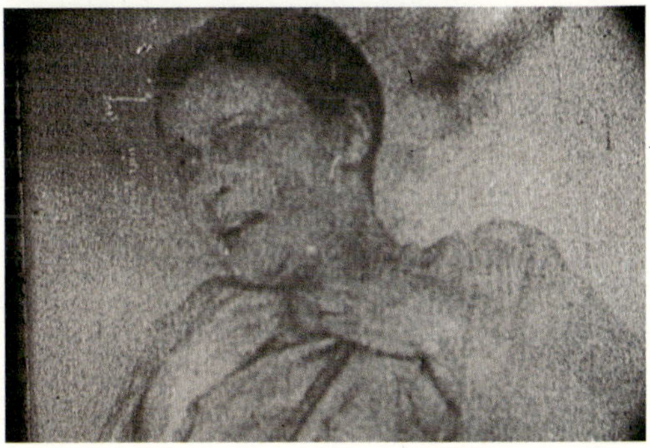

Part of the final sequence of *Joan of Arc*. Even without the soundtrack, these gritty, documentary-looking black-and-white stills deliver a powerful message.

In a very real sense, Colin and Tim have contributed as much to the programme as I have. Though the original idea and most of the visuals are mine, Tim's music has given the programme a shape, and Colin's performance — and his darkroom work — have given that shape its final form. Without them there would have been no programme.

Teamwork is the norm, even in professional circles. One man cannot produce programmes efficiently on his own. A professional producer is likely to call on a scriptwriter, a graphic designer, a photographer, photographic models, a professional voice, a sound engineer, a music library and a slide-duplication service in the course of making even the simplest programme.

So when you've made a few programmes of your own, sit back and decide what you can do, and what you want to do. Obviously you may want to try something new — scripting, for instance, or graphic design. And unless you try these things, you will never find out how good you are. More to the point, unless you *keep* trying you will never learn to do them. But after a while you will reach your own decisions about your capabilities. You may decide that scripting is not for you. You may decide that your voice is simply not up to the job of reading commentaries. You may decide that your photography isn't good enough to match your own original ideas. Whatever you decide, if you're still interested in slide shows then the time has come to look for partners — friends and acquaintances who share your interest and can add the missing pieces to your production jigsaw.

Finding and meeting these people can be a pleasure in itself. You will need to look in all sorts of fascinating places: the local camera club for photographers, the amateur dramatic group for voices, art classes for graphic designers, and (perhaps) hospital radio stations for your recording engineer, or even a good narrator. It's a search that will yield its own harvest of new friends and new interests, even if you don't always find what you are looking for. But if you are patient, you will finish up with an enthusiastic team of like-minded people who will share your interest and complement your own skills. And the result can be some first-rate programmes.

I can recommend teamwork because my own professional audio-visual partnership depends on it — and was built up, initially, from a chance succession of meetings with like-minded people. Today we are producing full-scale audio-visual presentations for major national clients.

In a word, teamwork pays.

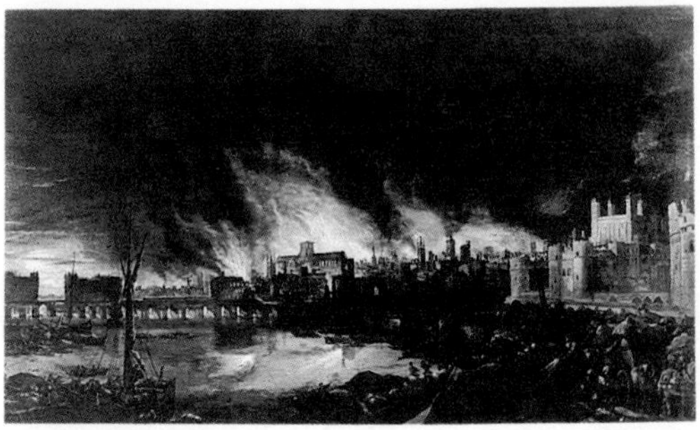

And finally . . .

Whatever direction you take — into the touring circuit, into commercial audio-visual, or simply into the living room with a new, improved holiday programme — I hope you will find, as I have, that slide-tape can be one of the most rewarding and enjoyable hobbies there is. Because it covers so many different areas, there is something in it for almost everybody. Even if you never took a decent slide in your life, there is nothing to stop you writing scripts or making soundtracks. In the end, your enjoyment is what really matters. I sincerely hope that this book has given you some new ideas — about making programmes, and about subjects for them. I hope that you're feeling ready to go out and set the world on fire.

And if you manage *that* — well, don't forget the camera.

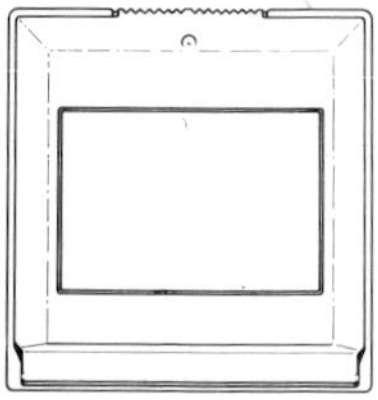

Appendix 1

Slide shows and the Law of Copyright

Copyright law is an extremely confusing subject — and it's becoming more confusing every year as methods of breaching copyright become more sophisticated. Even so, a few basic principles are fairly clear.

Copyright in photographs belongs to the photographer, unless he was specifically commissioned to take them by someone else and gave up his copyright as part of the contract. If you have paid a fee to a museum, gallery or house to take pictures there, then copyright in those pictures is yours unless you have surrendered it — just the same, treat these people with consideration, and remember that there may be a copyright in the object you photograph (e.g. a modern work of art).

Copying pictures out of books and then using them for your personal profit is, of course, illegal — however, no one is likely to complain if you do so for your own personal use, or as part of a show for friends or a local club.

Similar rules apply to sound recording, though the copyright position here is far more complicated. Suppose, for instance, that you wanted to use the current number one hit single as a soundtrack for a slide show. To start with, there are two lots of copyright to deal with — the author's copyright, in this case the copyright of the person who wrote the song, and the recording company's copyright in the actual sound recording of the song. Both copyright owners might well require a fee for your use of the song — and an additional fee might be payable to the Performing Rights Society if you wanted to present the show to an audience made up of the general public.

Depressed? Don't be. The Institute of Amateur Cinematographers can issue you with a blanket license that allows you to use recorded music in your shows subject to certain clear restrictions. The main restriction is that you yourself do not make money out of the show, and that it is not used to advertise a product or service. (Yes, I know . . . more about how to get round these problems later.) You can then show the programme at your club, at slide-tape festivals, and at most other venues suitable for amateur work. Full details from the I.A.C. (see Listing in Appendix 3).

But suppose you want to make some money?

If this is how you feel about copyright, contact the I.A.C!

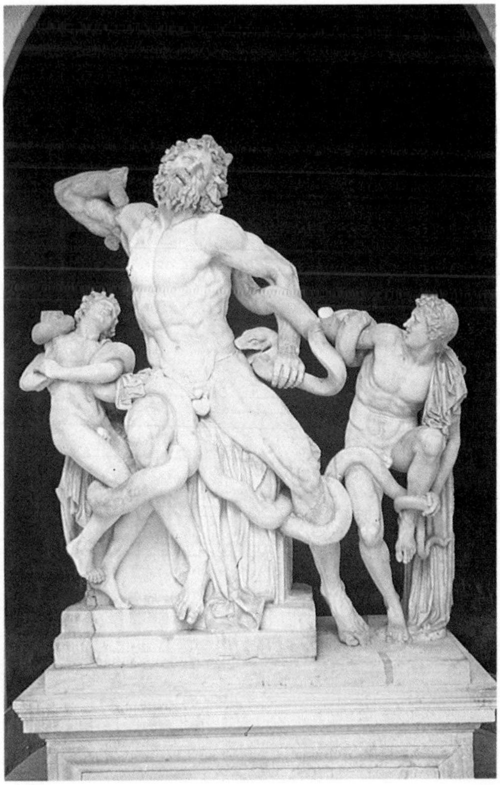

The obvious answer is to use library music which is composed especially for commercial soundtracks. To do this, apply first to the libraries themselves (see Appendix 3) and then to M.C.P.S. (the Mechanical Copyright Protection Society) who will arrange the necessary licenses, and invoice you accordingly. Fees are normally on a standard scale, and though M.C.P.S. will try to be helpful, you may not find this a particularly cheap way to buy your music. Just the same, for professional work these are the fees you must expect to pay. Unless . . . .

Those of us who have no prejudice against classical and early modern music often find it useful here: most of it is out of copyright (though do check, especially if the composer died in the 1920s or 1930s), so you only have the copyright in the *recording* to deal with. If *that* is more than 50 years old, then it's out of copyright anyway — not that it'd be too much use to you! The point is that record companies can be quite approachable. You could, for instance, approach a very small company and offer to sell their records at each of your venues — but you will have to prove that you are sufficiently businesslike to make the arrangement worth their while, so don't expect them to leap at the idea. And watch out for performing rights — check that you are clear in that department, too, or you might face prosecution!

For further advice about specific problems, talk to the I.A.C. or M.C.P.S. — I have found them considerate and more than helpful, and I'm sure you will too.

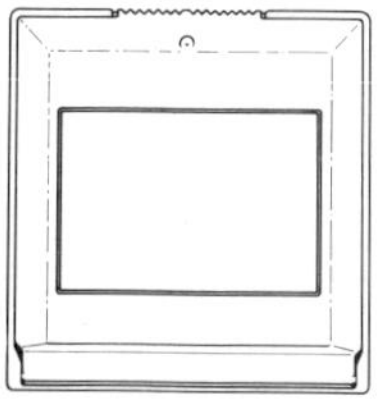

Appendix 2

Some Further Reading

Books on slide-tape are few and far between. Good books are even rarer. Focal Press publish a series of books on particular aspects of audio-visual work, including photography, scripting, lighting, and one on slide-tape as such. These are a bit dry but detailed, competent and accurate. Pick the ones you think you might need from their extensive list.

Balls, Colin, *The A to V of Slide-Tape.* Copies available from the author (38 Fieldside Avenue, Buxton, Lancashire) or from Pollock Audio-Visual. A quirky book, expensive and rather badly produced, but full of useful information from an experienced slide-show maker.

The following books on photography may be useful to the comparative newcomer:

Kilpatrick, David (Ed.), *Successful Creative Photography* (Collins, 1983)
Hedgecoe, John, *Introductory Photography Course* (Mitchell Beazley)
Langford, Michael, *The Step by Step Guide to Photography* (Ebury Press)
How to take Good Pictures A Kodak photo guide (Collins, 1982)

After an extensive hunt, I can really only recommend one book on tape recording. It is:

Gardner, John, *Master Creative Tape Recording* (Newnes Technical Books, 1977).

However, Agfa may be able to supply you with three excellent little booklets if you contact them at the address in Appendix 3. The booklets are:

Tape Recording Manual (Order No. 701E)
Recording with Compact Cassettes (Order No. 702E)
Tape Recording Technique

Useful Magazines

There is no shortage of enjoyable and readable photography magazines on the market, but I would particularly recommend *Amateur Photographer* (still pretty much the market leader), and (for single-lens reflex owners) *SLR Camera*. If you are looking for a more advanced magazine with startling and original ideas you might try *Camera and Creative Photography*, sister magazine to *Practical Photography*, which also gives regular coverage of slide-tape events.

Good news for home recording enthusiasts is a recent arrival on the news-stands, *Home Studio Recording*. On the basis of its first issue, released shortly before this book went to press, it will be a useful and informative magazine that deserves to do well and should be required reading for all home recording enthusiasts.

The magazine for the professional AV market is *Audio Visual*, but this can be hard to get on news-stands. For a subscription write to Audio Visual, P.O. Box 109, Croydon CR9 9DD.

Reading magazines is the only sensible way to keep up to date with changes, improvements, and new arrivals in the wide range of equipment available for slide-tape. Any book — including this one — can only hope to give you an idea of what is available in this expanding and very profitable market. The magazines also publish regular reviews of cameras and projectors — a field so huge I have not even tried to cover it!

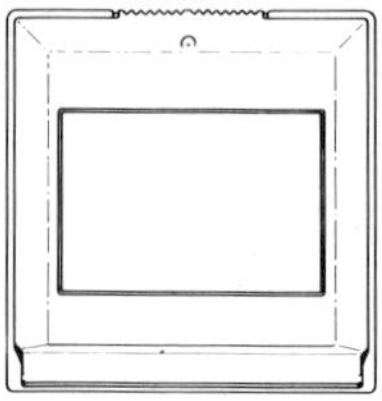

Appendix 3

Address List

Dissolve units and projector control equipment

Diafade Ltd
10 Cowbridge
Hertford
Herts SG14 1PQ

Electrosonic Ltd
815 Woolwich Road
London SE7 8LT

H.B. (Photo Services) Ltd
Arndale House
Sheep Street
Wellingborough
Northants NN8 1BG
(suppliers of the Royale dissolve system)

Imatronic Ltd
Dorian House
Rose Street
Wokingham
Berks RG11 1XU

Kodak Ltd
P.O. Box 66
Kodak House
Hemel Hempstead
Herts

Pollock Audio-Visual
138 South Street
Dorking
Surrey

Screens

Cine Screens Ltd
Leighton Road
Leighton Buzzard
Beds LU7 7LP

Harkness Screens Ltd
The Gate Studios
Station Road
Boreham Wood
Herts WD6 1DQ

Specialist Slide Mounts and Accessories

A.V. Slide Work Ltd
42–44 Beak Street
London W1R 3DA
(Wess slide mounts and accessories, including the Splitter)

R.C.W. Colour Slides
P.O. Box 4DL
7A Livonia Street
London W1A 4DL
(soft-edge masks)

Both these companies are also 'facilities houses' with their own rostrum cameras, able to provide a full range of creative services to the slide show maker. For a complete list of companies carrying out work of this kind, contact the A.V.A. at the address given under *Societies and Professional Bodies*.

Projector stands

Unicol Ltd
Church Lane
Marston
Oxford OX3 0PT

Photographic and Audio materials

Agfa-Gevaert Ltd
27 Great West Road
Brentford
Middlesex TW8 9AX

Kodak Ltd
P.O. Box 66
Kodak House
Hemel Hempstead
Herts

Ready-made colourslides and slide-tape programmes

Woodmansterne Ltd
Greenhill Crescent
Holywell Industrial Estate
Watford WD1 8RD

Music Libraries

Bruton Music
19 Upper Brook Street
London W1Y 1PD

Chappell Music
129 Park Street
London W1

De Wolfe Music Ltd
80/88 Wardour Street
London W1

Josef Weinberger Ltd
24 Vivian Avenue
London NW4 3XP

Copyright clearance

Institute of Amateur Cinematographers
63 Woodfield Lane
Ashtead
Surrey

Mechanical Copyright Protection Society (M.C.P.S.)
Elgar House
41 Streatham High Road
London SW16 1ER

Societies and Professional Bodies

Audio Visual Association (A.V.A.)
Secretary (1984) A. K. Boyle
46 Manor View
London N3 2SR
(The professional body for AV producers and all companies and individuals working in the field)

British Association of Picture Libraries and Agencies (B.A.P.L.A.)
P.O. Box 284
London W11 4RP
(Of special value to those planning to set up their own picture libraries)

British Institute of Professional Photography
Amwell End
Ware
Herts SG12 9HN
(Professional body)

Bureau of Freelance Photographers
Focus House
497 Green Lanes
London N13 4BP (Advisory service)

Master Photographers' Association
TMT House
1 West Ruislip Station
Ickenham Road
Ruislip
Middlesex HA4 7DN

Royal Photographic Society
The Octagon
Milsom Street
Bath BA1 1DN
(A distinguished society whose Fellowships and Associateships are greatly valued)

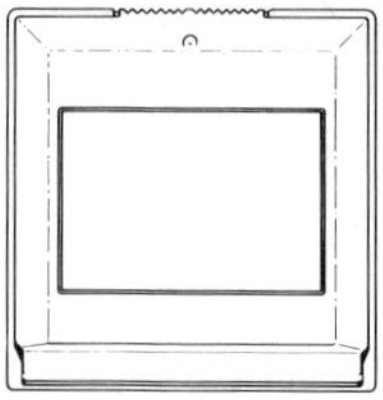

Appendix 4

Table of Projection Distances

All distances shown are for 35mm transparencies (frame size 24 × 36mm), and are approximate lens-to-screen distances. The height of a horizontal picture will be ⅔ of the screen width. (Reproduced by courtesy of Kodak Ltd.)

Screen width	Focal length of lens in mm				
	60	70	85	100	120
36″	5′ 4″	6′ 6″	6′ 10″	8′ 8″	10′ 5″
48″	6′ 11″	8′ 0″	9′ 3″	11′ 11″	13′ 11″
59″	8′ 5″	9′ 11″	11′ 11″	14′ 8″	16′ 11″
69″	9′ 9″	11′ 7″	14′ 10″	17′ 1″	19′ 9″
76″	11′ 0″	12′ 9″	16′ 6″	19′ 2″	21′ 8″
90″	13′ 3″	15′ 0″	19′ 5″	22′ 9″	25′ 9″
104″	15′ 1″	17′ 7″	22′ 2″	26′ 11″	29′ 7″
116″	16′ 10″	19′ 3″	24′ 7″	29′ 1″	31′ 7″
122″	17′ 5″	20′ 2″	25′ 8″	30′ 6″	34′ 8″

Screen width	Focal length of lens in mm		
	150	180	250
36″	12′ 6″	16′ 4″	22′ 2″
48″	16′ 11″	21′ 10″	29′ 3″
59″	20′ 8″	27′ 3″	36′ 1″
69″	24′ 5″	30′ 10″	41′ 0″
76″	27′ 6″	33′ 0″	44′ 10″
90″	32′ 5″	40′ 3″	53′ 2″
104″	37′ 5″	46′ 0″	61′ 10″
116″	41′ 9″	51′ 5″	68′ 6″
122″	44′ 2″	54′ 3″	72′ 2″

Index

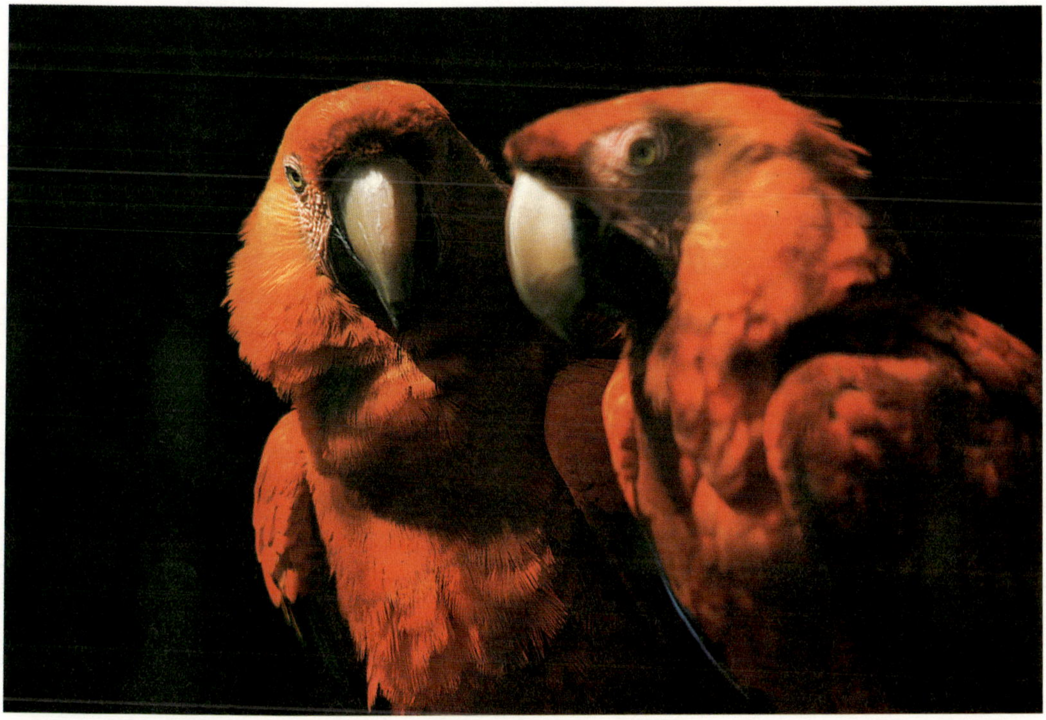

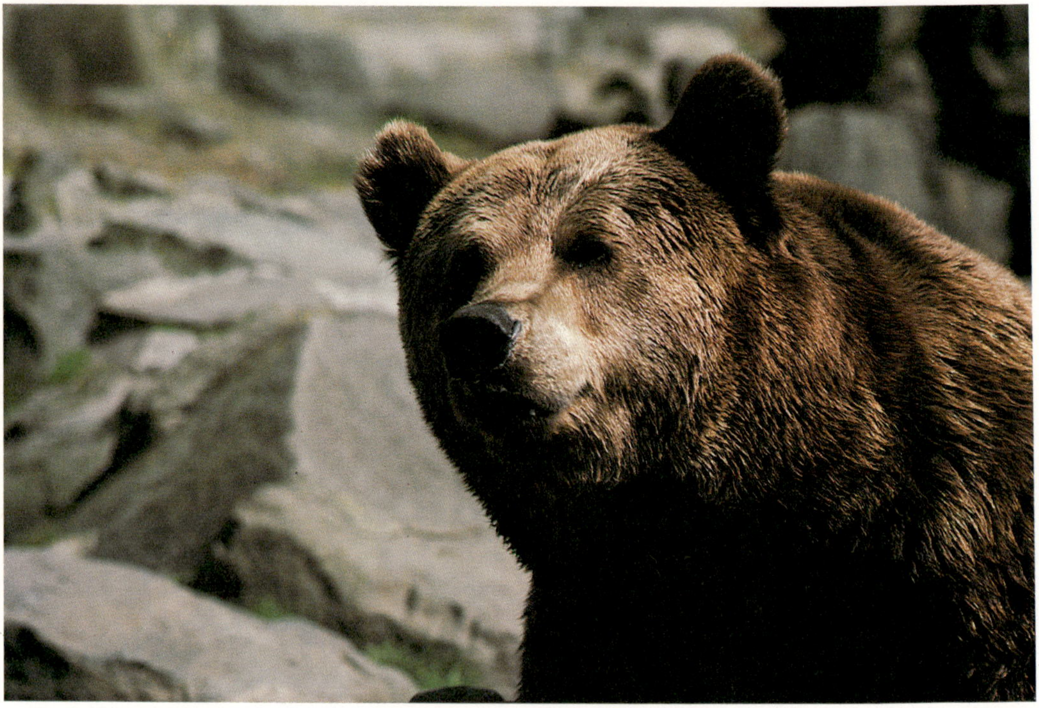

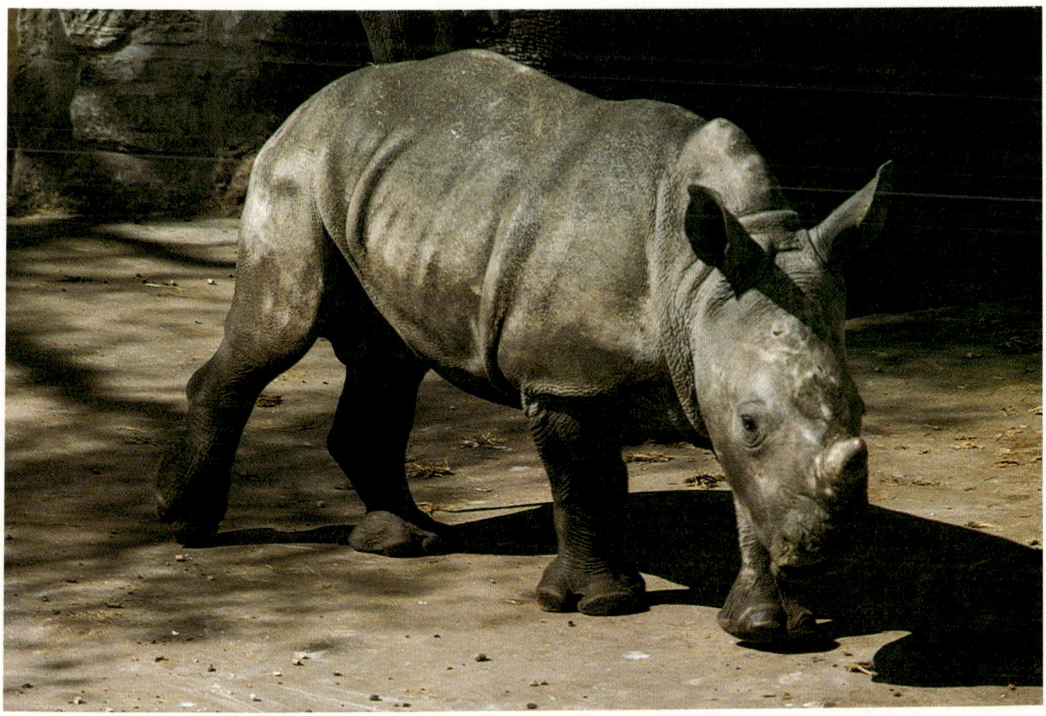